Double Blind

The Icelandic Manuscript Murders

a novel by Sara Winokur

Double Blind: The Icelandic Manuscript Murders

Anchor House Publishing

Publisher's Note: This book is a work of fiction. Any references to historical events, real people, or real places are used fictitiously. Other names, characters, places, and events are products of the author's imagination, and any resemblance to actual events or places or persons, living or dead, is entirely coincidental.

ISBN: 978-1-7334528-0-9

Published in the United States

Book Design by Felix Barca

Cover Design by Black Chateau Enterprises

ARCTIC CIRCLE

WEST FJORDS
ÍSAFJÖRÐUR

EYJAFJÖRÐUR
HRÍSEY
HÚSAVÍK
MÖÐRUVELLIR
MUNKATHVERÁ
AKUREYRI
LAKE MÝVATN

LÁTRABJARG

FLATEY
ISLAND

ICELAND

SKAFTAFELL

EAST FJORDS

THINGVELLIR

REYKJAVIK

SELFOSS

EYJAFJALLAJÖKULL

WESTMAN
ISLANDS

Sumardagurinn Fyrsti
is known from the earliest Icelandic records
when the year was divided in two.
Summer and Winter.

A child's age was marked not in years, but in winters.
In those days, when young death was so common, the
First Day of Summer was a celebration of survival.

Prologue

EYJAFJÖRÐUR, NORTH ICELAND
APRIL 1997
FIRST DAY OF SUMMER

Lúkas was seven winters that day, the day he froze in time and memory.

It was mid-morning when the children pressed their noses to the window, Lúkas in his Thor superhero jammies and Brynja in princess-pink. Below, an icy wind howled off the fjord, battering the red and white flaps of the carnival tent—a giant, striped bird that had landed on the snowy patch of farmland below their house. The townspeople were gathered at the fair, huddled in their heavy, gray overcoats, their chatter frozen in white puffs. Their neighbors, hardy farmers in rough-knit sweaters, stomped their boots and greeted one another with a clap on the back.

The two—twins and inseparable—bundled into woolies and raced across the hall. Brynja begged their father Pabbi to let them go down to the fair.

"Too young, my little lambs," he said. "Next year." He kissed the tops of their heads and shuffled back to Mamma.

Brynja poked her head into the kitchen, though she knew she shouldn't. Pabbi had just said no.

"Jónas?"

"Well, well, *litla mín*," he said, flipping slices of blood sausage in the pan atop the stove. "Breakfast will be ready soon."

Brynja clasped her hands together. "Can Lúkas and I go to the carnival first? *Please?* We'll watch out for each other. I promise."

The farm manager never said a lot, so she knew to be patient while he thought about it. "You'll have to ask your father."

"I did." Brynja turned and put her finger to her lips, daring Lúkas to stay quiet. She wasn't lying. She *did* ask Pabbi.

"Okay, then, just for a bit. But keep an eye on each other." Jónas shook his finger. "No pony rides or talking to strangers."

Brynja grabbed Lúkas's hand and ran to the entry. They hurried to throw on their winter coats, stuffed their stockinged feet into rubber boots, and quietly shut the door. Taking the long way around the house, they avoided Pabbi and Mamma's bedroom window.

Brynja held onto Lúkas as they tromped down the hill through snowdrifts piled high against the cliffs. They had to stop more than once to clear the snow from inside their boots.

Ducking under the carnival tent, they wandered among tables stacked with deep-fried *kleinur* and steaming pots of cocoa. They peeled off their icy-cold mittens and warmed their hands against the cups as they sipped the hot, sweet liquid. Nearby, the sizzle of grilled lamb mixing with the sulfur smell of manure made Brynja feel a little sick, but that didn't stop her from burying her face in sticky, pink clouds of cotton candy.

They had their pictures taken. Brynja put the tiny photos into the silver locket that hung about her neck. They painted their faces green and white, looking like the elves that roamed the highlands. They played ring toss and fed the newborn lambs. Tractors rumbled. Accordions bellowed.

Farmers raised their mugs and shouted, "*Skál!*" The old folks sang. A man tied balloons into monkeys and dogs. One popped in Lúkas's hand when he held it too tight.

Circus music piping through speakers drew Brynja to the up-and-down, round-and-round, every-color-in-the-rainbow carousel. Mesmerized by the wild eyes and flowing manes of the painted horses, she pulled Lúkas from the tent and ran across the clearing in the field.

"Two tickets," she said, digging deep for the *krónur* Jónas had tucked into her pocket.

Lúkas stomped his foot. "No. Jónas said not to go on any pony rides."

"Come on," Brynja pleaded, tugging his arm. "It's a merry-go-round. Not a real horse."

Lúkas folded his arms across his chest. "No."

"Please? We have to stay together."

He shook his head.

"Okay, then, wait right here. I'll only be a minute." She pulled the red ribbon from her braid and handed it to Lúkas before giving him a quick hug. "Take this. And don't worry. Wave to me and I will see you from the carousel."

She climbed atop a painted pony. The merry-go-round jerked, then spun about, faster and faster, until the waves of her hair flew with the horse's mane. Soaring above the crowd, she let go of the reins, lifted her face to the sun, and kissed the clear, blue sky.

With each exhilarating turn, Lúkas grew smaller and smaller, until, when the carousel slowed and the horses reared to a halt, he was nowhere to be seen.

Chapter 1

REYKJAVIK, SOUTHWEST ICELAND
JUNE 12, 2017

From the top floor of Legacy Genetics, Brynja watched the morning sun dance across Reykjavik. The tumultuous skies of last night's storm had given way to an alabaster dawn that slid down snow-capped Mount Esja and breathed a purple mist across the bay. *A good omen*, she thought.

As she turned toward her desk, she caught a spark on the distant horizon.

Brynja jerked her head back.

No. Not now. Not again.

She watched in horror as the delicate threads banded together into brilliant points of light that rode the ebb and flow of the open sea until, one by one, they converged, igniting a ball of flames. The blazing comet stormed across the sea, the harbor, the rooftops below—then burst through her office window, shattering the glass with a crackling explosion of fire.

Brynja's hands flew up to protect her face and she jumped back.

The pressure in her head throbbed as she lunged forward to shut the blinds. In the darkened room, she leaned against the wall, too frightened to move.

Brynja shut her eyes against the lingering headache. She was twenty-seven now and hadn't suffered a visual aura in years; she had hoped they'd been tucked away along with the painful memories of her childhood. The trauma of losing Lúkas two decades ago had brought on the first episode and, after suffering repeated auras, the doctor had determined that stress was likely short-circuiting the parts of her brain controlling visual and spatial perception. He had diagnosed her with Alice in Wonderland Syndrome, a disorder so rare that most people had never heard of it, much less believed that people afflicted with it were otherwise normal.

Brynja clenched her jaw and looked toward the office door. It wouldn't do for one of her colleagues at the biotech company to come in and find her disoriented, rubbing her face in a darkened corner of her office. A geneticist was expected to be a rational, analytical, unflappable scientist.

She pulled off her windbreaker and shook out the waves of her chestnut brown hair. In a small alcove to the rear of the office, she checked herself in the mirror, swept several loose strands of hair away from her sea green eyes, and swirled the rest into a loose bun. Fingering the silver locket that held the last photos of Lúkas and her together, she tucked it beneath the neckline of her silk blouse.

Crossing the room to her desk, she pulled a pair of tortoise-shell glasses from the drawer and adjusted the shiny, brass nameplate: Brynja Pálsdóttir, Director of Forensic Sciences. Just last year, the National Police Commission had made the decision to outsource all DNA forensics to Legacy and she'd been hired to head up the newly created department. She liked her job, her colleagues, the prospect of her future here and couldn't let the auras derail her life.

She sat down and booted up the computer. She took a deep breath, feeling more in control. Her role at Legacy was to oversee DNA analysis on evidence collected from crime scenes and report the findings to the authorities. She pulled up the file for a missing persons case the police were under intense pressure to solve, given that blood spatter had been found in the kitchen of the family's farm.

As Brynja studied the family's pedigree and the lab results, a loud rap on the door startled her. A young woman barely out of her teens and dressed in a tight, fish-leather miniskirt darted into the room, sweeping a fringe of tangerine bangs from her forehead with one hand and juggling an iPad and stack of folders with the other.

"Elly Sørensen?" Brynja said, forcing a smile. She didn't need—or want—an assistant to coordinate her forensics work with the police department, but the station had agreed to an intern-exchange program with the corresponding Danish office in Copenhagen and, apparently, this was the result.

"Yes, ma'am."

"Welcome. I wasn't expecting you quite so early."

"I'm not one to hit the snooze button, ma'am, er, Dr. Pálsdóttir."

"Please. Call me Brynja. Icelanders don't call each other by their last names. That'll probably take some getting used to, but you'll catch on. Even the prime minister is just Ari, not Prime Minister Ketilsson."

Elly nodded and plunked her slight frame down opposite Brynja. "I'm so excited to be here. Where do we get started?" She flipped open the cover of her iPad and promptly dropped the manila folders, spilling their contents clear across the floor. "I'm sorry, I'm so sorry." She knelt down and scrambled to pick up the papers. "There," she said, placing the jumbled stack on Brynja's desk and smiling sheepishly.

This could be a very long summer, Brynja thought.

Elly adjusted her skirt and flipped open the iPad again. "I've already downloaded a bunch of stuff on my way over from the police station." She tapped the screen. "Police Commissioner Skúlason asked me to arrange a meeting with you."

"Ísak," Brynja said.

Elly looked confused.

"You can just call him Ísak," Brynja said. "Police Commissioner Skúlason is a little formal for here."

"*Ja*. Right. Ísak." Elly looked down at the screen. "Ísak wants to go over that case you're working on with Detective Superintendent Henning Holt."

"Just Henning."

Elly shook her head. "I'm going to have to get used to this. Seems disrespectful. Anyway, are you available tomorrow at nine to meet with Ísak and Henning?"

"I am," Brynja said, already feeling uneasy about questioning the detective's handling of the missing persons case. She took a sip of water. "Anything else?"

Elly tapped the iPad and the stack of bangles about her wrist clanked against the screen. "Ísak also asked me to set up the police department with social media. Kind of an outreach thing. Public relations and all. Want me to do that for Legacy, too? My dad's a sergeant with Copenhagen's police department and I helped them get online, so I'm sure I can do the same thing here."

So, that's how Elly got the internship.

Elly scooted around the desk and opened the Facebook app. "See? I made you a forensics page already. It's not live till you give me the thumbs-up, though." She clicked on another icon. "And how's this for Twitter? @PartyintheGenePool? Cute, huh?"

Brynja tilted her head, rubbed the back of her neck, and smiled. "It's catchy, but I'm not sure the higher-ups will sign off on that one." She glanced up at the clock. "Listen, Elly, why don't you go ahead and get settled? There's a desk in the outer office you can use while you're at Legacy. In the meantime, did you meet Gréta? In Human Resources? She's offered to show you around."

Elly nodded. "*Ja.* Yep. She said to knock on her door whenever I've got a moment."

"Great. Gréta's a bit gruff but don't be intimidated. She's a sheep in wolf's clothing. I've got a bit of work to do but we can talk more in an hour or so."

"Shall I leave these files here?" Elly asked, pointing to the jumbled stack of papers and manila folders on Brynja's desk. "Ísak wants me to bring you a copy of the police log every day so you can keep up with what's going on over there."

Brynja nodded, then turned back to the computer and clicked on the circles and squares of the DNA pedigree.

Elly leaned over to look at the computer screen. "What game is that, anyway? Connect the dots?"

Brynja searched for signs that Elly was joking, but from the blank look on her face, she guessed not. Realizing she'd have to get Elly up to speed quickly if she was going to be any help at all, Brynja took a moment to explain what she was doing. "We've got a national database that contains DNA profiles of just about everyone in Iceland. It's not a criminal database like in many countries. It's a database of our collective DNA." She pointed to the monitor. "The family trees and DNA sequences are stored in a software program called GeneID."

"What are all those letters and bars?"

"Those are DNA sequences that allow us to see who's who. Every individual has a unique pattern of DNA sequences. Kind of a human barcode. Like a fingerprint."

"What do you do with it?"

"The police collect whatever evidence they can from a crime scene—bloodied clothing, cigarette butts, chewed gum—and send the samples to us. We analyze the DNA and run the sequences through the GeneID software. With any luck, we can identify the individual that committed the crime. And if the victims are mangled beyond recognition, we can use DNA to identify them as well. Even if we think we know who the victim is, we confirm their identity by DNA fingerprinting. DNA doesn't lie."

"So, after the police collect evidence and send it to Legacy, how do you actually get the DNA?"

"We isolate DNA using a variety of methods depending on what the sample is. Bone, blood, and hair all require different approaches. Pretty much anything will have at least some trace of genetic material. After we isolate the DNA, we analyze the sequence and run the results through the GeneID database. Hopefully, we come up with a match."

Elly smiled broadly. "So, you *do* connect the dots."

Brynja laughed. "In a sense, I guess we do." She paused and looked up at Elly. Maybe this girl would work out just fine. She was asking all the right questions.

Elly swept the bangs from her face and pointed at the pedigree again. "What are all those circles and squares?"

"GeneID also gives us information about how individuals are related. These are family trees, or what we call pedigrees. The circles are female, the squares male. We need to know how closely related people are because sometimes samples are contaminated with DNA from relatives they live with. They might share clothing, or hairbrushes, or any number of items. So, we need to know exactly whom the DNA belongs to."

"Cool."

Brynja nodded. "Anyway, you go ahead and have Gréta show you around." She waved a hand at the files Elly had put on her desk. "And thanks for bringing these over. I'll let you know if I think we should follow up on anything."

"Sure thing."

The metal heels of Elly's harness boots clanked against the polished, concrete floor as she left the room.

Brynja turned to the police log and took a quick look. No major crimes had been reported last night: no homicide, assault, battery, kidnapping, arson, robbery, or rape. No wonder Iceland ranked number one on the Global Peace Index.

But when the midsummer sun didn't set until midnight and the tourists outnumbered Icelanders five to one, the activity log was never a dull read. Last night, a French backpacker had climbed onto an iceberg at Jökulsárlón Glacier Lagoon and been stranded for hours before Iceland Search and Rescue had brought him into the ER with frostbitten feet. A squad of Belgian footballers had staggered out of the Lebowski Bar at three a.m. and banged on every door up and down the street until one of them recognized their hostel. And an American couple had ignored the warning signs at Geysir and suffered third degree burns while taking a selfie, apparently not realizing that steam and scalding water could erupt at any moment.

Elly poked her head through the door. "Dr. Pálsdóttir? Sorry. Brynja? I forgot to give you this." Elly waved a paper scroll overhead as if conducting some invisible choir. "Here," she said, plunking the paper baton down on top of the police log.

Brynja's eyes widened. She looked up at Elly and then down again at the scroll.

It was tied with the same type of ribbon she had worn in her hair as a child. The same type of red, velvet ribbon her mother had cross-stitched tiny, white flowers onto before going completely mad and abandoning all pretense of caring for her children. The same kind of ribbon Brynja had pulled from her braid so her brother could wave to her as she rode the carousel on the day he disappeared.

Chapter 2

Out of habit, Brynja pulled a pair of latex gloves from the drawer; she never touched any unfamiliar object with her bare hands. DNA analysis was so sophisticated these days that even picograms could be detected and she couldn't risk contamination with her own DNA.

She reached for the scroll, but misjudged the distance and her hand landed on the empty space in front of it. She glanced up. Had Elly noticed?

She reached for the scroll again, managed to grasp the edge of the paper, and pulled it toward her.

Her hands shook as she picked at the tight knot in the red ribbon. She unfurled the paper and stared at the drawing and inscription. A stem of black leaves crept up the edges of the page, framing a handwritten poem in bright, red ink. She pushed the glasses up the bridge of her nose and squinted to read the words.

Upon the madder mead
Where the sagas planted seed
Arose the Book of Möðruvellir.
Tear the wheat from the chaff
And you will find your other half
In the ink of Gloom's root cellar.

Brynja jerked her head toward Elly. "Who gave this to you?"

"The detective—Henning. He said it was delivered to the police station by mistake."

"Who sent it?"

"Henning didn't know, so I asked the mail clerk. He said it was in a package that came addressed to you and that he opened it like he's supposed to open all packages but couldn't remember exactly where it was mailed from. He was sure it was posted from a foreign country. Said he'd look at his stamp collection—he keeps all the unusual ones." Elly cracked her fingers. "I've never really gotten why people collect stamps."

Brynja had stopped listening. She stared straight through her intern then looked down at the poem again.

And you will find your other half . . .

In a daze, Brynja reached for the locket about her neck and clutched the silver heart.

Her other half. Her twin. Lúkas.

She walked to the window, put her hands to the cold glass, and scanned the horizon. The wind had kicked up, roiling the deep blue waters of Faxaflói bay.

Brynja turned abruptly and marched back to her desk. "Elly, I'm going to need you to contact Ari Ketilsson over at Parliament."

"The prime minister?"

"That's right."

"Really? The prime minister will take a call from me?"

Brynja nodded. "Tell his secretary Fríða you're working in my office."

"You actually know the prime minister?" Elly brought her right hand to her left and began wringing the bangles on her wrist. "I can't believe it. That is so cool."

"It's a small country," Brynja said, looking down at the desk to hide the flush in her cheeks.

She hadn't told anyone, including her own father, that she and Ari were engaged. Pabbi hadn't even wanted her to date Ari; a thirty-eight-year-old suitor just wouldn't do for his daughter, even if he was a lawyer, history professor and, now, prime minister. Brynja was just as glad to keep the relationship secret if doing so warded off the hostility of people who might think Ari had influenced Legacy to hire her.

She looked squarely at Elly. "Call the front desk at Parliament. They'll connect you directly with the prime minister's office."

"Okay. Sure thing. Will do. Let me see if I have the number." Elly scrolled through the contact list on the iPad. "What do I tell Ari?" She shook her head. "That sounds so weird to me. We'd never call the prime minister of Denmark by his first name." She swept the bangs from her forehead. "Anyway, what do you want me to ask him?"

"See which manuscripts he's planning on displaying for the exhibit at Parliament." Brynja tried her best to sound matter-of-fact, but her heart was beating fast. Somehow, in some way that she didn't yet understand, the poem was saying that her other half—Lúkas—could be found in the pages of the *Book of Möðruvellir*, the medieval manuscript that was the heart of Iceland's past.

"Manuscripts?" Elly looked confused. "What do you mean manuscripts?" Her face brightened. "Oh, wait a minute, I get it. You mean like binders on crimes you've solved. Or maybe cold cases?" She bobbed her head. "But why would you let the public in on the evidence?"

"No, Elly. They're not police binders. Nothing to do with cold cases. I'm talking about ancient manuscripts handwritten by monks nearly a thousand years ago. They're the closest things we have to a national treasure."

"That's pretty cool."

"The prime minister arranged to put some of them on display for National Day and I just want to know if the exhibit includes the *Book of Möðruvellir*."

"The book of what?"

"It's a mouthful. The *Book of Möðruvellir*. The *Möðruvallabók*. The most complete collection of the Icelandic family sagas. You *do* know what the sagas are, right?"

"Sure, I do. *Saga*. It's a space opera fantasy comic book series. Brian K. Vaughan. *Star Wars* meets *Game of Thrones*. Love it!" Elly grinned, clearly teasing.

Brynja shook her head. "Got me."

"Seriously," Elly said. "You mean the stories of when the Vikings settled here."

"That's right. *Saga* is the Icelandic word for story. They're really quite dramatic—epic tales based on actual historical events. Family feuds, love affairs, poetry, justice, tragedy—the Icelandic sagas have it all."

"I don't actually know much about them," Elly said, "being raised in Denmark and all."

"The manuscripts are Iceland's most valued possession," Brynja said. "More than that, they're masterpieces of world literature. Back in the 1600s, when Iceland was a Danish protectorate, Nordic antiquities were all the rage in Europe. Denmark scoured our country for all the medieval manuscripts they could find and then brought them to Copenhagen. They only returned the books in the nineteen-seventies. There was huge controversy over whether Denmark or Iceland owned the manuscripts and the debate over whether to return them to Iceland or keep them in Denmark stirred up some pretty heated protests on both sides."

"Didn't know that," Elly said. "Before my time, I guess, but I'm on it, Brynja. I'll call over to Parliament right away and find out which manuscripts will be at the exhibit."

She started toward the outer office, and then turned back. "What was it called again? The *Möðru—Möðru...*"

"The *Möðruvallabók.* Mooth-ru-valda-book."

When Elly left the room, Brynja turned back to the computer and opened the online Icelandic Saga Database, sagadb.org. Although she remembered reading many of the sagas in school, the poem Elly had handed her didn't seem familiar. She entered the site, clicked on 'Search,' and typed in the words from the scroll, hoping to find some clue as to the origin of the poem. After scanning through all thirteen sagas found in the *Möðruvallabók,* she leaned back in her chair. Nothing.

"Brynja?" Elly was standing in the doorway. "The prime minister says the *Möðruvallabók* is slated to be at the exhibit." She broke into a small, delighted smile. "And he'll see you tonight."

As difficult as it was, Brynja forced herself to focus. She had work to do. She would tell Ari about the poem tonight. She would also call Pabbi and Jónas to see if they could make any sense of it. Pushing aside the familiar pang of guilt that knocked deep inside her whenever her thoughts drifted to her family, she slid the poem into a clear, plastic evidence file and put it in her tote. She turned back to her computer and the missing persons case.

Several days ago, the police had received a call from a frightened, young girl at a farm near Selfoss. An argument between her parents had escalated to physical blows and she hadn't seen her mother, Inga Grímsdóttir, since. Inga's husband insisted his wife had fled to her parents up north, but Inga hadn't been heard from in days and the young girl was sure something had happened to her mother; she never would have left her daughter behind.

Henning had gone out to the farm and noted blood spatter on the kitchen cabinets. Following procedure, he had collected the blood samples and sent them to Brynja at Legacy for analysis.

Brynja clicked on Inga's file and studied the family's pedigree. Inga, her husband, their daughter, and two cousins that lived in the home had banked their DNA in Legacy's database. The pattern of DNA fragments extracted from the blood samples did indeed match Inga's, but Henning seemed to accept the husband's claim that Inga had simply cut herself with a kitchen knife. Brynja wasn't at all sure: the woman was missing, she'd had a fight with her husband, and her blood had been found on cabinets far from where she'd been carving a lamb shank.

Brynja shook her head. Rather than being strictly objective, Henning was too often swayed by those that carried a Y chromosome.

As if on cue, a cloud of smoke blew into the office and Henning stood in the doorway, a cane hooked over his arm. The detective's eyes flashed beneath a shiny helmet of nut-brown hair gelled firmly into place.

"Here," he said, plunking a specimen bag down on her desk. "We found the kitchen knife Inga was using stashed below the sink." He took a swig from his coffee mug and extinguished the cigarette in the remaining dregs. "Ísak tells me we've got a meeting tomorrow at nine. Would've been nice if you'd let me know about it."

Brynja suppressed the urge to fire back. Six months ago, with budget cuts looming in the public sector and the police outsourcing DNA forensics to Legacy, Henning had hoped for a career change. He had applied to head the effort at Legacy, but the job had gone to Brynja. With her medical degree and training in forensic genetics, she was clearly more qualified. Nonetheless, Henning was bitter the position had gone to someone nearly thirty years his junior. And a woman at that. It was no secret he'd rather have seen her fall through thin ice than crack the glass ceiling.

Brynja took a breath. She had to stay calm to avoid triggering another aura; any sign of illness would only give him an opportunity to undermine her.

"I just learned about the meeting myself," she said, motioning to Elly, who was standing in the doorway, bouncing on her toes like a marionette on strings. "You've met Elly Sørensen? She's an intern here for the summer. I'm sure she'll be able to keep us up to date with joint meetings going forward."

With an all-too-obvious look of disdain, Henning took in Elly's choice of clothing. "Yes, we've met. Next time be sure to ask me first. I'm a busy man." He thumbed the suspenders that held up police-issued trousers too large for his slight frame.

The color rose in Elly's cheeks. "Sorry, sir."

He turned to leave.

Brynja called after him. "Henning?"

He stopped. Kept his back to her, turning his head just enough to indicate he was listening.

"You know there's no smoking here," Brynja said. "And I'll be over ten minutes early tomorrow morning. Eight-fifty. We need to go over your report on the Inga Grímsdóttir case."

He left without a word.

Chapter 3

Across the street from Ari's apartment, the bells of Domkirkjan Cathedral struck six on Tuesday morning. Brynja was already wide-awake, having spent much of the last five hours staring down the white night of Midsummer, picking apart the clues in the poem she had received the day before.

Beside her lay Ari. She was tempted to burrow into his bare chest and lose herself once again in the heat of his embrace. She knew she should have told him about the poem last night, but something kept her from confiding in him. She told herself it was because Ari was busy preparing for National Day and he shouldn't be bothered at the moment. But, in truth, she was worried that he'd think her too obsessed with the past. She had followed false leads before, and, each time, come to a dead end.

Sitting up in the platform bed, she looked around the modern apartment Ari had settled into when he was appointed prime minister two years ago. The studio space was small, furnished only with a brushed, stainless-steel dining set and two sleek, wishbone chairs. Ari needed the warmth of people, not things.

They were different in so many ways. She liked people, yes, but could only get so close. Ari needed a crowd to recharge his battery; she needed solitude. Brynja could count on the fingers of one hand the people she allowed into her world: Ari, her fiancé; Pabbi, her father; Jónas, the man who had basically raised her and Lúkas; and Stína, her childhood friend. Of course, if her brother Lúkas were alive, he would make the fifth, and her hand would be complete.

Perhaps if Lúkas hadn't been torn from her as a child, she would have learned to trust in others. But, deep down, Brynja knew that love could be ripped from your heart in the time it took a carousel to grind to a halt. Even her own mother had abandoned her, committing suicide by swallowing an entire bottle of antipsychotics a few months after Lúkas disappeared.

She peeled herself out of bed and tiptoed over to pick up the clothes Ari had stripped from her just hours before. She slipped into her bikini briefs and camisole, wrapped herself in Ari's bathrobe, and sat down at the kitchen table. A bowl of green apples sat next to a plate of cinnamon rolls; Ari had baked them gluten-free, knowing she loved the pastries but couldn't eat them at coffee shops because of her allergy.

Brynja took a bite from one of the rolls and reached into her tote for the poem, wondering why it had been delivered to the police station instead of to her office at Legacy Genetics. She'd called the mail clerk, Baltasar, to inquire about the stamp but had been told he was away on vacation. When she had asked the temp about dates, she had learned that Baltasar had received the package a week ago and given the scroll to Henning, knowing that the detective collaborated with her on forensics. Apparently, Henning had been in no rush to pass it on to her; days had passed before he thought to have Elly bring it over to Legacy.

Brynja put the poem on the table and pondered the meaning of the words.

Did the poet know where Lúkas actually was? Or did they mean that she could discover what had happened to him?

You will find your other half....

She had long questioned whether Lúkas was alive, yet she still continued to search tirelessly for him. Had he wandered off, fallen into the icy waters of the fjord? Had he been kidnapped? Had he been killed, his body dumped somewhere in the remote highlands? Brynja had searched through every public record—births, marriages, deaths—looking for any mention of his name. She had scrutinized missing persons reports, records of passports and drivers' licenses, enrollment lists of schools and colleges. Nothing. Five years ago, the bones of a small child had been found buried behind an abandoned sheep shed, and she'd followed the news closely. But DNA analysis had revealed the child to be a girl, a diploid for genes on the X chromosome.

She looked back down at the poem. *You will find your other half...in the ink of Gloom's root cellar.* She shuddered. Did that mean that Lúkas was dead? Buried in a root cellar somewhere?

"Brynja?" Ari mumbled, turning over in bed. "What's that you're looking at?"

"Oh, nothing, really." She stood quickly and moved to the kitchen area to make a pot of coffee. "Just some lab results. Go back to sleep, *elskan.*"

Ari sat up and ran his hands through the tousled strands of his toffee brown hair. He reached for his glasses on the nightstand and gave her his trademark cockeyed grin. "Well, I have to say, Brynja, there aren't many people who would look straight into the prime minister's eyes and tell such a bold-faced lie."

She pulled two cups from the shelf. "Want some coffee?"

"Come here, gorgeous." Ari patted the empty space beside him.

Something inside melted. She put the poem on the nightstand, slipped off the bathrobe, and climbed back into bed.

Ari pulled her close and wrapped his arms around her. "Tell me, what's up? Are the forensic lab reports written in cursive script now? With pretty little doodles of leaves on the borders?"

"I'm sorry. I should have told you earlier," Brynja said, stroking his chest. It seemed she couldn't help but keep her distance. "It's a poem someone delivered to the police station by mistake. My new intern brought it over to Legacy yesterday."

Ari ran his finger down the smooth skin of her breasts. "Aha! Should I be jealous? *How do I love thee? Let me count the ways. I love thee to the depth and breadth—*"

She stifled a laugh. "It's not that kind of poem."

"Oh." Ari pretended to pout. "That's no fun. Read it to me, then, would you?"

Brynja slipped out of bed, walked to the table, and returned with the poem. She read the words to Ari.

> *Upon the madder mead*
> *Where the sagas planted seed*
> *Arose the Book of Möðruvellir.*
> *Tear the wheat from the chaff*
> *And you will find your other half*
> *In the ink of Gloom's root cellar.*

Ari was silent for a moment. "Bizarre. Is that why you had the intern call to ask which manuscripts would be at the exhibit? Because you wanted to know if the *Book of Möðruvellir* would be on display?"

Brynja rested the poem in her lap, looked at Ari, and nodded.

"All right then." He sat up. "Let's think. First of all, isn't your family from Möðruvellir?"

"Yes. Well, close by. I grew up on a farm south of Möðruvellir. In the Eyjafjörður valley."

"So that's where—"

"Yes. That's where Lúkas disappeared. Just down the hill from our house at Munkathverá."

"Your other half."

She nodded again.

"Does your father know about the poem? Maybe he'd have some idea what it all means."

Brynja bit her lip. "I must have called the house ten times yesterday before I finally got an answer. Pabbi was asleep but I read the poem to Jónas and made sure he wrote down every word."

"What did he think?"

"Same as me. That it's strange but definitely worth trying to figure out what it means. I told him I'd be up soon for a visit and we can talk about it then."

Ari brushed a lock of hair from her forehead. "Any idea who sent the poem?"

"No clue."

"Well, someone at the police station must know. It didn't just appear out of thin air."

Brynja shook her head. "No one knows. The mail clerk who received it is away. I can't reach him." Her voice trembled with frustration. "Why would someone send me such a strange poem? Why not just tell me what happened to Lúkas? They obviously know."

The gold in Ari's hazel eyes darkened with concern. "If he's out there, we'll find him. I'll have the editor at *Morgunblaðið* publish the poem. Maybe someone will come forward."

"Oh, God, no." The last thing Brynja wanted was the public reading about her life in the morning paper. "I mean, thanks, but no. I lost Lúkas; I'll find him."

"You can't keep blaming yourself, Brynja. You were only seven years old." Ari kissed her gently on the forehead. "I still can't believe your father let you two go to the carnival alone."

"He didn't. Pabbi thought we were too young and told us we couldn't. So, I asked Jónas. Of course, I left out the little detail that Pabbi had said no. Jónas said we could go to the carnival but made us promise that we'd watch out for each other." She lowered her head and spoke softly. "I didn't watch out for Lúkas. I left him alone while I rode the carousel. It's all my fault—don't you get it?"

Ari took a moment to adjust the pillow behind him.

"I'm sorry," Brynja said.

He lifted her chin and kissed her warmly on the lips. "You've got to find a way to forgive yourself."

They lay against the headboard in silence for a while.

"Ever feel like we're being watched?" Brynja asked, gesturing at the galaxy of eyes peering out from the signed movie posters lining the walls of Ari's studio. There were scavengers and extraterrestrial invaders descending into the post-apocalyptic world in *Oblivion*, alien intelligence creating a wormhole in *Interstellar*, and humanoid aliens from *Prometheus* swallowing dark liquid and disintegrating into the crash of waterfalls.

"Hey, they're some of my best friends." He laughed. "But, seriously, it's good for the economy. Iceland's the new Hollywood."

Brynja kissed him. "I need some air. I'm going out for a walk before work."

"I'll come with you," Ari said, rising out of bed.

Admiring his backside as he walked to the closet, Brynja considered pulling him back under the covers. She and Ari had been together for six months now, ever since Ísak had introduced them at a benefit concert. Each time she and Ari made love, it felt like the first time. He made her feel like she was the only woman on earth. He'd been burned many times before by women flaunting the status of dating the prime minister or seeking political favors, but in Brynja, he'd found a soulmate; she was a strong, independent woman who wouldn't add to the list of titillating scandals that had landed him in the tabloids more than once.

A minute later, he stood at the bedside, dressed in a leather, flight jacket over a linen, V-neck tee and slim-fit jeans. "Here, you'll need this."

He tossed an oversized, Icelandic wool sweater onto the bed. "It's too cold outside for that blouse and tight skirt you wore yesterday. I've got hundreds of these sweaters. Every member of Parliament thinks it's the perfect gift when Christmas rolls around. And my sister left these." He held up a pair of worn, black sweatpants. "Don't worry," he said, noticing her reluctance. "You'll look gorgeous. You always do."

"All right," Brynja said, managing a faint smile. "But I hope we don't run into anyone we know."

Brynja and Ari stepped out of the apartment and walked the few steps to Austurvöllur Square. She loved the defined space of the public garden, its emerald green grass bordered by the charcoal gray basalt of Parliament House and the elegant, ivory façade of the Hotel Borg.

The fresh air lifted, and she locked arms with Ari. He could easily be mistaken for one of the leading men in the films he so admired: hair glossy as a thoroughbred's coat, sparkling eyes, and a smile that melted snow from the mountaintops.

A voice called out from across the square and a Norse goddess straight out of Valhalla descended on them. She reached for Ari's hand, her cornflower blue eyes dancing as they touched.

"*Góðan daginn.*" The woman's cherry-tinted lips looked ripe in the early morning light. "Remember me?"

Ari beamed. "Of course, I do." He kissed her on the cheek.

Brynja reined in the oversized sweater with one hand and extended the other to shake hands. "I'm Brynja Pálsdóttir. I don't believe we've met."

"Ásta."

Brynja took in the beauty's lush, blonde hair, spike-heeled boots, and sleek, fitted coat, opened just enough to reveal Rubenesque breasts that almost spilled out over her low-cut, silk blouse.

"Ásta...?"

"Just Ásta." The goddess turned back to Ari. "I want to thank you for everything you've done. Allowing us to film on the glacier."

"Absolutely." Ari looked up at the gathering clouds. "Hope the weather holds for you, though. What are you shooting today?"

"The sequel to *Thor: God of Thunder*. I'm the Asgard goddess Sif." Ásta peeked up through thick eyelashes. "Thor's lover."

"Got a minute to walk with us?" Ari said. "We're just wandering."

Ásta motioned to a van parked outside Hotel Borg. "I can't. We're leaving soon for Skaftafell." She looked back at Ari. "We're filming a documentary in town tomorrow. Maybe we could grab a bite then?"

Ari turned to Brynja.

"I think you've got a dinner with the Nordic Council," Brynja said.

It wasn't a total lie. Ari did have a dinner. But she was pretty sure it was *next* weekend.

"What's the documentary about?" Brynja asked.

"Genetic privacy." Ásta lifted her chin, a touch of defiance. "Everyone seems to think Iceland is some sort of genetic jackpot they can mine for their own purposes."

Brynja forced a polite smile.

"I've been asked by RÚV News to do the film as a public service," Ásta added. "I'm happy to. The company that's collecting DNA on Icelanders supposedly for the greater good...ha! Doesn't fool me; it's for their own good. They don't have any qualms about making a profit by using us like guinea pigs."

Brynja's smile tightened. Ásta was talking about her company, Legacy Genetics. In addition to their forensic work, Legacy had developed a software program, LinX, to track DNA mutations in families and link that genetic data to medical records. They had been able to identify several genes that cause disease and were hoping to profit by selling the information to pharmaceutical companies.

Brynja couldn't help coming to Legacy's defense. "They're actually doing a lot of good. Knowing what genes underlie disease will lead to treatments and alleviate a lot of suffering. Iceland is the perfect place to do these studies. We're such a small country and everyone's related—"

"But whose DNA is it, anyway? My DNA doesn't belong to Iceland. It belongs to me. I wish I'd never donated my DNA."

"I see," Brynja said.

Ásta batted her eyes at Ari before turning back to Brynja. "Do you work for them? That company? My uncle does." Her voice trailed off. "Our family has a genetic disease and I definitely don't want the whole world knowing about it."

The sky blackened and a gusty wind blew over the square.

"They can't publicize your name—" Brynja began.

"They don't have to. Anyone can figure it out from the database. If one person in the family has the mutation, we're all suspect. Guilt by association. Our family line goes all the way back to one of the Viking settlers here, so they've got plenty of data on our family tree." Ásta rattled on, the words tumbling out of her. "Apparently that guy had a bone disease that also affected some of his relatives. People now think it was Paget's disease. Since he's my ancestor, anyone can figure out I might have the gene, too. Legacy could prove it by poking around in my DNA. If I've got Paget's, my bones will continue to grow and grow until I turn into a lumpy, gruesome mess."

Brynja studied the goddess's beautifully structured face, with its high cheekbones and ivory skin.

"It's *my* DNA. Nobody else's business," Ásta said, putting her hands on the curve of her hips. "I'm going to have that database shut down if it's the last thing I do."

Ari reached for Ásta's arm. "I don't believe you have anything to worry about. Legacy's disease database is secure; not even the police can access the files without a warrant since it contains private health information."

Ásta made an effort to restore a congenial facade before leaning toward Ari. "I've got to run. Call me later?"

Brynja scowled. Call me later? Who did this woman think she was?

With a final glance at Ari, Ásta ran off, hopscotching over the cobblestones in her impossible heels.

Chapter 4

It wasn't long before the black clouds made good on their threat and the deluge brought an end to their walk. Taking leave of Ari and bracing against the pelting rain, Brynja hurried from Austurvöllur Square to her office. She'd rather think about work than the unsettling experience of bumping into Ásta. She took refuge in logic, in the analytics of solving a crime. And something about the missing persons case just didn't sit right.

Why was Inga's blood found on the cabinets on the far side of the kitchen?

After peeling off Ari's rain-soaked sweater and brushing out her hair, she changed into one of the blouses and skirts she had hanging in the alcove. She sat down at her desk and scrolled to an article from Legacy's website: *DNA and RNA Markers for Forensic Identification.* This was one of several updates Legacy posted about their research and its applications in order to ease public concern about the use of their DNA. Although a complicated topic, the article on forensics was written for the general public and gave an introduction to genetics in terms of a common cooking metaphor:

DNA to RNA to Protein

Suppose you want to concoct a Viking feast and decide to make *Hákarl*—cubes of fermented shark—in the traditional way. The only original recipe you find is in the book *Viking Cookery,* located in the Reykjavik City Library. In this metaphor, the library building represents the nucleus of a cell, the books contained within the library represent the genome (all the genes in a cell), and the recipe represents the DNA instructions from one particular gene to make one specific protein... in this case, *Hákarl.*

DNA (recipe)

Gut and behead a Greenland shark and place in a shallow hole dug in sand at the tideline. The shark cannot be eaten fresh because of toxic levels of urea in the meat. Cover the shark with sand and gravel, and place stones on top to force the fluids out. Ferment for 6-12 weeks. Dig up the meat, cut into strips, and hang to dry.

RNA (copy of recipe)

Fine. Now you know how to make *Hákarl.* However, the librarian will not allow you to check out *Viking Cookery* since it is the only copy and for reference use only. The DNA—the gene—must stay in the nucleus of the cell. She does, however, allow you to make a copy of the recipe to take home with you. This copy is the RNA in our metaphor. You read the recipe (DNA), make a copy of it (RNA), and take it out of the library (nucleus) to your home (the cell's cytoplasm), where the real work can be done to make *Hákarl*.

Protein (*Hákarl*)

The final step is to make the *Hákarl*. The fermented shark protein is assembled by translating the instructions on the messenger RNA (nucleotides) into amino acids (protein). Cut into cubes and serve at room temperature.

Bon appétit!

Brynja wondered why the authors had used such an unappetizing metaphor. No one ate fermented shark any longer. No one, that was, except for tourists eager to prove just how adventurous they were. She had to admit, however, the metaphor did get the point across. It relayed the central dogma of genetics: DNA to RNA to protein.

She scrolled through the article, skipping the section on DNA forensics, which she knew inside and out. DNA was pretty straightforward. Analyze the sequence and lengths of DNA fragments, match the pattern to someone in the GeneID database, *et voilà*, you had your individual, which in a crime could mean your culprit or victim.

But RNA was another matter. *These things are never simple*, Brynja thought. RNA forensics couldn't tell you *who* the culprit or victim was, but only what part of the body a blood or tissue sample came from.

"Yes. Fine job."

Brynja appreciated the comment. Ísak had been a member of the highly trained counter terrorism unit Viking Squad before taking on the role of police commissioner for Greater Reykjavik. His direct manner left little room for praise, but he always seemed to have a kind word or two for her.

"Thank you. Henning did an excellent job collecting the evidence—"

"Just following protocol," the detective said, turning from the window. "I spoke with Inga's husband. He says she's not the tidiest cook and that after preparing the lamb shanks and cutting herself with the knife in the process, she didn't wash her hands before opening the cabinet for a roasting pan. He's assured me Inga's up north visiting her parents' farm."

Ísak ran his fingers over his bald scalp. "Have you been able to reach her?

Henning shook his head. "Apparently they don't have a landline. But the husband said he spoke to her via cell just yesterday."

"Did you check the phone records? Verify the call?"

Henning stiffened. "Not yet."

"And Inga's parents live where up north?" Ísak stood to examine the laminated map of Iceland behind his desk.

"I—I'm not sure precisely. Somewhere outside of Húsavik."

Brynja wondered whether Henning was so embittered by being passed over for the job at Legacy that he was losing a grip on his ability to pursue a proper investigation.

Ísak picked up a black marker. "Call the station up in Húsavik," he said, circling the area on the map. "Get an officer out to the farm immediately. And bring the husband into the station. The blood is Inga's. That we know. But did she cut her hand? Or was foul play involved? We need answers. Now."

Brynja stepped forward. "I've had an idea."

After explaining the potential of RNA forensics to determine whether Inga had cut her hand or whether she'd been the victim of a crime, Brynja returned to Legacy. She spent the remainder of the morning reviewing results from a paternity case. A cleaning woman had demanded child support from her boyfriend, insisting he was the father of her newborn baby. DNA analysis revealed otherwise. After filing the report, Brynja met with Stefán, the lead laboratory technician, to discuss microRNA techniques. She directed him to rerun Inga's blood samples and analyze the RNA in order to determine just where in the body the blood had come from.

Between the recurrence of her auras and the cryptic poem she received yesterday, the past twenty-four hours had left Brynja shaken. She decided to work the rest of the day from home where she could read over the lab results from her only remaining case—a residential burglary in Seltjarnarnes —in solitude. She left the office and walked to the renovated carriage house she shared with her friend Stína Finnsdóttir. The small cottage sat on the grounds of one of Reykjavik's hilltop estates and, even though it was only three blocks from downtown, provided a peaceful refuge from the city.

She fumbled for her keys and unlocked the door. Inside, she kicked off her heels and called out to Stína.

Only the cat answered back.

Brynja tossed her tote onto the entry table, knocking over the framed photo of a pair of nesting puffins. She propped it back up and remembered Stína's plans. She'd left early to guide a group of German photographers intent on filming the circus of puffins on the Westman Islands.

Minutes later, Brynja sat down with a cup of hot cocoa at the small kitchen table and gazed out of the crown-glass windows onto Tjörnin Pond. A bank of gray clouds rolled across the sky and an easterly wind scattered the flocks of waterfowl that nested there each summer.

Brynja reached for the binoculars that hung on the wall and brought a pair of Arctic terns into view. She enjoyed watching them. The terns migrated all the way from Antarctica to Iceland—the longest distance traveled by any creature on earth—to breed with their mates and nurture their young.

Her thoughts drifted back to the square and the awkward meeting with Ásta. She forced herself to admit that Ásta had done the fawning, and Ari had been no more than courteous. He was naturally warm and outgoing, but that didn't mean he was unfaithful.

Brynja finished the last of the cocoa, grabbed her laptop from her tote, and climbed the ladder to her attic room. She flopped down on the antique sleigh bed and stared up at the low, wooden beams beneath the pitched roof.

She was reaching for her cell to call Pabbi and Jónas when the front door slammed.

"Brynja? You here?" Stína's voice boomed up from the floor below. "Tour was cancelled. Seas are too rough. I'm coming up, ready or not."

Brynja burrowed beneath the covers, hoping Stína would think she was sleeping. She wanted to be left alone. If Stína saw her face, she would know in an instant that something was wrong, and the last thing Brynja wanted to do at the moment was talk about Ari.

"Up and at 'em, girl," Stína said, reaching the loft and pulling the duvet off Brynja's head. "Carpe diem."

Brynja opened one eye to find her friend, all of five-foot-two and a hundred pounds, hovering over her. Stína reminded her of the black and white barnacle geese that swept through Iceland each fall; her dark eyes flickered beneath a feathered fringe of jet-black hair, and although Stína spent most of her days photographing in the outdoors, her skin was white as the Arctic winter.

"Rise and shine, girl," Stína said. "Early bird catches the worm."

"I'm not hungry," Brynja mumbled. "And it's one o'clock."

Stína studied her friend's face. "What's wrong?"

Try as she might, Brynja just couldn't hide her feelings from Stína. They had grown up together, living on adjacent farms, and no one knew her better than Stína did. On top of that, Stína had more empathy than most people, having been left behind at four years old with her grandmother after her parents divorced; her mother had taken off with a shipping magnate and her father had packed his bags for Denmark to pursue his dreams of singing for the national opera.

As children, Brynja and Stína had both suffered the loss of family, although they had dealt with it in different ways. Brynja lived with the oppressive weight of 'what-if,' the constant worry about what could go wrong, what might happen in the future. Stína was spontaneous; she relished the present and, although she could be a bit flippant at times, she had an irresistible, easy-going, so-what attitude. Life was unpredictable and, damn-it, meant to be *lived*.

Brynja looked her friend in the eye. "Ari and I were out on Austurvöllur Square this morning. We ran into a beautiful actress, Ásta—"

Stína cut her short. "Oh jeez, 'nough said. She's a pain in the ass, that Ásta. A real prima donna." She looked closely at Brynja. "Don't tell me you're jealous? Your eyes are greener than ever."

Brynja ignored the comment. "How do you know Ásta?"

"I met her yesterday. She came waltzing into our office demanding that we arrange a photoshoot for her. She wanted some stills for a documentary she's working on. Of course, all the guys dropped everything for her." Stína laughed. "Including their pants."

Brynja shot her an icy look.

"Sorry. Not funny." Stína went over to the closet. "Brynja, you've gotta know Ari loves you. You just need to trust him." She pulled a cotton tunic and jeans off the shelf. "Look, you can't bury your head in the sand all day. We're getting out of town. I'm going up to Akureyri and you're

36

coming with me. You'll visit your Pabbi and Jónas. I'll stay at my grandma's. I've already called Amma to say we're coming."

Stína tossed the clothes onto the bed and her eyes narrowed into the *I-won't-take-no-for-an-answer* stare that Brynja knew all too well. On the playground, at school—as far back as she could remember—Stína always got her way.

Stína kicked a pair of shoes toward her. "Road trip!"

"Stína, it's Tuesday. I can't just take off."

"It's just for the night. We can leave at the crack of dawn tomorrow and you'll be back at work before anyone even knows you're gone. Bring your laptop and cell. C'mon. Please?"

Maybe Stína's plan wasn't such a bad one, Brynja thought. The farm belonging to the parents of Inga Grímsdottír was in Hùsavik, not far from her father's. She could ask Ísak for permission to accompany the officer out to their farm. Perhaps she'd be able to determine the timeline of Inga's movements over the past few days.

And she would have a chance to discuss the poem with Pabbi and Jónas.

Chapter 5

After phoning the office and instructing Elly to call with any urgent matters, Brynja was speeding north along the Ring Road with Stína at the wheel. Just outside Reykjavik, a bank of low, gray clouds hovered over vast, craggy fields of black lava, broken only by patches of green clinging for life among the sharp crevasses. Living in the city, Brynja could easily forget what a harsh land this was: a land of extremes, born of fire and ice. Not everyone survived the elements here. Many had gone down in the cold, dark sea, and others had been caught in fast-moving blizzards and frozen to death upon the moors.

Some, like Lúkas, had simply disappeared.

Brynja flipped through the radio stations, searching for the soothing sounds of Sigur Rós or Tonik Ensemble. Stína rattled on about the ducks she was eager to photograph up at Lake Mývatn. Three male mandarins with their red beaks, iridescent, green stripes, and feathered, orange whiskers had recently been spotted among the harlequins and ring-necks at the volcanic lake.

Brynja's eyes grew heavy. Lulled by the rumble of Stína's jeep, she tucked a cashmere throw under her head and fell asleep.

Hours later, Stína shook her awake.

Brynja sat up and rubbed her eyes, glancing at her watch. "I'm sorry. I can't believe I slept that long."

"No worries," Stína said. "You were mumbling in your sleep, though. Something about planting seed and tearing wheat." She nudged Brynja with her elbow. "What's that all about? You going into farming now? Had enough of all that genetics stuff?"

"I'm sure I was dreaming." Brynja hesitated before confiding in her friend. "Truth is, I received a weird poem yesterday. Someone mailed it to the police station, but it was addressed to me. I'm pretty sure whoever wrote the poem is trying to help me find Lúkas."

"*What?*" Stína took her eyes off the road and narrowly missed steering them into a ditch. "When did this happen?"

"I should have told you about the poem earlier." Of all the people she knew—apart from Pabbi and Jónas, of course—Stína felt the pain of losing Lúkas just about as much as she did. Stína and Lúkas had been nearly inseparable as children. Boy and Tomboy.

Stína shook her head. "I don't get it. Someone sent a poem to you at the police station? About Lúkas?"

"Yes. Obviously, whoever wrote it doesn't know I'm at Legacy. The mail clerk at the police station gave it to Henning and he had my new intern bring it over."

"Oh."

"What do you mean, oh?"

"I don't want to ruffle your feathers, Brynja, but there's something about Henning I don't trust. Remember your holiday party? Maybe he just had too much to drink but he seemed more interested in impressing women than keeping his detective work confidential. I overheard him bragging that he knew who had kidnapped that little girl out at Gulfoss a couple of years ago."

"Impossible. That case was never solved. We have no idea what happened to her other than she was last seen holding hands with someone in an oversized, green parka."

"Exactly." Stína pulled a bag of licorice from the center console, tore it open with her teeth, and spat out a small piece of loose plastic. "Anyway, who wrote the poem?"

"I don't know. There's no name on it and I can't get hold of the mail clerk to know where it came from."

"What does it say?"

Brynja recited the poem and studied Stína's face.

"Hmm," Stína said, popping a licorice into her mouth. "The *Book of Möðruvellir* is the *Möðruvallabók*, right? I know a guy who works in manuscripts at the Árni Magnússon Institute. Maybe he'll know what to make of it. He owes me big time after our little smash-and-dash last week."

"Smash-and-dash? Did you get into an accident?"

Stína rolled her eyes. "No, it's, you know, shoot-and-scoot, pounce-and-bounce. A one-night stand, my friend. Screw-and-shoo. I'm not sure I remember the guy's name, but I have his phone number."

"You've got to be more careful, Stína."

"Hey, what's good for the goose is good for the gander." Stína slammed on the brakes to avoid a flock of sheep crossing the road. She reached for another licorice. "Kind of weird your poem is written like a riddle. If someone really wanted you to find Lúkas, why would they be so mysterious? Why not just tell you where he is?"

"I don't know—"

"Well, I think it's chicken shit. A hoax. Take that last line, something about a gloomy cellar. What the hell does that mean?"

"It says we can find Lúkas *in the ink of Gloom's root cellar.*"

"Who's Gloom?"

"I have no idea."

"Well, nobody uses a root cellar anymore," Stína said. "Amma had one on the farm before she got a fridge, but that was back in the seventies."

"I don't think Pabbi ever had a root cellar. Not that I can remember, anyway. I'll ask him."

Just before Akureyri, they veered off the Ring Road and took the smaller, two-lane causeway across the fjord. Turning south, they headed toward her father's farm at Munkathverá, past the field where Lúkas had disappeared from the carnival. Brynja turned her gaze away from the window.

Stína pulled up to the rural, turf house. "Say *halló* to your dad," she said, rolling down the window and poking her head out to take a look around. "And Jónas. Tell him I'll come see the greylag geese he was so excited about when I was here a couple weeks ago. Guess they're nesting down by the river. We had some big discussion about how they shed their feathers after breeding and don't fly for a full month. He wants me to take some pictures of them."

"Really? I don't remember him being so interested in birds."

"Remember that old Polaroid camera Jónas gave me when we were little?" Stína said, lifting her Nikon off the seat. "I think that's how I got started." She zoomed in on a meadow pipit perched on the rusty, blue truck to the right of the house. "Doesn't look like Jónas or your dad has bothered to fix that old bucket-of-bolts. The door's practically hanging from the hinges. I'll take a look at it when I stop by later."

"Thanks, Stína. That'd be great. Give Amma my best." Brynja climbed out, glad to be free of the car after the long drive.

She waved goodbye, walked up the path to the front door, and stood for a moment under the layer of sod that shielded the entrance from winter storms. Now that she was here, she couldn't deny the guilt she felt for not having been in contact with her father for almost a month. She had called, but if anyone answered, it was always Jónas on the line, not Pabbi. Her father was constantly busy with chores on the farm. And, of course, being the stubborn ox that he was, Pabbi had refused to call her, saying, last time she'd asked, "Talk doesn't plow the field." When she had suggested he get a computer and set up an email account, his response was: "Much doesn't always long for more. I don't need one of those contraptions."

But deep down, Brynja believed the real reason her father never called lay buried in the memory of Lúkas. Pabbi tried to pretend otherwise, but she knew he had never completely forgiven her for losing sight of her brother.

Brynja blinked back a tear and opened the door. "Pabbi?"

No response. The only sound was the familiar clatter of Jónas's 1930s Royal typewriter echoing through the hallways. Jónas kept meticulous records of the farm's flock of sheep—breedings, births, illnesses, feedings, shearing schedules. When she and Lúkas were born, Jónas had been hired to manage the family farm and had helped raise them. In fact, Brynja often felt as if Jónas were their real father; Pabbi had been too busy taking care of their mother to pay them much attention. Even after Mamma died a few months after Lúkas disappeared, Pabbi continued to rely on Jónas to manage the farm and tend to his daughter. After she'd moved to Reykjavik for medical school, Jónas had agreed to stay on and now it was just he and Pabbi in the old, turf house.

Brynja tiptoed through the living room into the kitchen and patted Jónas's shoulder.

He reeled around and stared at her in disbelief. "Where did you come from?"

"Sorry. I didn't mean to startle you," Brynja said, giving him a gentle peck on top of his head. She noticed for the first time that streaks of gray had crept into his sandy blond hair. "Stína drove me up. Just a short visit, I'm afraid."

Jónas smiled. "I'm happy you're here, but you should have called, *litla mín.*"

She put her hand lightly on his bony shoulder. She loved that he still called her 'my little one,' even though she was in her twenties. He was twice her age, nearing fifty-four. *I suppose I'll always be little to him.* "I called from the road, but I guess you didn't get my message."

Jónas was wearing denim overalls and the *lopapeysa* sweater she had knitted for him years ago. One day, when she was just a child, after a long day shearing Munkathverá's sheep, he had patiently explained to her why Icelandic wool was so special. Over more than a thousand years of exposure to the sub-Arctic climate, the fleece of Icelandic sheep had evolved into a two-layer fiber that produced a kind of parka even Shackleton would envy. The long, glossy, and coarse upper layer, the *tog*, was waterproof, and the shorter, soft wool of the lower layer, the *thel*, provided insulation. Brynja had been captivated by how clever the sheep were, making their own special coats to keep warm in the winter. Even though Jónas's explanation of genes and evolution had been too much for her to understand at the time, Brynja could trace her fascination with genetics back to that day.

"What do you say I knit you another *lopapeysa*? This one's looking a bit threadbare."

"No need, *litla mín.* You're too busy for that now."

Brynja winced. How had she become too busy for Jónas and her father? Both of them were getting older, and they needed her.

"How's Pabbi?" she asked.

"Sleeping."

Brynja shot a quizzical look at the grandfather clock. "Sleeping? Already? It's only seven."

"Your father's napping. Been under the weather a bit, I'm afraid. His fever's down but he's still not himself."

Brynja took off her jacket and hung it on the hook by the entry. She glanced at the framed photos lining the wall, stopping at a faded photograph from 1971. The image captured the throngs of spectators crammed into Reykjavík harbor, watching the Danish coastguard vessel *Vaedderen* deliver the first of Iceland's national treasures, its medieval manuscripts, home from Denmark. Many of the older Icelanders still resented the Danes for rounding up their precious books more than three centuries ago. Even after Iceland had gained its independence from the Danish Crown in 1944, they had refused to return the manuscripts. Finally, after much protest, they had relented, and the books came back to Iceland.

Brynja had never really paid much attention to the photograph before, but now she felt a rush of adrenaline. Had the *Möðruvallabók* been on that ship? Was the poem telling her that Lúkas had been taken away by sea? Her pulse quickened. She hoped Stína would remember to call her smash-and-dash pal at the Magnússon Institute. He was sure to know something about the *Möðruvallabók*'s journey from Iceland to Denmark and back again.

To the right was a photograph of several hundred people cheering and waving Icelandic flags. Someone had scrawled: *Akureyri Botanical Gardens, 1989,* on the bottom. Brynja felt a heavy weight settle in her stomach. 1989. Pabbi and Mamma had been there that day, celebrating the anniversary of the return of the *Möðruvallabók*. Why had they kept that photo on the wall? It was a constant reminder of a celebration that had ended in disaster.

Brynja sat down at the table. "Do you remember that day, Jónas? In 'eighty-nine?"

She covered his hands with hers. Even in June, his hands were cold. They always were. Especially his left hand, missing a thumb and the tips of two fingers. Jónas always complained that the circulation in that hand had never been the same after a sheep-shearing accident he had suffered as a young boy.

"I don't remember it so well, *litla mín*. Nineteen eighty-nine was a long time ago, and my memory's not so good anymore."

Really? How could he not remember that day? True, not everyone had been as affected as her parents had been. An explosion had marked an end to the celebration. Mamma had been thrown to the ground and had lost her unborn child. The police discovered a grenade had been thrown into the crowd, but the perpetrator was never caught. The explosion had put an end to her parents' happy marriage. Even after Brynja and Lúkas arrived the following year, Mamma had spent her days in bed, wracked with fear and paranoia.

Brynja choked with recognition. Only a few hours ago, hadn't she been doing that very thing—wallowing in bed? Annoyed over the encounter with Ásta?

She looked into Jónas's tired eyes. His responsibilities had clearly taken a toll on him.

"I want to talk to you about that poem—the one I left a voice mail about," she said in a soft voice. "Did you listen to it?"

"Yes. I was going to call you but got tied up with everything around here. The poem's very strange. What do you think it means?"

"It seems to say we'll be able to find Lúkas in a root cellar somewhere. Do you think he's dead? Buried in a root cellar? Or maybe he's alive and he's being held somewhere out of sight? I don't understand the meaning exactly but we've got to pursue this."

"Ah, *litla mín*. I don't want to see you get hurt again. We've been disappointed so many times."

"I know but I can't ignore this one. It's definitely some kind of riddle with clues to finding Lúkas. What if the poet really knows where he is?"

Jónas pulled a sheet of paper from his typewriter and put it aside. "Read it to me again."

She reached into her tote and laid the poem on the table.

Jónas looked down. "Why is it in a plastic bag?"

"I'm planning to do some forensic analysis."

"Of course, of course, that's right." Jónas rubbed the stubble on his chin. "Strange the poem mentions the *Möðruvallabók*. Why would that have anything to do with Lúkas?"

"I don't have any idea. But there's a manuscript exhibit scheduled at Parliament on National Day this Saturday. First time the old books have been taken out of the archives in I don't know how long. Everyone's going to get a chance to see the *Möðruvallabók*." Her voice quickened. "Even better, Ari's arranged for a guard to come by my office before taking it over to Parliament. Isn't that great? I don't know what I'm looking for, but the manuscript's got to have something to do with Lúkas's whereabouts. I'm hoping maybe I can find some clue in the actual book."

Jónas's eyes glazed over. Had he heard a word she said?

"I'm sorry." She touched his hand. "I know this is overwhelming. And, as you say, we might be in for another disappointment."

"No, no, I'm fine." Jónas took a deep breath and exhaled slowly. "I just don't understand what the words mean."

Brynja nodded. "Maybe if I read it out loud, something will come to us." She looked toward the staircase. "Let me see if Pabbi is up. Maybe he'll have some ideas."

"Not right now, *litla mín*. He's sleeping. Your father is—"

"Is everything okay?"

"Pabbi—"

"What is it, Jónas? Is something wrong with Pabbi?"

"He hasn't been well the past few days."

A loud crash sounded through the ceiling above.

Brynja looked up. With one last glance at Jónas, she turned and hurtled up the stairs to her father's bedroom.

Brynja found her father lying on mounds of pillows, fitfully tugging on the buttons of his pajama top. He lifted his head and his vacant eyes looked not at her but through her. Matted strands of oily hair stuck to his pale forehead and the corner of his lips glistened with saliva.

Brynja swallowed her shock. "Pabbi! Are you all right?"

An oil lamp lay shattered on the floor, its wick extinguished. She gently pushed aside the larger pieces of the glass shade and approached his bedside. She stroked his arm gently and peered into his eyes.

A faint glimmer of recognition swept across his face. "You're back."

"Yes," she whispered. "It's me, Pabbi."

"It's been so long." His weakened voice rattled from deep within his throat. "Come closer."

She kissed his cheek. "I'm here."

He reached out to her, his withered fingers in a knot. "Where have you been?"

Brynja smiled softly.

He *had* missed her after all.

A tear rolled down his cheek.

"It's okay, Pabbi, it's okay," Brynja whispered.

Slowly, he opened his fist and a small, wooden truck tumbled to the floor.

"Lúkas," he mumbled. "My son. You've come back."

Chapter 6

Early the next morning, the back door slammed shut and Brynja heard the rhythmic stomp of Jónas's boots on the floor mat in the hallway. He was already up, collecting logs from the woodpile. It might be June and light outside, but even in summer, the cold air swept across the fjord and pinched the air inside until a fire was lit.

She pulled the covers up and stared at the ceiling. She was still angry. Why hadn't Jónas called her about Pabbi's illness? Did he not want to worry her?

She slipped out of bed, pulled on a pair of jeans and a fleece, and made her way to the kitchen where the earthy smell of oats simmering in a pot of *hafragrautur* warmed her bones.

She found Jónas in the kitchen, hunched over his typewriter. A large bowl of berries sat in the center of the table. Bilberries. Her favorite. Jónas gathered the ripe berries each fall and froze them so that she would always have a treat whenever she came home. The knot in her gut loosened; it was hard to stay angry with him.

She rested a hand on his shoulder. "*Góðan daginn.*"

Jónas jerked his head back. "I didn't hear you come in, *litla mín.*" He walked to the stove and lifted the lid off the pot. "These oats will take a while longer I'm afraid. Would you like some *skyr* instead?"

"No, I'm fine. I can wait. I'll go check on Pabbi."

She kissed Jónas's cheek and turned to climb the stairs to her father's room. She sat down on the bed and stroked his cheek. The years of sorrow had clearly caught up with him; he was shriveled—dry and frail as an autumn leaf. But this was more than that. At only fifty-six, his mind was not right. He seemed unaware of her presence. Had he suffered a stroke?

She glanced at her watch. She had called the doctor last night and was told he would be in his office at nine. She could call in an hour.

Brynja sat by her father's bedside, quietly reading aloud from his favorite book, *The Poetic Edda.* He loved the stories of Old Norse mythology and had often read the poems to Brynja and Lúkas before bedtime.

A few minutes later, Pabbi sighed as if exhausted, and she left him to sleep.

In the kitchen, Jónas was at his typewriter again and Brynja sensed that he was better off left in peace until breakfast was ready. She saddled up her mare Drífa and headed south along the riverbank toward Amma's farm. Stína wasn't answering her cell and she needed to know what time they'd be driving back down to Reykjavik.

Overhead, the morning sky was laced with delicate threads of polar white. As Brynja rode across the pasture, she breathed in the bloom of buttercups and purple lupines scattered over the rich soil. Every corner of the farm held memories of her early childhood at Munkathverá: the old barn teeming with bleating lambs that she and Lúkas had fed with handfuls of hay in winter; the granary with its bales of barley upon which she and Stína had giggled, gossiped, and dreamt of one day moving to the city; the stone corral awaiting *réttir*, the annual roundup of sheep after their summer spent grazing upon the moors.

Out on the open fields, Brynja's tension gave way to the fluid motion of Drífa's ambling gait. In contrast to the chaos of the past couple days, the farm seemed to breathe a quiet serenity. Not much had changed here in a very long time. The ground she rode on had been christened a Benedictine monastery in 1155. *Munkathverá. Monks' river.* Her ancestors had purchased the land after Iceland's conversion to Lutheranism in 1550, and generations of her family had raised sheep and planted barley in its rich, glacial soil ever since.

The wind picked up. Strong gusts sent ripples across the river that she and Lúkas had splashed in while Jónas fished for Arctic char and brown trout. She fastened the collar of her fleece and reached down to stroke her mare's flaxen mane. Even her Icelandic horse, her precious Drífa, belonged to an ancient time, a breed of horse lost everywhere but here. Drífa's genes led back to the Asian steppes, to the Mongolian horses that had carried Genghis Khan to victory. The horses spread to Russia and Norse settlers brought them to Iceland in the ninth and tenth centuries, where they mixed with breeds imported from the British Isles. Along the way, Drífa's forebears had developed mutations which, instead of causing disease, adapted the horse to the harsh conditions of the Icelandic landscape, granting the creature a sure-footed gait, a thick mane and tail, and a double-coated hide for insulation against the cold.

Survival of the fittest.

Brynja gave her mare a gentle kick and Drífa accelerated into a *tölt,* the four-beat, ambling gait unique to her breed. She felt a sudden surge of pride. Just last year, her fellow geneticists at Legacy had identified a mutation, a change in the DMRT3 gene that allowed Drífa's spinal cord neurons to coordinate fluid movements and cross rough terrain with such ease. The *tölt* had evolved here over the past millennium, as the Icelandic horses had bred amongst themselves, isolated from the outside world.

But this, she knew, could also be a problem.

Iceland's governing body had ruled in 982 AD that livestock could no longer be imported, which meant her precious Icelandic horse had never acquired immunity to equine diseases. Drífa's genes would not be able to defend against foreign invaders; an outbreak on the island would devastate the breed.

Brynja shivered and patted Drífa's neck. They were both vulnerable: Drífa to some pathogen introduced from abroad, and Brynja to the dread of what she might discover about Lúkas.

She pushed the worries out of her head and focused on her father. *How could he not have recognized me?*

Even though she and Lúkas were twins, they were fraternal, not identical, twins. Their physical resemblance had not been striking. She had been a swirl of chestnut brown waves and sparkling, green eyes. He, a blue-eyed boy with honey-colored hair.

Through the dense fog gathered beneath the looming peaks of Tröllaskagi, she could barely make out Litlihamar, the neighboring farm owned by Stína's grandmother. As children, Brynja and Lúkas had been constant fixtures at the farm; Stína's grandmother had been the only maternal figure truly present in the twins' lives and they had taken to calling her Amma—grandma.

The old woman was sweeping away the dirt kicked up by the sudden windstorm when Brynja arrived. As she perched the broom against the door, her lace cap slid off, revealing a bun as white as the snow that lingered on the mountaintops.

"What on earth are you doing out riding in this cold, dear?" Amma said, grabbing hold of the bridle. "Come in."

Brynja slid off Drífa and left the mare to roam. She hugged

Amma and followed her into the kitchen of the small, stacked-stone farmhouse Stína's grandfather had built in the seventies after he and Amma immigrated from Denmark.

Brynja glanced at the recipe book that lay on a polished, stone counter next to the cast-iron stove.

ICELAND MOSS SOUP
Fjallagrasamjólk

1 cup loosely packed, dry Iceland moss
4 cups milk
1 teaspoon salt
1 tablespoon brown sugar

Briefly soak Iceland moss in lukewarm water.
Rinse, then chop roughly.
Bring the milk to a boil in a saucepan.
Add Iceland moss and simmer for 5 minutes, stirring often.
Remove from heat.
Season to taste with salt and sugar.

"Is that for spackling the walls?" Brynja teased, although she knew full well that the 'moss' was really a nutritious lichen, seldom used now.

"You can make fun all you want, dear, but it keeps these old bones strong," Amma said.

Brynja took off her fleece and combed her windswept hair with fingers chilled by the crisp, morning air.

Amma stirred the soup and leaned over to spoon a taste. "This will be done soon. Why don't you warm yourself by the fire in the sitting room?"

Brynja glanced toward the stairs that led to Stína's bedroom.

"I'm afraid it's just me, dear," Amma said. "Stína left quite early to drive to Lake Mývatn. She wanted to capture the birds at sunrise."

"Did she say when she'd be back?"

"I don't imagine it'll be long."

Brynja nodded. "All right then, if you don't mind, I'll wait."

"Make yourself comfortable. I'll put on a pot of tea," Amma said.

Brynja smiled and then walked down the hall to the sitting room. She plumped up the pillows on the threadbare couch, moved a pair of knitting needles and a ball of gray, woolen yarn to a bench, and sat down.

The warmth of the fire enveloped her.

Amma soon appeared with a tray of *rúgbrauð* and a pot of angelica tea.

"There we go," she said, pouring Brynja a cup. She offered her a slice of the rye bread, then quickly put it back on the tray. "That's right. I'd forgotten you don't eat such things. Let me get you some berries—"

"I'm fine, Amma. Tea is perfect."

Amma patted Brynja's knee, then leaned in and whispered, "Stína told me the news."

Brynja raised her eyebrows. "The news? Did Stína tell you about the poem?"

"The poem? No, I don't know of any poem." She patted Brynja on the knee again. "But what a romantic, that Ari Ketilsson. Did he write a poem for the big occasion?"

"Amma, I'm not sure what you're talking about."

"Your engagement, dear. Stína told me you and Ari are engaged."

Brynja's teacup rattled in its saucer. She forced a weak smile, wishing Stína could have kept that bit of information to herself.

"It's a wonder you two have any time for romance. You being head of forensics at that company, and Ari, well, running the country." She chuckled. "He must be pleased his Independence Party is back in power with all those new parties springing up every day. Pirates, Bright Future, Rainbow, Solidarity…"

"How do you keep track of it all, living out here in the country?"

The old woman pointed at the Bakelite radio sitting atop a doily. "With you and Stína gone, that old box keeps me company." She paused and looked at Brynja with concern. "My, my, listen to me chattering away. Is everything okay, dear?"

Brynja put the teacup down on the bench. "I'm worried about my father. Pabbi's not himself."

Amma's finely wrinkled face broke into a knowing smile. "Well, who is? Everyone wants to live long, my dear, but no one wants to grow old. I'm creeping toward eighty-six myself." At Brynja's lack of response, she reached over and took her hand. "But your father's still young. Tell me, what's wrong?"

"It's not his age. It's his mind. Pabbi didn't even recognize me yesterday."

Amma pushed herself up from the armchair and walked to the bookshelf beside the fireplace. She picked up a framed photograph and dusted it off with her hand. "Your father and I have never been particularly close, even though we've been neighbors all these years. My mother had a saying: 'When your neighbor's wall breaks, your own is in danger.' In such a small community, we all need to watch out for each other. But Páll's always kept his distance. Months go by without us seeing each other. Not that I blame him. He was so overwhelmed taking care of your mother and then you children—"

Brynja fingered the locket around her neck.

"I'm sorry, dear," Amma said. "Lúkas was such a darling boy." She sat down on the couch and patted Brynja's knee again. "I'm not sure it's the right time to tell you this, but I think I might know why your father didn't recognize you." She handed Brynja the framed photograph.

Confused, Brynja looked at the image of three people in front of the barn at Munkathverá. She recognized a younger Amma and her father peering into the camera.

"Do you remember him?" Amma pointed at a middle-aged man slumped in a wooden wheelchair.

Brynja shook her head. "No. Who is he?"

"It's your grandfather Björn, Páll's father. Björn and I were great friends back then."

Brynja strained to reconcile the image with other photos she had seen of Pabbi's father as a healthy, young man.

"Björn passed away just a few years before you and Lúkas arrived," Amma said. "According to the doctor, he died from some debilitating dementia."

Brynja stared at the crumpled figure in the wheelchair. "His hair isn't even gray. How old is he in this picture?"

"As far as I know, this is the last picture of your grandfather. It was taken when Björn was in his late fifties."

"That's so young."

"After Björn died, your father broke down at the funeral and confided in me. He thought your family was cursed. You see, Björn wasn't the first in your line to die young. Björn's mother—Páll's grandmother and your great-grandmother—also suffered the loss of her mind early on and died at a fairly young age."

Brynja froze. When she had told Pabbi about her job and asked him to contribute his DNA to Legacy's database, he had refused. He wouldn't even discuss the matter and she had given up trying to persuade him. At the time, she'd thought it was just his usual preference for privacy. But now she thought otherwise. Could these family deaths be the reason? Did her father fear he had inherited one of the genes for dementia? Did he fear the test would let the world know what he carried in his genes?

When Brynja had sipped the last of her tea, she thanked Amma and asked her to have Stína call as soon as she returned from Lake Mývatn. Bidding the old woman goodbye, she called to Drífa and climbed into the saddle.

The wind was gusting hard now, whipping south off Eyjafjörður's waters and whistling through the valley. Brynja wrapped her scarf around her neck and reached into her fleece pocket for her cell phone. She steered Drífa into the empty barn on Amma's farm and dialed her boss at Legacy.

A gruff voice came on the line. "Dr. Bragason here. Chief scientific officer."

Brynja rolled her eyes. Rúnar never missed an opportunity to boast.

"*Halló*, Rúnar. It's Brynja," she shouted over the wind howling through ruptured slats in the barn.

"Are you in the office?"

"I'll be in later this morning. For the moment, I just need to know who's working on dementia at Legacy."

Rúnar sneezed and blew his nose. "I thought maybe you hadn't been quite right lately."

She ignored the jab. "I'm curious to know what Legacy's found out about the genetics of dementia."

"Why do you ask?"

She had to think fast. "I'm working on a case and I need to know if the testimony of an elderly witness is reliable. Seems they have dementia running in the family."

"Well, I probably know more about disease genetics than anyone on the planet, but most cases of dementia are not genetic. They're not inherited."

Did he really think she didn't know anything about genetics?

"Yes, Rúnar, I know. But what about in people you're tracking that *do* have inherited cases? You know, like families with early-onset Alzheimer's? How accurate is genetic testing in those families?"

"It's true people suffering from Alzheimer's in their fifties and sixties often have defined genetic mutations. It's usually a defect in the presenilin 1 gene, sometimes presenilin 2. There's also a link with ApoE4 mutations." Rúnar coughed. "But there's some good news on the Alzheimer's front as well. We've discovered a protective allele, A673T, in the amyloid-β precursor gene. You can thank me for finding that one.

It's rare, but Icelanders who inherit that mutation are five times more likely to reach old age without any signs of Alzheimer's."

"Good to know. Thanks, Rúnar. I appreciate the info."

"Need me to check your witness for any of these mutations?"

"That would be great. I'll get a sample if he consents and send it to you. Thanks again. Talk to you later."

"Wait—Brynja?"

"Yes?"

"The lab ran the RNA analysis you requested on the blood from Inga's kitchen. I called your office, but you weren't in, so I rang the police station and gave the results to Henning."

Brynja cringed. She should have told Henning she'd driven Jónas's truck out to Húsavik late yesterday evening and met an officer at Inga's parents' farm.

They had found it deserted. After inquiring with several of the neighbors, they'd learned that Inga's parents had moved to Canada several months ago to be near their son.

Inga could not have been visiting her parents up north.

"You know you could have called my cell, Rúnar. Tell me the results."

"It's liver RNA. And some from the lining of the small intestine."

Brynja's pulse quickened. The poor woman must have been stabbed in the gut.

Inga wasn't missing; she was dead.

Chapter 7

Brynja punched off her cell phone, ending the call with Rúnar. She guided her horse back through the barn door and rode against a chill wind toward Munkathverá. In the distance, smoke rose in a thin stream from the kitchen chimney. Jónas would have breakfast ready by now.

She would need his help to get a sample of Pabbi's DNA and test it for any of the Alzheimer's mutations.

Brynja mentally checked off a list of the best samples for DNA isolation.

Her father would refuse a cheek swab. Whole blood was obviously not an option, and semen—ugh—was out of the question. Perhaps Jónas could pick up some of his fingernail clippings, or, though not as reliable, hair from his brush? Pabbi didn't smoke nor chew gum, so cigarette butts or a wad of gum were out of the question. Did he chew hard candy? Maybe she could collect some saliva? But how?

She gave Drífa a gentle prod and hurried toward home. The yew trees bordering the farm to the north began to sway wildly in the wind, then grew twice their size. Four, ten, a hundred-fold. She blinked. Gnarled limbs clawed the air, blackening the sky. A torrent of razor-sharp leaves swirled overhead, ripping the yew's bright, red berries from their stems.

She jerked the reins. Drífa reared her head, trumpeted, and stopped short.

Brynja shut her eyes and waited for the aura to pass. When she opened them again, the skies had cleared. Ahead stood the turf house. She wouldn't tell Pabbi and Jónas the auras were back. They needed her now more than ever. Pabbi was sick and Jónas was frail. She would deal with the visions. On her own.

She gave Drífa a gentle kick and continued toward Munkathverá. At the farm, she led the mare into the old barn, unbridled her, and brushed her down. She patted Drífa on the neck and then hurried to the turf house.

Brynja stomped the dirt off her boots and pushed open the front door. The muffled tap of Jónas's typewriter echoed through the three-foot-thick blocks of sod that formed the walls and roof of their home. Back when Pabbi was a young man, he had been so clever, studying the layout and construction that Icelanders had used to build their homes up until the twentieth century. This archaic dwelling, testament to his pride in Iceland's past, could just as well have been a remnant from centuries ago, when the Vikings settled in this remote and harsh land after fleeing the iron rule of Norway's King Harald Fairhair.

As she moved through the turf house she knew so well, she could feel its origins in the one-room Viking longhouse. The dwelling had evolved over time into a structure of several small A-frames linked together by stone passageways and a common sod roof. In the early eighties, Pabbi had constructed their home in this style, each section of the turf house joined together under one roof. It was during this time her father had first met Jónas. Pabbi had gone out to Glaumbær Farm to survey the historic site's turf homes and he'd struck up a conversation with a young student studying ancient farming techniques at Hólar Agricultural College. A year or two later, after Mamma had taken to her bed, when Pabbi needed someone to manage the farm, he thought of the young man he had met that day and hired him to help raise the children and manage the farm at Munkathverá. Jónas had stayed on ever since.

Brynja hung her jacket on the hook in the entryway and squinted to adjust her eyes to the darkness of the largest room, the *baðstofa*, with its sitting area, games table, and stone fireplace. Dim shafts of light filtered from above through *vindauga*, small openings high up on the walls. The *vind-auga*, the wind's-eyes or wind-ows, allowed the smoke and stale air to escape from the *baðstofa* in winter, when the door was shut tight against the cold.

Brynja was on her way to the kitchen when her cell phone rang; she fumbled in the darkness to retrieve the device from her jacket pocket.

"Stína?" she answered, seeing her friend's name on the screen.

"Hey, girl, you won't believe it," Stína yelled above gusts of wind. "I actually got a pair of gyrfalcons on film. Pretty early in the season for them."

"Hold on." Brynja hurried through the passageway to her room, the one she had shared with Lúkas so long ago. She dropped her voice. "Can I call you back in a few minutes? I've got to take care of something."

"Sure, but we're going to have to leave soon. The tour company called, and I've got to meet some birdwatchers at Flói nature reserve. Apparently, the red-necked phalaropes are nesting in droves there. It's not every year you see that. I'll stop by Reykjavik first, pick up some binoculars, and drop you at Legacy."

Brynja didn't know a red-necked phalarope from a red kangaroo, but she admired Stína's enthusiasm. Her friend was all about capturing the moment, with both her often-inappropriate hook-ups with men, and her ever-present companion, her camera. Nothing made her happier than capturing a bird in flight, a chick breaking through its shell, a pair of puffins nesting. She could hold onto those images forever.

"That's fine," Brynja said. "Give me a minute to sort something out?" She cupped her hand over the phone and whispered. "Pabbi's not doing very well."

"What's wrong?"

"He didn't recognize me. I'm hoping his confusion is due to fever, but I can't rule out he has some type of dementia, maybe Alzheimer's. I've got to take care of something quickly, but I'll tell you more when you get here."

"I'll be there as soon as I can," Stína said.

Brynja changed into a clean pair of jeans and a pullover and walked back through the *baðstofa* to the kitchen.

She stopped short in the doorway. Jónas was still hunched over his typewriter and seemed as ancient as the house itself. Even though she was upset Jónas hadn't informed her of Pabbi's declining health, it was hard to stay angry with him.

"Hey, Jónas." She sat down at the farm table.

He jumped up. "Why were you gone so long?" Without waiting for an answer, he went to the stove and pulled a pot from the cupboard. "You must be freezing. I'll warm you some milk."

Brynja smiled. She was an adult now and Jónas was still getting her a glass of warm milk.

She leaned over to see what he was typing.

SKYR with BILBERRIES
Skyr með bilberjum

2 quarts sheep's milk

1 cup sour cream

1 tablespoon calf stomach rennet or crushed butterwort

1 teaspoon salt

1 tablespoon brown sugar

Bring milk to a boil without burning it, and then cool to blood heat.
Whip sour cream and mix with milk until thin and smooth.
Add rennet or butterwort, salt and sugar. Stir well.
Let stand at room temperature for 24 hours.
Strain through cheesecloth.
Save whey for pickling and storage.
Top with bilberries.

"I don't remember you typing up recipes when we were children," she said.

"I thought I'd type up my favorites. I won't be around forever, you know."

"Don't be silly," Brynja said. "You're not going anywhere. But I am concerned about Pabbi. How long has he been like this?"

Jónas stood up, lifted a copper ladle from the hook over the stove, and stirred the pot of milk. "Just a few days now. The flu's knocked him down but I expect he'll be better soon."

"The flu?" Brynja shook her head. "I really don't think so. I know a little about medicine, remember?"

Jónas put the ladle on the counter, sat down, and put his head in his hands. "I'm doing everything I can, *litla mín*."

A flood of guilt washed over Brynja. "I know you are. You must be exhausted."

She swallowed her hesitation. Jónas was used to being in charge of the family and the farm and wouldn't like what she was about to say. "I'm not sure we should keep Pabbi here. I wonder if we should bring him down to Reykjavik so I can help care for him; his symptoms look a bit like dementia. I'd like to get his DNA tested."

"You're overreacting, *litla mín*. I called the doctor. He said to give it a couple more days. If your father's not better soon, I'll take him to the clinic."

"Actually, I called as well. The doctor's coming by this afternoon."

Jónas nodded and turned his back to her. "If you think that's wise." He opened the refrigerator and pulled out a large bowl. "You were gone so long I burned the oats. How about some *skyr* instead?

Brynja looked at the bowl of *skyr*. *That's it. I can get Pabbi's DNA without Jónas's help.* His saliva—and his DNA—would be left on the spoon after he ate.

"Maybe we could all have breakfast together," she said. "In the kitchen, like old times."

Jónas shook his head. "Páll's too weak to climb up and down the stairs."

"Would you mind bringing the *skyr* up to his room, then? And let's use the silver spoons. It'll make Pabbi feel special."

"Of course," Jónas said. "And Amma brought over some *vínarbrauð* just the other day. She's been a godsend, helping me with the sheep since Páll's not been able to do much." He reached into the cabinet for a plate and arranged some of Amma's Danish pastries on it. "I'll bring these up. I know you can't eat them, but it might do your father well. Between Amma and the ladies from the church, we've got more food than we know what to do with." He wiped his hands on his overalls. "Though, honestly, it's been more company than I'd like."

Brynja hardly heard a word Jónas said. Energized by her plan to get her father's DNA, she took the plate of *vínarbrauð* from Jónas and hurried up the stairs to his room.

"What on earth are you doing here?" Pabbi said. He sat up in bed, smiled, and reached for her hand.

She hurried to his side, gave him a big hug, and stood back to look him in the eye. "Pabbi, it's me, Brynja. I came last night. Do you remember?"

"No. You and your pranks. You can't pull the wool over my eyes. I'd remember that."

She swallowed hard. "Well, I'm here now, Pabbi. I've missed you terribly. Maybe you'd consider coming down to Reykjavik for a while."

She heard Jónas climbing the stairs. "Let's open these curtains and let some light in." She moved aside the heavy drapes and looked about the room for his brush. "Here, let me get that hair off your face so you can see better." She brushed his thinning hair, tucked a few strands in her pocket, and gave him a kiss on the forehead. If her father's saliva on the spoon didn't provide enough DNA, she could use the hair follicles as backup.

Jónas handed them each a bowl of *skyr* topped with dried bilberries and sat down in the wicker chair to eat his.

Pabbi picked up the spoon and examined it closely. "Why, I remember these spoons." He ran his finger over the embossed 'B' on the handle. "Must not be mine, though." He took a bite of the Danish and several spoonfuls of *skyr*.

"Pabbi," Brynja said gently. "The 'B' is for Björn, your father. He left the spoons to you, remember? You were his only child, Páll Björnsson."

His eyes clouded over and a rivulet of *skyr* dripped down his chin. "Mamma? Is that you?" He fiddled with the buttons on his pajama top.

Brynja's heart sank. Dementia was the ultimate identity thief.

She got up slowly and put her bowl of *skyr* on the nightstand. "It's Brynja, Pabbi. Back home with you."

Jónas ate silently in his chair, but Brynja had lost her appetite.

She wiped the drool from her father's mouth with the spoon and placed it on the tray along with the bowl. "You should get some rest." She tucked his comforter up under his chin and kissed his forehead. "I'll be back in a little while." She offered the serving tray to Jónas so he could place his bowl alongside the others. "I'll do the dishes."

On her way down the stairs, Brynja's cell phone rang. She hurried to the kitchen, put the dishes near the sink, and reached into her pocket for the phone.

"*Halló?*"

Ari's voice boomed on the other end. "Brynja, what happened to you? I hear from your intern that you went up north to see your father."

Ásta's face was still fresh in Brynja's mind. "I did, yes."

"I miss you," Ari said. "When will you be back?"

"Later today."

"Any chance you can meet me at Thingvellir? I've got a ribbon cutting at noon."

"I've got a meeting with Ísak and Henning at three."

"It'll only take an hour. We'll get you back in time."

Brynja agreed. She missed him, too. She said goodbye and called Stína. "Change of plans. Can you drop me at Thingvellir? And take something to Legacy before meeting your tour group?"

"Thingvellir? Why there? Hot on some case?"

"I'm meeting Ari."

"Hot on the prime minister, then. Good girl. You've got some warm blood running through your veins after all. I'll swing by in a few minutes."

Brynja rushed to the sink. Pabbi had drooled all over his silver spoon, and, with any luck, he had left enough saliva on it for DNA analysis. She carefully wrapped the spoon in a piece of foil and tucked it into her backpack.

She washed the breakfast dishes and quickly put away the rest of the spoons. Jónas wouldn't notice one was missing since they only used them for special occasions.

The sudden change in her plans left her conflicted about leaving, but there wasn't much to be gained by staying longer. She returned to Pabbi's bedroom to explain that something had come up and she had to return to Reykjavik sooner than expected. Outside, Stína's jeep snaked up the dirt drive toward Munkathverá. She gave Jónas a hug, leaned down to kiss Pabbi on the forehead, and hurried down the stairs.

Soon, she would have an answer to a question she didn't want to ask.

Stína turned the jeep south along the Ring Road toward Thingvellir National Park. On the long, quiet drive, Brynja reexamined her decision to leave so abruptly. Perhaps she should have stayed, waited for the doctor, and taken more time to observe her father for signs of other causes that might explain his bizarre twists of memory. Or maybe that was just wishful thinking. She swung back and forth. But in the end, she found some comfort in knowing the doctor had promised to contact her after examining Pabbi and advise her how best to proceed.

She looked at her watch. "Hope the weather holds. I told Ari I'd be there by noon."

Stína tapped the steering wheel. "It's good to keep a man waiting."

Brynja didn't want to keep Ari waiting. When she imagined him looking to the road for signs of her, pacing and growing impatient, she had a vision of Ásta suddenly appearing to soothe him. She tried to calm herself, rationalizing she had misinterpreted his kindness toward Ásta. He was just being a gentleman, as usual.

They drove through a valley ringed by the snow-capped mountains. The dense fog at their base had lifted and the sun warmed an endless tapestry of purple lupines, a kaleidoscope of violet petals perched like butterflies on tall stems that swayed in the breeze, their roots anchored deep in the crevasses of jet-black lava.

Brynja breathed in a lightness she hadn't known for a very long time. Everything would work out. *Thetta reddast*. She just had to give it time. Pabbi would get the help he needed. Henning would eventually accept she'd been hired instead of him. Ísak would be impressed with her analysis of the Inga Grímsdóttir case. She would find Lúkas. Dead or alive. At the very least, she would know what had happened to him.

Chapter 8

Stína sped up to pass a slow-moving horse trailer. "That reminds me, I didn't get a chance to fix the door on the pickup. I can't believe your dad and Jónas still drive that thing."

"I got out to Husavík with it yesterday to check on a case," Brynja said, zipping her fleece. "Pretty shaky ride."

"Well, I hope they never get rid of it," Stína said. "I can still picture Jónas beaming out the driver's side when he picked us up from school every day." She popped open a bottle of *Egils Appelsín* soda. "Remember Lúkas always called shotgun? Truthfully, I was glad he sat in front so he could yap away with Jónas about the drawings he did in school and I could just watch the birds whiz by in peace."

Brynja's hand rose to the locket about her neck.

"What's this super-secret package you want me to smuggle into Reykjavik?" Stína said, taking a swig of the orange soda. "I'll have time to drop it off before picking up the binoculars from the office."

"I'm worried Pabbi has dementia and I need to have his DNA tested in the lab at Legacy. Most cases of dementia aren't genetic, but early-onset Alzheimer's can be."

"No way your dad's got dementia. I just saw him a couple of weeks ago. He was fine."

Brynja struggled to reconcile this with her own experience. "He didn't recognize me yesterday."

"You said that, but I can't believe it." Stína looked over at Brynja. "Maybe he just had too much to drink?"

"No. His speech wasn't slurred, and he didn't smell of alcohol. Maybe he's just sick and disoriented but Amma told me this morning that both my grandfather Björn and my great-grandmother had dementia at a young age. I'm worried it might be inherited."

Stína nodded. "So, that's why the DNA. How the heck did you get a sample from your dad?"

Brynja dug into her bag and showed Stína the foil-wrapped package. "This is the spoon he had breakfast with. It's got enough of his saliva on it to extract DNA."

Stína studied her face. "You must be pretty worried."

"Watch it!" Brynja screamed, as three young lambs skittered across the road.

Stína slammed on the brakes and honked the horn. "Damn sheep. Get the flock outta here." She shook her head. "Why do they have to have so many goddamn lambs?"

"Thoka."

"Thoka?" Stína looked over.

"Thoka. It's a fertility gene. Icelandic sheep were bred for it. Allows them to have multiples. Triplets, sometimes even quads. More milk, wool, and meat for the Vikings."

Stína rolled her eyes. "Is everything always about genetics for you?" She put the car back in gear and started down the road.

"I've got an intern for the summer," Brynja said. "Her name's Elly. If you can give the spoon to her, I'd really appreciate it. I'll call and let her know you'll be coming by."

Brynja picked her phone up from the console and dialed her intern, who answered after just one ring. "Brynja? You back? Henning's been asking about you. He texts me like every hour wondering where you are."

"I see."

Elly couldn't have missed the change in Brynja's tone.

"No problem. I told him you were following up on something important. That I didn't quite know all the details, but even if I did, I wasn't at liberty to discuss what you were working on. I was just about to call you and give you a heads-up."

Brynja smiled. Elly could easily have been sleeping in this morning after a night out partying with the other millennials in Reykjavik's hormone-infused bar scene this time of year, but she clearly took her role as intern seriously. It boded well for their summer together.

"Thanks, Elly. I know you set up a meeting with Henning and Ísak at three this afternoon. Could you confirm that?"

"Actually, Ísak said he'd be out until tomorrow. He took his daughter to some summer program up in the Westfjords."

"Okay, then. Guess I'll see you at Legacy instead of the police station."

"Sure thing. But hey, Brynja, what's the scoop on that painting?"

"What painting?"

"I overheard Henning talking to Ísak yesterday afternoon about a painting that's missing from the Kjarval Art Museum. I think Henning sent some evidence to Legacy for forensics. Didn't he call you about it?"

Brynja frowned. "No, not yet."

She paused to consider this new development. Henning seemed to be taking every opportunity to undermine her position.

"Elly? Would you arrange a meeting with Ísak as soon as he's back?"

"*Ja.* Will do. I'll check his schedule."

"In the meantime, I'll need you to take something over to the lab. My friend Stína has a spoon wrapped in foil. I know that sounds weird. Please ask the lab to extract DNA from the saliva on it and do some analysis. I'll call them with the details. Don't unwrap the foil; we don't want any contamination with your DNA."

"Spoons and spit. Evidence, right? Cool. I'm on it."

"No, it's not evidence, but I do need you to take the spoon directly to the head technician, Stefán. No need to tell Rúnar about it. The sample's actually from my father."

Elly gasped. "My God, is he all right?"

"He's fine. The DNA isn't for a criminal case; it's to check for a couple of specific mutations." Brynja paused to consider the other side of Elly—on the one hand she was an eager worker and enthusiastic, but on the other she jumped much too fast to conclusions. "I'll call Stefán and tell him which DNA loci to look at. And you'll have to let him know that my father's one of the few people who doesn't have his DNA banked with Legacy. Tell Stefán his name is Páll Björnsson."

Elly was silent for a moment. "I hope he's okay. Björnsson, though? I'm confused. Is he your stepdad?"

"No, he's my father." Brynja realized why Elly was confused. "Children are named after their father's first name and then we add '*son*' or '*dóttir*.' My father's first name is Páll, so I'm Pálsdóttir."

"Oh, okay, then, I'll be here when Stína arrives. But wait, Henning—"

"Yes?"

"Henning's name is Holt."

"His father's Danish. Or Norwegian. I don't remember. Anyway, that's why there's no
'*son*' at the end of his name."

"Ah, okay, got it. And, Brynja?"

"Yes?"

"It's a good thing you told me not to discuss the sample with Rúnar. I might've mentioned it since I see him so much when I'm over at the station."

"At the station? Rúnar's at Legacy."

"Well, he's been over to the police department so many times you'd think he's running the place. Earthing up potatoes."

"What?"

"Earthing up potatoes. Sorry. It's some weird Danish saying. It just means he's digging around in the dirt. Seems like he's snooping around for something."

Brynja felt like a leather strap had tightened around her chest.

"Rúnar's been over at the police station four or five times the last two days talking with Henning. Maybe more. I've seen him in the hallway a few times and wondered who he was. I haven't actually been introduced to him but Ísak told me his name."

"What were they talking about?"

"I don't know. He just goes down the hall to Henning's office and shuts the door."

Brynja tried not to sink into paranoia, imagining the worst possible motives on Rúnar and Henning's part, but it was hard to think of any reason for the two men to be meeting so often and in private. She didn't know what they were up to, but Ísak would have to be informed. At the very least, he wouldn't tolerate a civilian—any civilian—waltzing in and out of the police station like that.

"Thanks for the update. Stína should be in Reykjavik by one or so."

"I'll be here. Call me if you need anything else."

Brynja punched off her cell and leaned back against the headrest. She had a lot to think about.

"Mind if I close my eyes?" she asked Stína. "I didn't sleep much last night."

Stína pulled the open bag of licorice buttons from the center console and popped one in her mouth. "Hopefully, you won't get much with Ari tonight, either."

Two hours later, a series of loud blasts jarred Brynja awake.

"Let's go, chicken shit," Stína yelled out the window, honking the horn and gesturing wildly for the hay-laden tractor in front of her to pull over to the side of the road. She sped up to pass the front-loader and looked over at Brynja. "Good timing, girl. Five kilometers to Thingvellir."

Stína turned into the national park and drove toward a cluster of men and women gathered in front of a stone building. The park was unusually quiet this afternoon, save for a number of government officials, police officers, and journalists milling about the park's visitor's center after the ribbon cutting. Brynja scanned the group for signs of Ari. As soon as she spotted him, she felt the familiar struggle between desire and jealousy throbbing in her heart, waiting for her to choose between them.

Stína nudged her friend. "Well, what are you waiting for?" She practically pushed Brynja out of the car. "A bird in the hand is worth two in the bush. If you catch my drift."

Brynja laughed. "You're incorrigible." She opened the car door. "Thanks for the lift. I'll call you later. And I appreciate your taking the spoon to Legacy."

She got out, said goodbye, and zipped her fleece against the cold front that had swept over the island last night.

Ari separated himself from the group and waved to her. Trying her best not to appear overly excited, Brynja walked casually toward him, threading her way through the sawhorses in the empty parking lot.

Ari threw his arms around her and kissed her with a warm, wet passion that took her breath away. "If we hurry, we can have the hot springs to ourselves." He waved at two security officers. "The guys promised to keep everyone out."

"I didn't bring a bathing suit."

"You wouldn't have it on for long anyway, my sweet."

She felt her resistance melting even as her mind conjured up a vision of Ásta, interrupting the much more pleasant thought of being naked in the pools with her fiancé.

"It's cold, Ari." She tucked her scarf beneath the collar of her fleece.

"Not for long." He put his hand around her waist and steered her in the direction of the hot springs.

They walked down the path beneath steep cliffs of black, volcanic basalt into the great, rift valley formed by the separation of the North American and Eurasian Plates, which served as the original site of Iceland's Parliament, the Althing. The towering wall of columnar basalt formed a natural amphitheater where the chieftains and judges debated and enforced the law. There had been no king. The only elected official was the lawspeaker whose sole duty was to recite portions of the tenth-century Law Code from memory.

"This is where it all started," Brynja said, stopping at a rocky outcrop that marked the spot of Lögberg, the Law Rock.

"Yes indeed," Ari said with a note of pride. "Thing-vellir. Assembly-Fields. Imagine holding Parliament out here in the open air for almost a thousand years. Not sure if the MPs these days would be tough enough for that."

"Actually, I didn't mean where Parliament started; I meant my career. The first case I solved after coming back from the forensics program in New York was here. Henning was originally on the case, but I figured it out."

"Is that where his animosity began? You think he resents your success? Trying to make you fail?"

"I don't know about making me fail but he does make things hard. He's always throwing up obstacles to make me look bad."

"Maybe he's just awkward, inept."

She pulled a face. "Maybe, but I don't think so. Apparently, there was a break-in at the Kjarval museum that he neglected to inform me about. Sent the evidence to the lab at Legacy without my knowledge. Anyway, I'm sure you have to deal with your fair share of obstructionists in Parliament—"

A reporter from RUV News came out of nowhere and approached Ari with a microphone. "Prime Minister, any comment on plans to unfreeze the *kronur*?"

Ari cleared his throat, squeezing Brynja's hand in apology for the interruption.

She stepped a few feet away.

"The time is right," Ari answered, "to lift capital controls. The financial crisis of 2008 is well behind us and we're seeing a return to economic normality and a prosperous future. I'll address this in my speech on National Day. Until then, if you'll excuse us."

He smiled and thanked the reporter, then turned and subtly motioned to the security patrol to keep the press away.

They headed back down the path.

"What do you think is the most common motive for murder?" Brynja asked.

"I don't know. Money?"

"Nope. It's passion."

"Are you trying to tell me something, Brynja? Because, I swear, I've got nothing going on with Ásta."

Brynja stopped in her tracks. "Am I that obvious?"

"You left so abruptly during our walk when she came up to us. I know what it looks like, but I have to talk to people. If I could put her off, I would. I want nothing to come between us."

"Then let's not discuss Ásta." Embarrassed, Brynja cast around for something else to talk about. "I was telling you about the first case I cracked using DNA. It was here, at Thingvellir."

"Yes, tell me."

"It started when some college students decided to reenact one of the sagas. The idea was to educate the public about what took place during the parliamentary assembly at Thingvellir."

"I'm sure it was one hell of a Viking party. Thousands of folks meeting up for two weeks in summer after being stuck in a musty, turf house with the same stinking people all winter long."

Brynja had to laugh. "Well, the law students got that part right. They drank bucket-loads of beer, partied all night, and, then, in the morning, stumbled through a live performance of parts of *Njál's Saga*. Njál was the wisest man in Iceland. Knew a lot about the law."

"Brynja, you forget I was a history professor. I've read *Njál's Saga* cover to cover. Blood feuds. Minor insults that escalated into murder. The kinsmen of the victim were duty-bound to kill someone in the *first* family out of revenge, and then the family of *that* poor chap had to defend *his* family's honor by murdering a kinsman of the fellow who had hurled the insult in the first place. And so on and so forth. A bloody domino effect."

Brynja nodded. "That's pretty much it."

"So, what happened in your case?"

"Well, after partying all night, the girlfriend of the student playing Njál accused him of sleeping with her best friend and clubbed him over the head with a beer bottle. Classic crime of passion."

Ari was silent. "I don't understand how Henning came into it."

"Henning fell into a crevasse trying to retrieve the beer bottle as evidence. He cut himself on the lava and was in the hospital two months with a terrible infection. Almost lost his leg."

"That's hardly your fault," Ari said. "His pride must have been hurt."

"Henning hasn't gotten over the fact I solved the case without him, even though it was pretty simple. Blood on the glass shards from the bottle showed DNA from the student but also from his girlfriend."

"Do you think it's a coincidence?" Ari asked slowly.

"What do you mean? The chance of that blood sample *not* matching the girl's DNA was more than one in a trillion."

"No. I mean, do you think the fact that the first crime you solved here revolved around *Njál's Saga* is a coincidence?"

"I don't understand. What's the coincidence?"

"*Njál's Saga* is the first saga in the *Möðruvallabók*. Your poem mentions the *Book of Möðruvellir*."

Brynja gasped. "I never thought about it like that."

"Do you think Henning had anything to do with writing that poem to you?"

"Why would he do that?" She looked into Ari's eyes, as though he had the answer.

"Maybe to distract you from focusing on your job?"

Brynja paused. "I don't know…that would be quite a stretch."

Ari reached over to smooth her tousled hair and kissed her lightly on the lips. "Let's forget about work for a while, Brynja."

He motioned to the officers to stop following them and to keep the area clear of passers-by before slipping an arm around her waist and guiding her behind the rocky outcrop that shielded the hot springs from view.

Brynja hesitated, glancing around before stripping off her clothes and gliding into the thermal water. The heat soothed her, and she began to relax.

She watched Ari peel the clothes from his chiseled frame. He slid into the pool, trailed his fingertips down her back, and pulled her close. She wrapped her arms around his broad shoulders and nuzzled the base of his neck. His hard chest pressed against her breasts and she quivered with desire. They kissed and teased one another until they were both shaking.

"Brynja," he said, his voice husky. "Bryn—"

She arched her back and allowed a wave of pure ecstasy to pulse through her body.

Chapter 9

Brynja arrived at her office early Thursday, eager to catch up on work and microRNA report. The results confirmed Inga had indeed been stabbed in the abdomen. Ísak had elevated the case from that of a missing person to suspected homicide and had issued an all-points bulletin for Inga's husband, who had not been seen in several days.

After thanking Stéfan in the lab for expediting the microRNA analysis, Brynja discussed her father's DNA sample with him. Pabbi's doctor had called last evening, suggesting that a diagnosis of dementia was premature. He suggested Pabbi be referred to a neurologist for a full evaluation. After ending the call, Brynja dialed the clinic in Akureyri and made an appointment for her father. Nonetheless, she couldn't shake the worry that he—and, therefore, she—may have inherited some form of dementia.

Brynja felt a sudden empathy for Ásta, who herself was concerned she had inherited a disease. Paget's in Ásta's case. Brynja stared at her desktop computer; she was tempted to study the confidential information on Paget's disease in the LinX database and determine whether Ásta had indeed inherited the mutation. She was well aware that, in addition to the GeneID database that matched DNA samples to individuals, Legacy had a second database called LinX. This system contained data that linked DNA mutations to medical records. If a specific DNA sequence occurred only in family members affected by a certain genetic disease, that information could lead to a better understanding of the disease mechanism. Muscular dystrophy, breast cancer, neurofibromatosis, Huntington's disease…the list of genetic conditions with defined mutations was long. Legacy could pass that information on to pharmaceutical companies interested in developing treatments.

Ásta's words echoed in Brynja's mind: 'My DNA doesn't belong to Iceland. It belongs to me. Our family has a genetic disease and I don't want the whole world knowing about it.' Brynja understood her concern, but the LinX database was confidential. No one outside of Legacy would know the identity of individuals with disease mutations. In fact, not even anyone at the company was authorized to access personal information unless it pertained to a criminal case.

Brynja looked around the office. She was alone and she knew she shouldn't. The hunger to find out if Ásta had truly inherited the Paget's gene—or whether she was merely using her family's plight as a ploy to win Ari's sympathy—rumbled inside her. A couple of clicks on the keyboard and she would know. The first would bring up family pedigrees with no identifying information and the second would reveal the specific individuals with mutations for Paget's.

Her guilty conscience was overshadowed by a deep pride in her country's heritage. Only in Iceland could you trace a family tree back a thousand years. Detailed records of each person's genealogy—from the original settlers onward—were meticulously recorded in the *Landnámabók*, the *Book of Settlements*, and the *Íslendingabók*, the *Book of Icelanders*. Unfortunately, all that inbreeding in such a small population meant that not every day at the gene pool was a sunny one. Harmful mutations trickled through generations like magma, threatening to seal the fate of those unlucky enough to have inherited them.

Brynja took a breath and then typed 'Paget's disease.' Six pedigrees popped up on the screen. One more tap on the keyboard and she would know which of the affected families Ásta belonged to.

Brynja stopped. Put her hands in her lap. This was not a criminal case. There was no justifiable reason, no ethical reason, for her to reveal the identities of individuals with Paget's mutations. A sudden sense of shame overwhelmed her.

"Still working out all that geometry?" a voice called out from the doorway.

Brynja bolted upright. She hadn't noticed Elly come into the office and now here she was, peering over her shoulder.

"You really should knock first, you know."

Elly shuffled her feet and looked down, fidgeting with the bangles around her wrist.

Brynja smiled apologetically. "Sorry for being short. I didn't sleep well last night."

"*Nej*, my bad for barging in like the wind blowing half a pelican."

Noticing the confusion on Brynja's face, Elly said, "Danish for being in a rush. Anyway, here." She put a binder on Brynja's desk. "Ísak wanted me to bring you a copy of the log from last night." Her eyes widened as she glanced at the file on the screen. "Are we on some case involving Paget's? That's not the GeneID database you're always checking. That's LinX, right? The database you need special permission to look at because it shows which diseases run in families?"

Brynja cringed.

Elly's eyes glittered. "I remember some CSI episode when they found out the murder victim had Paget's. I think it was *Youngblood*. Are you thinking one of your victims has Paget's, too?"

Brynja swallowed. She had come so close to compromising her morals. Guilt and fear and shame came rushing back with a vengeance.

"I'm working on something I need to keep confidential for now," she said. "Let's keep this between us, okay?" She motioned to the log Elly had put on her desk. "Anything I should know about in last night's report?"

"Not really—"

An incessant knocking on the outer office door interrupted their conversation.

"Someone's sure going berserk out there," Brynja said. "Would you see who it is?"

"You bet."

A few seconds later, Elly popped her head back into the office. "Brynja? Tómas, the guard from the manuscript institute, says he's here with the book."

Brynja's pulse quickened. The *Möðruvallabók*.

Ari had kept his promise. He must have pulled more than a few strings to ensure she could take a look at the manuscript before the guard delivered it to Parliament. Why had she ever doubted his devotion to her? The thought of him sent a rush of heat through her.

She shut the computer down and forgot about Ásta and Paget's disease. Finding Lúkas was the only thing that mattered now. It had colored every part of her life in the years since he had disappeared: the guilt that kept her at arm's length from Pabbi, the fear of abandonment that sometimes held her back from Ari, the hope that a career in forensic genetics would lead her to back to her brother.

"Brynja?" Elly was standing in the doorway, looking back over her shoulder. "Shall I send him in?"

Before she could answer, a portly man in his mid-twenties or so wrestled himself through the doorway, cocooned in an oversized vest dangling an extendable baton and a can of MK-4 OC-spray. He struggled with the weight of a large, wooden box the size of a shallow milk crate.

"Tómas Gylfason, ma'am."

Brynja scrutinized his gear.

"I think it's a bit much, too, ma'am," Tómas said. "The Magnússon Institute just wouldn't let the book out of their vault otherwise. The prime minister instructed me to bring it here first thing this morning. He said you might want to examine the *Möðruvallabók* before it goes on display at Parliament. Something about an old case involving *Njal's Saga* and I—I'm not sure, exactly."

Brynja smiled as she eyed the wooden box. Ari had certainly been inventive in coming up with a plausible if outlandish reason for giving her time to examine the treasure privately. "Yes. Thank you for bringing it by. Here, put it on my desk. It looks heavy. Would you leave it with me for a bit?"

"Of course, ma'am." Tómas placed the box on a table next to Brynja's desk. "I have a pair of gloves everyone is required to use when handling the book. I'll leave them with you."

"Thank you." Brynja reached for the white, cotton gloves. "Can you give me a few minutes?"

"Of course. Take your time. Any chance you've got some coffee?"

Brynja glanced up at Elly and nodded in the direction of the outer office.

Elly stepped toward Tómas. "Come with me. We've also got some doughnuts if you're hungry."

Brynja raised her eyebrows. "We do?"

"*Ja*. Yep. Someone mailed you a box of *kleinur*. The delivery boy brought it up this morning."

"Really? Who sent them?"

"I don't know. There's no return address."

Tómas piped up. "I'd love some *kleinur*. My little doughball loves company." He chuckled and grabbed the tire around his stomach.

"Can I get you one, ma'am?"

Brynja shook her head. "Thanks, but no. Gluten allergy. Maybe Elly would like one?"

Elly took the hint and motioned to Tómas. He followed her out of the office, squeezing sideways through the doorway. As the two disappeared behind the closing door, the office grew quiet.

She had the room and the manuscript to herself.

The *Möðruvallabók*. The *Book of Möðruvellir*.

Brynja cleared her desk and then pulled on the cotton gloves. She unclasped the hinge of the wooden box and opened the lid. The ancient book sat wrapped in velvet fabric, nearly filling the box. She lifted the heavy tome from its cradle and laid it on her desk. She ran her fingers over the smooth, wooden cover and down the spine.

Squeezing her eyes shut, she felt the warmth of Lúkas's hand as they stood in line at the carousel. Why had she let go?

Having the book here on her desk, holding and touching it, made the treasure seem all the richer, more extraordinary. The leaves of parchment were folded and carefully gathered into sets, or quires. The quires were threaded onto leather cords, the cords secured onto burly, wooden boards that served as the book's cover, and the boards then fastened with a thick, lead clasp. The sagas—the stories of Iceland's past, the stories of their ancestors—were protected within.

The thrill at touching the *Möðruvallabók* quickly turned to confusion and empty desperation. She brushed back a tear. If only she could have gathered her brother's leaves into quires and bound them to safety forever.

She didn't know whether to look for the passages from the poem she had been sent about Lúkas or for something else. She pulled the poem from her bag and set it beside the manuscript. *Upon the madder mead...*

She shook her head. It made no sense.

Brynja pulled the desk lamp closer to the book and examined the cover. A large but faded, golden 'M' was painted on its surface. Plant-like vines wound about the pillars of the letter, while delicate flowers sprouted from above, and a tangle of roots was painted below.

She unbuckled the clasp and lifted the cover. A woody aroma, musty but sweet, filled the air. As she woke them from their long and silent slumber, the stiff pages rustled like fallen oak leaves. On each, two columns of text were written in Old Icelandic, a language that had changed very little over the thousand years since the settlement of Iceland. Even so, she strained to read the words written in a deep brown ink that had faded into the toast brown of parchment. Before her eyes, the letters swirled in the gothic script of monks straining to write in the dim candlelight of medieval monasteries.

Brynja glanced over at the poem about Lúkas. *And you will find your other half...In the ink of Gloom's root cellar.* She sat up straight. Was that it? If she examined the ink, could she solve the mystery of her brother's disappearance?

But who was Gloom?

The crisp swish of the office door shattered her reverie.

"Ready for Tómas to take the book over to Parliament?" Elly asked. "He's getting antsy."

"Can you stall him a little longer?"

"Well, he's already eaten half of the *kleinur*. No wonder he's so pudgy, scarfing down all that flour and butter. My mom makes those doughnuts back home, but with cardamom. It's a Danish thing." Elly paused for a moment. "You know, Tómas seemed kind of annoyed when I told him I'm Danish. He started spouting off about how the Danes stole the manuscripts from Iceland. How we had no right to scoop them up and ship them off to King Christian V and the royal antiquarian, whoever that was. I know you told me about the controversy, but I didn't realize it was still such a big deal."

At that moment Brynja saw Elly for the stranger she was. She wondered how it was possible Elly had grown up unaware of the undercurrent of hostility that existed among some people in their two nations. She may not have learned in school how poorly the Danish Crown had treated Iceland. Although the people of Iceland had long ago adapted to the wrath of nature—volcanic eruptions, the plague, the Little Ice Age, a climate nearly incompatible with life—the Crown had added to their woes. The Danes had imposed severe trade restrictions, dismissed the Icelanders as a bunch of incompetent farmers, left them vulnerable to invasion of Barbary pirates in the 1600s, and carried off Iceland's manuscripts to Copenhagen.

Brynja heard these snippets of her heritage rattling through her head and forced herself to set them aside. She would be no better if she focused on the age-old twinges that sometimes rankled in the hearts of Icelanders.

"Don't take it personally, Elly. Sometimes, we Icelanders get a little fired up over the Danes. You'd think we'd let it go after so many years."

"Well, Tómas was practically foaming at the mouth. His face was red as a fisherman's neck. I had to calm him down with more *kleinur* and some whipped cream and blueberries I found in the fridge."

Tómas coughed loudly in the outer office.

"Think maybe you could keep him occupied a little longer?" Brynja asked.

"As long as there are some *kleinur* left, sure."

Brynja turned back to the manuscript. She leafed through the pages, noting that some were marked with vertical slits through which fine strips of rope were threaded. Was that a kind of bookmark? She read the headings on those pages: *Njál's Saga; Egil's Saga; Kormák's Saga; Víga-Glúm's Saga; Laxdæla Saga...*

She lifted the pages and scanned the parchment for anything unusual—a drawing, a picture, a map. Anything at all that might give a hint as to the meaning of the poem.

Her heart leapt at the sight of a scribbled note in the margin of one of the pages. She peered closer. The note was in Old Icelandic and in the same brown ink as the text of the *Möðruvallabók*, but written in a sort of scrawl, not the carefully crafted script of the sagas. She squinted to make out the words: *Have Gauk's Saga Trandilssonar written here. I am told that Grímur owns it.*

Had that been written by the owner of the book? Or had the abbot or prior at the monastery instructed a scribe to copy *Gauk's Saga*?

Brynja fought back tears of frustration. If that was a clue, it sure wasn't obvious. She made a mental note to ask Stína if her connection at the Institute knew anything about it.

Disappointed, she turned through a few more pages. Seeing another note, she braced herself. In bold strokes, someone had scratched deep into the parchment in a shiny, black ink. The words could not have been written since the manuscript arrived back in Iceland in the 1970s; the Magnússon Institute would never have allowed such a desecration of the priceless heirloom.

Was this the clue she was looking for? She pushed her glasses up the ridge of her nose.

May 3, 1628. Here I sit in the large dwelling-room at Möðruvellir. Magnús Björnsson.

1628? So long ago. Magnús was a very common name, especially in earlier centuries when seemingly every other person was named Magnús. And any son of a man named Björn would have the patronymic Björnsson. Björn's son. Her own father was a Björnsson.

Even so, Brynja took a photo of the inscription with her cell phone. She would check the register of Icelanders living at that time for anyone with that name. And she'd need to ask the scholars in the university's Medieval Norse Studies Department for help in examining the manuscript.

Elly rapped on the door. "Ready? Tómas is getting really antsy. He won't leave the office without the *Möðruvallabók*."

Brynja nodded. She closed the cover over the parchment leaves and secured the clasp.

"Tell him—"

A thunderous crash against the outer door made Brynja jump. "What the—?"

She nearly collided with Elly as they both rushed to the antechamber door.

Tómas lay collapsed on the floor, staring up at them. Wide-eyed, he strained to move his hand toward his mouth and then belched a stream of yellow vomit. His eyes rolled up behind curtains of fear, the corpulent flesh about his belly bounced in a convulsive frenzy, and then he was still.

Brynja raced to his side. She fell to her knees and checked his pulse. Nothing. She pumped his chest, then tilted his head back and pinched his nose. Swiping away the vomit, she covered his mouth with hers, and blew two sharp breaths into his lungs.

She checked his pulse again. Nothing.

"Elly, call Emergency—112." She leaned in to pump Tómas's chest. "Get an ambulance."

Chapter 10

The pulsating flash of ambulance lights snaked away through traffic toward Landspítali Hospital. The high-pitched wail of the siren faded. Brynja watched the ambulance disappear, already fearing the worst. She had failed to revive Tómas.

She slumped down in her chair just as a knock sounded on the door.

"Henning is here to see you," Elly said.

The detective pushed Elly aside and marched into the room. "What the hell just happened?"

Brynja looked him squarely in the eye. "Please, keep your voice down. No need to shout. What can I do for you?"

He glanced at the manuscript on her desk, took a long drag of his cigarette, and blew a cloud of smoke in her direction. "What was that security guard doing over here?"

She ignored the question. "Do you have something to say? Perhaps why you didn't inform me of the evidence collected at the Kjarval museum?"

"I took matters into my own hands since you were out of town." He tapped his cane on the edge of her desk. "A woman in your position should take the job more seriously, don't you think?"

"Henning—" Brynja stopped. In time, he would accept her. Until then, there was nothing to be gained by berating him. "I'll discuss the Kjarval case with you later. At the moment, I'll have to ask you to leave. I've got others matters to tend to."

Henning grunted and left the room, pushing past Elly, who dawdled in the doorway.

Brynja slumped back in her chair and buried her head in her hands.

Elly brushed the cigarette ash from Brynja's desk into an empty paper cup. "The paramedics said you handled everything perfectly."

"I tried to get a pulse. I really did."

"You can't blame yourself for Tómas's heart attack."

"I'll go over to the hospital later today." She should call Ari. How was she going to tell him the guard had just collapsed in her office? "In the meantime, would you call over to the Arne Magnússon Institute? Another guard will have to come get the book. And then ring maintenance to clean up the mess."

"Will do." Elly started toward the outer office but stopped short in the doorway. "Brynja?" Her voice was shrill.

Brynja hurried over.

"Look." Elly pointed at a chunky pool of vomit, littered with packaging from the syringes, bandages, and breathing tubes the paramedics had used. "There's a piece of paper there. It looks like it's from the book. That stiff kind of paper."

Brynja grabbed a pair of latex gloves from the cabinet and retrieved the yellowed paper from the sticky mess. The sheet was roughly the size of a small index card, with a note scrawled across its surface. And Elly was right; it was stiff, just like a strip of parchment from a page of the *Möðruvallabók*.

She stared at the dark brown ink.

Be warned by another's woe.

Be warned? Be warned about what? *Another's woe?* What was that about? Tómas's heart attack? Brynja struggled to make sense of the note, though it seemed simple enough.

Elly read over Brynja's shoulder. "That must have fallen out of Tómas's pocket when he fell. I saw him pick a piece of paper out of the box of *kleinur* and stick it in his shirt pocket."

"Are you saying Tómas found this with the doughnuts?"

Elly nodded.

"Didn't he think that was strange?"

"I don't know. He didn't read it out loud. He just shrugged, stuck the note in his pocket, and kept eating until the box was empty. When I went to throw the box in the trash, though, I noticed a second piece of paper. I didn't have time to read it because, by that time, Tómas was rummaging through the drawers looking for some sugar to put in his coffee and I didn't want him coming across anything confidential, so I took him down the hall to the lunch room and he got some sugar there." Elly was speaking so quickly she ran out of breath.

Brynja slipped the parchment into a plastic evidence bag taken from the cabinet. "I doubt we'll be able to learn anything from forensics on this, since it's covered in vomit. I'd sure like to know who sent the *kleinur*, though." She took off the latex gloves and threw them in the wastebasket.

"I'll get the other note from the box," Elly said.

"Wait." Brynja put on a clean pair of gloves. "I don't want us to contaminate it."

As they turned to Elly's desk, Brynja pointed at a crumpled wad of moss green paper in the waste paper basket. "What's that?"

"It's the paper the box of *kleinur* was wrapped in. I looked for a return address so I could send a thank-you note, but I didn't find one anywhere on the package."

Brynja retrieved a large evidence bag from the cabinet, folded the green wrapping paper, and tucked it into the bag.

She took off the latex gloves and reached for a clean pair in the cabinet. "Never thought I'd need so many evidence gloves in my own office." She turned her attention to the box that had contained the *kleinur* and plucked the second slip of parchment from underneath the doughnut crumbs. "This is the other paper you were talking about?"

"*Ja*. That's it."

Brynja read the note aloud.

> *At the Thing there is a throng*
> *Past all bounds the crowding comes*
> *Hard 'twill be to patch up peace*
> *'Twixt the men: this wearies me.*
> *Worthier it is for men to bear*
> *Weapons red with gore.*

"Why on earth would someone put this in a box of doughnuts? *Weapons red with gore?*"

The words were penned in the same brown ink found on the parchment Tómas had in his possession when he collapsed. Beneath the words was a drawing of a sword. Drops of blood appeared to fall from the blade onto the words: *Njál's Saga.*

Brynja reread the poem. Those lines seemed familiar. She put the parchment in another evidence bag, peeled off the gloves, and raced to her computer. She clicked on the bookmark for sagadb.org and opened the text of *Njal's Saga.* Just as she thought. A quick search confirmed the passage was indeed from *Njál's Saga,* the first saga in the *Möðruvallabók.* And so was the threat: *Be warned by another's woe.*

Were these warnings intended for her? Did whoever mailed the box of *kleinur* know she'd have the manuscript in her office this morning? If the threats *were* meant for her, was the box of *kleinur* itself dangerous?

Her brain reeled with questions, with all the dark pathways opening up before her.

Who knew that the *Möðruvallabók* would be in her office today? Ari, of course. He had arranged for it to be delivered. And she and Ari had just spoken about *Njál's Saga* at Thingvellir.

The folks at the Magnússon Institute knew. Ari's secretary Fríða knew. Stína knew. And Stína had probably told Amma just as she herself had confided in Jónas that Ari was arranging the manuscript to be delivered to her office before the exhibit. But Amma and Jónas didn't count, and she chided herself for wildly listing everyone she could think of. She had to be rational to figure this out. Clear thinking and logical.

So, who else? She drew a blank.

The real question was, why would someone want to threaten her? And why would someone mail a box of *kleinur* to her at Legacy? It had to be someone she didn't know well or at all, someone on the outer perimeter of her life. Anyone who knew her would surely be aware that, with her gluten allergy, she couldn't eat the doughnuts. She might not even look through the box and find the note. The more she thought about the *kleinur*, the more worried about Tómas she became.

"Elly, would you call the hospital and find out how Tómas is doing?" Brynja said, pouring herself a glass of water from a pitcher on the counter. After draining the glass, her mouth was still dry. "Hold off on calling the Institute, though. I don't want them picking up the book quite yet. I need to check something first before they take it over to Parliament."

She walked back to her office, gripped the edge of the desk, and took a series of quick, shallow breaths. Did Tómas actually have a heart attack or was it something else? Was her office a crime scene now?

She squeezed her eyes shut and tried to calm herself. Should she show the warning parchments to Ísak at the police department? Or would he take over and send the *Möðruvallabók* back to the vault, shutting down her access to it? She reached for the phone to call Ari, wanting to hear the reassurance in his voice, but stopped when she remembered he was in a planning meeting for National Day. He was under a lot of pressure right now, so perhaps she should wait to tell him.

Her phone rang, a call on line three, Ísak's direct line to her office.

"Brynja? Rúnar just called. Terrible thing, that young man falling sick in your office. You okay?"

"We're fine, thanks. Just hoping the guard recovers."

"Must have been a terrible shock. I hear he wasn't a picture of health. Heart attack waiting to happen with all that weight." He coughed. "Listen, I'm sure you're rattled, but what's your take on the museum theft, the Kjarval painting?"

"Henning hasn't briefed me on the case yet."

"Why would Henning need to brief you? I had Elly take the file to your office, not his. The case is primarily a forensic one at this point."

Brynja took stock of everything on her desk: the computer monitor and keyboard, the *Möðruvallabók* with the box it came in on the side table, the cotton gloves, notes on the Grímsdóttir case, the latest activity logs, a coffee cup, the childhood photo of her and Lúkas standing in the doorway of Munkathverá bundled in their woolen sweaters, a pitcher, an empty glass, her landline and cell phone.

"I don't have the Kjarval file here."

"Maybe Elly still has it?"

"I'll ask her." Brynja hesitated. "Ísak?"

"Yes?"

"I wonder if we could discuss Henning at some point. He seems to be uncomfortable working with me, and I want things to go smoothly."

"Of course."

She looked at the clock. "I'll be over after I take care of a few things."

"Anytime."

Brynja hung up, anxiety burning her insides like acid. What more could happen within the space of an hour? She would have to ask Elly about the file. She couldn't even remember if she'd seen it on her desk this morning.

She took a deep breath. One thing at a time.

Once again, she put on the cotton gloves. She lifted the cover of the *Möðruvallabók* and turned to *Njal's Saga.* As much as she hated the idea, someone in recent years might have left a mark or sign of some sort on the manuscript, something that could give her a direction to follow. It was an idea born of desperation, but she was determined. She scanned the pages again for anything unusual: a drawing, a scribble in the margin, an asterisk, an underlined word…anything that might be a clue as to why she had been sent the warning. Any clue as to how, according to the poem, Lúkas could be found in the *Möðruvallabók*.

Nothing.

No notes in the margins other than the two she had found earlier in other parts of the book. No markings, no torn bits of parchment, no pressed bits of leaves or flowers, no scratch marks.

Was she missing something?

The words began to blur upon the page, shifting shape and giving rise to the boyish curls and wide-eyed smile of a young boy. She and Lúkas had been climbing the tree out past the corral when the limb had snapped, and she had fallen. Lúkas had scrambled down the trunk and stood over her, wiping the tears from her face. "*Ég er hérna*, Brynja. I'm here. You'll be all right." And, at the time, she had felt as if things *would* always be all right. She and Lúkas would always be together, watching out for one another.

Brynja reached for the locket around her neck. Opening the pendant, she slowly ran her finger over the tiny photo that was nestled in one half of the silver heart.

What happened to you, Lúkas? Where are you? She sighed and squeezed the locket shut, tucking it under the neckline of her blouse.

She closed the cover of the *Möðruvallabók* and reached for the poem she'd received about her brother. She laid this next to the parchment found in the box of *kleinur*—the warning about weapons red with gore—and compared the two. First, the inks were different: The poem was in red with black ink at its edges and the warning was in brown ink. Second, the writing styles were quite distinct: The poem was written in a modern-day cursive, similar to the handwriting she had been taught in primary school, while the warning was penned in a rigid, Gothic style, nearly identical to the script in the *Möðruvallabók*. Third, the messages were different: The first merely referred to the *Book of Möðruvellir* but the second was taken entirely from one of its sagas.

The poem and warning seemed to have been sent by two different people.

Who had sent the poem? And who had sent the warning? One person seemed to want to help her find Lúkas and someone else was trying to frighten her.

Brynja pressed the intercom. "Elly, would you come in here?"

Not a second later, her eager intern dashed into the office.

"Were you able to find out how Tómas is doing?"

"Unfortunately, no," Elly said. "I told the hospital I was calling on your behalf, but they wouldn't give me any information over the phone."

"I'll get over there myself. Thanks for trying." Brynja looked again at everything on her desktop. "Have you seen the file for the Kjarval Museum theft? Ísak said he asked you to give it to me yesterday, but I can't find it anywhere. Did you move it by any chance?"

"No. I left it on your desk."

"When?"

"Yesterday."

"Was Henning in my office while I was gone?"

"Not that I know of."

"I don't seem to have it here," Brynja said, lifting her notes on the Grímsdóttir case and looking under the activity logs. "Anyway, would you call the Institute now and have them send someone over? We need to get the manuscript over to the exhibit."

Elly nodded and excused herself. She made a quick phone call from the outer office, and then came back in. "Someone will be over shortly."

Brynja motioned for Elly to sit down. "Ready for a crash course in forensics? We've got a few minutes before they pick up the book."

"Sure thing. I've been reading up on forensics and, besides, I've seen *CSI* a million times."

Brynja pointed at the two papers on her desk—the poem about Lúkas and the parchment with the creepy warning about *weapons red with gore*. "We've got to figure out who wrote these. I think the poem has something to do with finding my brother—"

"Your brother?"

"Yes. He disappeared when we were children."

Elly stepped back. "*Nej!*"

"It was a long time ago, but the poem refers to finding my other half. We were twins." Brynja paused. "Are twins," she said, correcting herself.

"I'm so sorry," Elly said, brushing aside her bangs. "Do you think those parchments are about him, too?"

Brynja shrugged. "I don't know. They may have to do with my brother. Or with the guard. Or…I just don't know. That's why I want to examine both the poem and the parchments. Identifying who wrote them may well give us the answer."

Elly sat down. "That parchment—the one about *another's woe*— is too mucked up with puke to be useful, right?"

"I'm afraid so." Brynja pushed her glasses up the bridge of her nose. "So, we'll focus on the poem about my brother and the parchment you found in the bottom of the box of *kleinur*. The poem is written in red ink with a drawing of leaves in black. It was addressed to me but mailed to the police station by mistake."

"I remember."

"Let's call it Exhibit A."

"Okay. Exhibit A. Poem. Red and black ink. Paper. Mailroom."

"Next, Exhibit B. This one is on parchment. A passage from the sagas. Seems like some sort of warning."

Elly nodded. "Exhibit B. Brown ink. Box of *kleinur*. B, B, B."

"Right."

Elly cracked her knuckles. "Two things that have nothing to do with each other."

Brynja cocked her head.

Elly explained, "That's what Grissom says in *CSI*. 'Two things that have nothing to do with each other.' And then his colleague Sara says, 'Or everything.'" She smiled. "Get it?"

Brynja wasn't quite sure she did.

"So, I mean, like, the poem and the warning could have nothing to do with each other, or they could have everything to do with each other."

Brynja nodded. Elly was going to work out just fine. "Right. Was it the same person, or two different people?" She leaned back in her chair. "How do you think we should proceed?"

"I'm guessing, since you're a geneticist, the first thing you're going to want to do is DNA analysis?"

"Right again."

Elly pointed at the poem about Lúkas. "A ton of people have already touched that one. The mail clerk Baltasar gave it to Henning; I brought it over here and handed it to you. You put on gloves, though, so it doesn't have your DNA on it."

"Just a second," Brynja said, checking her phone to see if Baltasar had called back about the stamp. He hadn't.

Elly's voice escalated. "And that's not even counting the person who actually *wrote* it. How are you ever going to tell whose DNA is whose?"

"It'll be a pretty complicated picture as far as DNA fingerprinting goes."

Elly pointed at the parchment with the brown ink. "But that one. Exhibit B. From the box of *kleinur*. I didn't touch it. And neither did Tómas."

"And I had gloves on when I lifted it out of the box," Brynja added. "With any luck, only one person's DNA is on that warning, the person who wrote it. By the way, we've also got to send the actual box and some of that green paper for DNA analysis. More people have touched those, I'm afraid, but it's worth a shot. Maybe we can match up the DNA fingerprints."

Elly nodded slowly. "I'm not really sure what you mean by DNA fingerprint. Is it the DNA in your actual fingerprint that we're looking at?"

"No, it's not a fingerprint in the usual sense, not the pattern of swirls on the skin of your fingertips. A DNA fingerprint is a metaphor. What we're referring to is the DNA isolated from skin cells left behind when you touch anything. Each person has a pattern of DNA fragments that's unique to them. We look at thirteen different regions in the DNA that contain STRs."

"And STRs are what exactly?"

"Short tandem repeats. Little bits of DNA that are repeated one after the other on a chromosome, kind of like a stutter."

"Okay…"

"The number of times that bit of DNA is repeated varies between individuals so that the STRs produce bands of different lengths. That allows us to identify people by the pattern those repeats make. The pattern is called a DNA fingerprint."

"Seems like there would be people with the same number of repeats."

"That's true if you look at just one STR region. But the chance of two people having the same lengths for each of the different thirteen STRs is about one in a billion."

"Got it. So, then, once you know the pattern of DNA, how do you match it to an actual person?"

"That's where the GeneID database comes in. Legacy's already profiled just about everyone in Iceland and stored those DNA fingerprints in their database."

Elly jangled the bracelets on her wrist. "We isolate DNA from the poem and the parchment, then determine the pattern of bands and look for a match in the GeneID database. Then we'll know who sent them. Got it."

"I'm most concerned right now with the parchment warning. We need to find out if it had anything to do with the guard's heart attack." Brynja took a sip of water. "All right, what else? What else can we do in terms of forensics?"

Elly leaned over. "The handwriting. The writing on the warning is written in some old- time, churchy style."

"Gothic," Brynja said.

"And the poem is in, like, cursive, or something."

"I'll have our specialist take a look." Brynja leaned back. "Anything else?"

Elly combed her fingers through her bangs.

"Think, Elly."

"Ink!" Elly beamed. "Your poem said something about ink, right?"

"Yes. We might be able to identify who wrote these by tracing where the ink came from. Let science help us. We'll have the lab examine the DNA. And the chemistry lab over at the university can analyze the ink by TLC."

"Tender loving care?"

Brynja shot Elly a look. "TLC is thin-layer chromatography. The chemistry lab basically dissolves the ink in a solvent and then drops it onto the edge of a sheet of glass covered with a thin layer of some absorbent material like silica gel. The components of different inks migrate by capillary action through the gel at different rates depending upon their solubility—"

Elly coughed. "You just went above my pay grade, Brynja. I think you're saying that we've got to cut off pieces of the poem and the parchment and send them to the chemistry lab so they can dissolve the inks and do some chemical voodoo on them."

Brynja smiled. "That's basically it. I'm going to cut off a small piece of the parchment you found in the box of *kleinur* and two small slips of paper from the poem you brought over from the police station. We'll send all three samples to the chemistry lab."

She was putting on a pair of latex gloves and opening a sleeve of sterilized scissors when her cell phone pinged. She looked at the screen; the message was from Ari.

Got a madman in the office.

Frowning, she removed the gloves and picked up the phone to text a reply. *Madman???*

Henning, Ari responded. *He's furious that I sent the Möðruvallabók to your office. Says he's going to bring charges against you for what happened to Tómas. Why haven't you called?*

Brynja's hands shook as she texted. *Charges? Against me?*

He's adamant that you've got something to do with it. Is he always like this?

Brynja gasped as she read the next line.

You do know Tómas is in a coma?

Chapter 11

Brynja pulled into the parking lot at Landspítali Hospital and sat for a few minutes to calm herself. How could Tómas be in a coma? He must have had more than a heart attack. Perhaps the heart attack had been so severe that he then suffered a cardiac arrest? She knew cardiac arrest often led to a coma. That was, if the patient was lucky enough to survive at all.

She was suddenly aware of her own heart beating much too fast as she shut the car door and headed to the entrance.

The automatic doors of the emergency room whooshed open. Fluorescent lighting buzzed in the waiting room and Brynja squinted in the bright light. Above the din of quiet conversations, an intercom crackled: *'Code White, Bed 3,'* signaling a pediatric emergency. A collective wail rose from the corner and a man and woman rushed past Brynja toward the swinging doors leading to the corridor beyond.

A jab of pain shot between her temples, fogging her thoughts. Twenty years ago. Akureyri. The carnival site, the fields, the riverbank, the village. Jónas clutching her hand. The hospital. The deserted waiting room. The acrid smell of bleach. The empty beds. The doctor shaking his head. The cold reality that Lúkas had simply disappeared.

"Ma'am?" A middle-aged woman in a gray, business suit was shaking her shoulder. "Can I help you? Get a glass of water? You look like you're about to faint."

Brynja drew a deep breath. "No. Thank you. I'm okay." She made her way to reception and said, "Here to see Tómas Gylfason."

Behind the counter, a bony clerk was filling out a large-print crossword puzzle. "No visitors allowed for Tómas Gylfason."

Brynja took out her Legacy ID and showed it to the man.

The clerk erased a few squares of the puzzle and blew the tiny specks of rubber from the page before looking up. "As I said, no visitors allowed. Why are you showing me your ID? That's a biotech company."

Brynja pointed to the official law enforcement stamp. "Legacy conducts forensic analysis for the police. I'm authorized to see the patient."

The receptionist examined the ID and then typed in a few keystrokes. He squinted to read the information on the computer monitor. "Tómas Gylfason isn't in the ER. He's in room 531, medical ward." He tapped his pencil. "That Tómas is a popular one. There's a detective up there already." He glanced at the visitor log. "Detective Inspector Henning Holt signed in an hour ago."

Brynja thanked the clerk and took the elevator up to the fifth floor.

At the doorway, she paused to study the room. Tómas lay motionless and sheet-white, enmeshed in a web of tubing. Henning stood next to the hospital bed, his nose buried deep in Tómas's medical file. He flipped through the chart, then scribbled in his leather-bound notepad. Brynja felt a heavy weight settle in her stomach and readied herself for a confrontation.

She knocked twice on the open door and walked quietly across the linoleum floor to Tómas's bedside.

Henning snapped the chart shut. "What are you doing here?" His Napoleonic frame stiffened in the starch of his police uniform. "I'll handle this case."

"Case? We don't know that Tómas is a case." She placed her hand on Tómas's shoulder and absent-mindedly adjusted his gown. "All we know at the moment is that the poor man is sick." She looked at Henning. "You do know his medical chart is confidential, don't you?"

Henning slid a pencil behind his ear. "This is clearly a criminal case. How else would you explain a healthy twenty-six-year-old frothing at the mouth like some rabid dog and damn near dying in your office? Pretty coincidental that Tómas just happened to leave you alone with the old manuscript you seem so interested in, wouldn't you say? What were you intending to do with it anyway? The whole thing reeks."

"Reeks?" Brynja pulled him aside. "Are you suggesting someone had a hand in this? For God's sake, look at him." She motioned to Tómas. "I feel horrible saying this, but he's obese. His heart—"

"That's not what the doctor's saying." Henning motioned to the hallway where a petite, young woman with curls of russet red hair was speaking with a nurse.

The doctor knocked on the open door and then entered the room.

"I'm Rakel Atladóttir," she said, extending her hand to Brynja. "I presume you're family?"

Brynja shook her head and showed the doctor her ID, explaining that Tómas had fallen sick in her office and that she was here to check on his condition. Henning grunted but otherwise remained silent.

The physician picked up Tómas's medical file. "Nurse shouldn't have left this here." She turned to the laboratory report. "Strange case. His blood sugar and electrolytes are all within range. And the cardiac enzymes are normal as well."

"So, not a typical heart attack, then?" Henning retrieved the pencil from behind his ear.

"Doesn't look like it." The doctor checked Tómas's cardiac monitor and then studied the medical chart further. "Patient resuscitated in ER, conscious but presented with muscle spasms, hallucinations, nausea, vomiting, and torticollis."

Henning tapped the pencil on his notepad. "Torticollis?"

"Wryneck," Brynja said, recalling a case study from medical school.

"That's right. Not many people have heard of torticollis, or wryneck, as you say." Dr. Atladóttir cleared her throat and turned her attention back to the chart. "Torticollis is a more or less fixed twisting of the muscles in the neck. I've seen it before." She reached up, standing on her tiptoes to adjust the flow of oxygen to Tómas's ventilator. "In fact, I've seen all of these symptoms together before, but that was in horses."

"In horses?" Brynja repeated.

"Yes. When I was thirteen, my parents sent me to Búðardalur to work on a farm during school break. It was a ridiculously wet summer, even for Iceland, and a number of horses fell ill. As far as I can recall, the horses had the same symptoms as Tómas here. Of course, you can't tell if a horse is hallucinating, but they sure were crazed. Poor farmer had to shoot the lot of them before they suffered any further."

"What are you saying?" Brynja asked. She looked over at Tómas and then back at the doctor. "What made them sick?"

"Turned out that the horses had been poisoned."

Henning's face brightened. "Poisoned?"

"Who would poison horses?" Brynja asked.

The doctor shook her head. "I just remember the adults saying they'd been poisoned. I don't remember how. I'm not sure I ever knew. I was young and more interested in the farmhands at that point. At any rate, we're doing a toxicology screen on Tómas and should have the results soon."

Henning was furiously scratching notes. "Doctor, I'm going to need a full report—"

The alarm on Tómas's heart monitor beeped loudly, and Brynja hurried to his bedside.

Tómas wrestled free of the sheet and flung his arms upward. He motioned toward his mouth and mucus gurgled in his throat.

The doctor raised the head of the hospital bed and listened to her patient's chest. Satisfied, she put the stethoscope back in her jacket pocket.

Tómas opened his eyes and looked around the room.

Relief washed over Brynja. Tómas was no longer in a coma; he was waking up. She gave Henning a subtle yet icy stare and moved to the opposite side of the bed.

She leaned in close to Tómas and touched his arm gently. "Tómas, you've had a fall. You're in the hospital now. We've all had a horrible scare, but you're in good hands, and you're going to be okay." She patted his arm. "You need to rest now."

Tómas grabbed Brynja's hand, weakly but with enough force to get her attention. He shook his head and words gurgled up from deep within his throat. "No. Not—"

He closed his eyes, took a halting breath, and fell silent.

More concerned than ever, Brynja returned to Legacy and waited in the lobby for Elly to arrive. She had asked her intern to make an appointment with Rúnar so that she could take the opportunity to introduce the young woman formally. At the same time, she planned to tell Rúnar about the warning she had received and inform him that the lab would be doing some analysis on the parchment.

She peeled off her rain parka, nodded at security, and looked up at the massive, helical sculpture of DNA in the center of the atrium. She had passed through the sky-lit lobby many times, but each time she marveled anew at how the steel plates reflected the changing world outside. Today, the sculpture mirrored the cold, gray clouds that hovered over the city—and the dread that had settled in her stomach. Did the warnings she'd received have something to do with Tómas's collapse or was that just a coincidence? Was she being warned to stay away from the *Möðruvallabók* or to stop her search for Lúkas?

A few minutes later, Elly flung open the lobby door and made a beeline for the reception desk. The tap of her boots reverberated off the marble floor and echoed against the glass walls. She didn't seem to notice Brynja was seated by the entryway.

Before Brynja could join her, Elly reached the receptionist. "Dr. Rúnar Bragason, please."

The wiry receptionist didn't bother to look up. "He's busy. You'll have to wait."

"But I have an appointment with him and Brynja. I called earlier."

The woman pursed her lips as if she had just chewed a lemon rind. "I'll call you when he's ready."

Turning, Elly spied Brynja and sat down next to her. "I'm so sorry. This is ridiculous. I really did make an appointment."

"I know you did. Rúnar keeps me waiting every time. It's just a little game he plays."

In truth, Rúnar annoyed the hell out of Brynja. He was an insecure, petty man.

"Just a heads-up," she whispered. "Don't be offended by Rúnar. At least, don't take anything he says personally. He's an equal opportunity chauvinist. Not a fan of women in the workplace, especially in the so-called hallowed halls of science."

"I know the type," Elly said. "Like that Nobel Prize guy who said women at work just cause trouble. *'You fall in love with them, they fall in love with you, and when you criticize them, they cry.'* Something like that."

"Exactly. Except I don't think anyone's ever fallen in love with Rúnar. You'll see."

"Can't wait," Elly said, adjusting her suede miniskirt. "I did get that impression when Rúnar was at the station. He's not super personable. Didn't even bother to introduce himself." She tapped her foot and glanced at the hallway leading to the labs. "By the way, I brought the spoon over to Stefán in the lab yesterday. He said it would take him a few days to get you the results. They're shorthanded because of National Day coming up."

The receptionist coughed, nodded, and motioned to the door.

"You can go in now," she mouthed, as if the inner sanctum were holy ground.

They were walking down the hall to Rúnar's office when Brynja heard his phone ring. She put her hand out to stop Elly from entering the room.

"*Halló?*" Rúnar barked into the speakerphone.

A raspy voice answered. "Detective Henning Holt calling for Dr. Rúnar Bragason."

"Yes, Henning, cut the formality. This is Rúnar."

"Oh, *halló*, Rúnar. Listen, we're not getting anywhere on the art theft at the Kjarval Museum. Any results yet? I was hoping the burglar might have left his DNA on the duct tape used to tie up the curator."

Brynja's muscles tensed. Why was Henning bypassing her?

"We're working on it," Rúnar said. "It doesn't look like the DNA is Icelandic stock, though."

"Stock?"

"The DNA doesn't have any of the SNPs we commonly see in Icelanders. The burglar might be Italian or Greek. I'm not sure yet."

"Keep me posted, will you? I've got to run. I'm at the hospital with the guard that came over to Legacy earlier. He's in a coma and I've got a meeting with Ísak about it. Seems your head of forensics is in hot water."

Brynja wanted to barge into Rúnar's office and grab the phone, but she restrained herself. Henning would have to be dealt with, and soon. Why was he still at the hospital with Tómas? And why was he spreading rumors about her being in hot water? Henning and Rúnar had been fast friends for more than four decades—ever since their school days—but this conversation breached all rules of confidentiality, not to mention professional standards.

"Henning?" Rúnar said.

"Yes?"

"Any idea why Brynja is interested in Paget's disease? Eric in IT informs me whenever an attempt to access the LinX database is made. Standard protocol. Seems Brynja started to download the file and then stopped. Is there some sort of investigation—?"

The piercing beep of a hospital monitor blasted through the speakerphone. *Code Blue. Fifth Floor. Code Blue. Room—*"

"I've got to go," Henning said and hung up.

Chapter 12

Brynja stood barely three feet from the door to Rúnar's office. She put a finger to her lips and motioned to her intern to back up. She had to think. Was that Code Blue for Tómas? Why did Rúnar tell Henning she'd attempted to access the Paget's file? If either of them asked why, what would she say?

As soon as Rúnar hung up the phone, Brynja and Elly approached the doorway.

They watched as Rúnar paced back and forth in front of plate-glass windows ablaze with color; yellow, orange, and red poppies bloomed from a row of potted plants on the windowsill. He methodically checked the soil with his fingertips and plucked leaves from one plant after another, putting them in the pocket of his navy sport coat.

"Looks like a jungle in there," Elly mouthed.

"Rúnar likes plants more than people," Brynja whispered. "He did his PhD thesis on the genetics of the Iceland poppy. They're quite toxic. Rúnar identified the compound. It's an alkaloid called chelidonine."

"Who knew?" Elly said.

Brynja knocked firmly on the door.

Startled, Rúnar whirled around. In a nanosecond, his expression changed from surprise to hostility. "Good. You're here. I have some questions for you. Come in." He waved them to chairs but didn't wait for them to be seated. "According to IT, Brynja, you attempted to access the Paget's file from the LinX Disease Database." He crossed his arms over the starch of his white, button-down shirt and scowled. "Is that correct?"

"I am the director of forensics, Rúnar."

"Going into that database—that's strictly against company policy. Is this for some case you're working on?" He didn't sound like he expected the answer to be yes.

Without warning, the walls began to cave in on her, squeezing the air from her chest. The poppies swirled in a kaleidoscope of colorful petals. She blinked. *No. Please. Not now.* Averting her gaze, she saw her feet plunge into the alternating black and white tiles that lined the floor. *Not now,* she begged her body, *not now. I need my mind—clear and whole. Let it pass. Please.* She counted. *One, two...*

A moment later, the walls released their grip, and she could breathe. Wresting her legs from the quicksand of the checkerboard pattern on the floor, she stood up and took two steps forward, stumbling slightly before collecting herself.

She stood up straight and looked directly at Rúnar. "In answer to your question, yes, I did have a pressing reason for accessing the database. A farmer up in Dalvik unearthed a skeleton while plowing his field. It had an enlarged skull, which I'm sure you know is indicative of Paget's. He wants to know if the bones belong to his great-grandfather, who wandered off decades ago."

She scrutinized Rúnar's face for signs he believed her story, but instead he looked confused.

"Are you okay?" Rúnar asked. "It looks like you lost your footing there."

"Yes, I'm fine, thank you."

"You sure? You don't look right."

"I'm fine."

"Okay, then, I'll let it go this time, but in the future, ask me directly before accessing LinX." Rúnar's tone softened when he noticed the fidgety shadow behind Brynja. He turned to Elly. "And, young lady, you are—?"

"Oh." Elly jumped. "I'm Elly, sir, uh, Dr. Bragason."

"Rúnar," he said. "I run the show here, but you can still call me Rúnar. After all, at the end of the game, the king and the pawn go back in the same box."

Elly nodded. "Yes, sir—er—Rúnar."

He frowned. "Are you new here?"

"I'm doing an internship in forensics and bouncing between the police department and Legacy," Elly said. "Brynja's assistant for the summer. I'm also getting some social media up to speed."

"Then you must've heard about the *Í-bók* app, eh?" Rúnar winked. "We sure got a lot of press over that."

"*Í-bók?*"

"You know, 'Bump the app before you bump in bed.'"

"Sorry. I don't know that one," Elly said.

Brynja stepped between them. Rúnar was practically drooling over Elly, who was half—no, one-third—his age. "Rúnar—"

He waved her off and moved closer to Elly. "The *Í-bók*. You know, the *Íslendingabók*, the *Book of Icelanders*."

"I'm from Denmark," Elly said.

"But you must know about Iceland's manuscripts?"

"I know about the *Möðruvallabók*," Elly stammered.

"Well, the *Íslendingabók* is even older. It's from the twelfth century." Rúnar cocked his head. "It's no wonder you don't know much about the Icelandic manuscripts. You Danes basically stole them from us, so I doubt you learned about them in school." He glanced at Brynja but quickly returned his attention to Elly. "Years ago, some kook set off an explosion to protest the fact that we finally got the manuscripts back from Denmark. Your boss here knows all about that. It was at an event celebrating the anniversary of the manuscripts' repatriation to Iceland. I was there when Brynja's mother—"

Brynja felt a flush rise from her neck to her face. What right did Rúnar have to bring that up? If it hadn't been for the explosion, her whole life might have turned out differently. Even though Rúnar had grown up in Eyjafjörður and was related to her family in some convoluted third-cousin-once-removed-godchild-of-an-uncle-by-marriage kind of way, they were *her* wounds, not his.

The families were not close—not even tolerating each other for the sake of appearances. Pabbi hadn't spoken a word to anyone in Rúnar's family since he and Rúnar's brother Axel had fallen out over property rights. The Bragason farm bordered Munkathverá to the north, and Axel had insisted a strip of Pabbi's farmland actually belonged to him. Pabbi had simply been too exhausted caring for Mamma to fight Axel's claim in court, and the property lines had been redrawn. Her father had refused to discuss the matter further, and Brynja had never learned just what piece of land the Bragasons had taken from her family.

"We don't need to talk about that right now, Rúnar." Brynja said. She wondered whether Rúnar knew more about the boundary issue than she did. But this wasn't the time to ask. "The return of the manuscripts from Denmark happened years before Elly was even born." She cleared her throat and forced herself to smile. She needed his permission to analyze DNA on the parchment since the warning was not officially part of a criminal case. "Speaking of manuscripts, though, I've got a favor to ask. I found a strange note written on parchment in the box of doughnuts the guard had helped himself to. I'd like the lab to analyze the DNA on it."

She would have to take things one step at a time; Rúnar would be hesitant to allow forensics on samples not referred directly from the police. But Tómas had fallen ill after eating *kleinur* and the doctor seemed to think he could have been poisoned. That was reason enough.

Rúnar looked puzzled. "Parchment? Why on earth would someone write a note on parchment?"

"I don't know," Brynja said. "I'm trying to figure out who wrote it. Then maybe we'll know why."

Elly stepped closer to Rúnar. "I bet you know how to extract DNA from parchment with that chemical magic Brynja told me you're so good at?"

Rúnar smiled.

Startled, Brynja watched the exchange with concealed amusement.

"Of course, I can extract and analyze DNA from parchment," Rúnar said, puffing out his chest. "Part of my research into agricultural genetics involved the interplay between plants and the farm animals that grazed upon them. Sheep, goats, cows. You do know that parchment is made from the skin of those animals, don't you?"

Elly gave the impression that she did.

"I'm sure I can even tell if your parchment is made from sheep, goat, or cow skin. Many people use the term parchment interchangeably with vellum, but vellum is strictly from cows. The word vellum has the same origin as veal, or calf. So," he rattled on. "We can test your parchment here to see what type of animal the DNA comes from. Maybe that'll help you narrow down where the person got the parchment from in the first place. In Iceland, parchment was made from calfskin—vellum— so if it's goat or sheep, it must have been sent from elsewhere."

Brynja interrupted his lecture. "That's great. That could be very helpful. But we're especially interested in the human DNA on it."

Rúnar nodded, stroked the hairs of his neatly trimmed goatee, and turned to Elly. "Your name again?"

"Elly."

"Well, Elly, you can be sure that I'll do my best to match any human DNA we find on the parchment to individuals in our database."

"Thanks, Rúnar," Brynja said, placing the bag with the warning on his desk. "I owe you one."

He wasn't listening. "Now, about that *Í-bók* App," he said to Elly. "The *Íslendingabók* is a book about the families that settled in Iceland. The *Í-bók* App was developed from the genealogies of those families and then extended to everyone living in Iceland now." He leaned in closer. "Since we Icelanders are all related, it's very useful as a dating app. In a couple of clicks on your iPhone, you can find out if the person you're stumbling home from the nightclub and tumbling into bed with is your second cousin, your father's step-brother, your wife's niece. Talk about great press! It was a hit, great public relations for Legacy. Thousands of people were suddenly interested in donating DNA to our database."

"Is that what you do here? Get everyone's DNA so they'll know who to f—er, sleep with?" Elly asked.

Brynja shot her a disapproving glance.

"I hope you understand, young lady," Rúnar said. "We do important work here, tracking the genetics of disease. Because of Legacy, Iceland is poised to solve the whole world's health problems. Diabetes, cancer, heart disease, you name it."

"Yes, sir."

"Iceland has an isolated population of only three-hundred-thousand-plus people who, for the most part, descended from a handful of Vikings that settled here a thousand years ago. So, we're all pretty much related. One person's DNA is very similar to another's." Rúnar walked over to the shelf of poppy plants lining the windows in his office. "Let me explain it in a way that you can understand."

Behind his back, Brynja and Elly glanced at each other.

Rúnar picked up a pot of white poppies. "Imagine you have thousands of white poppies covering the hillside in spring. Among them, you spot, say, three red poppies." He picked up a pot of red poppies with his other hand. "Those red poppies must have something different in their DNA that makes them stand out. They have a change in their DNA, a mutation, that causes the red color."

Elly was clearly doing her best to appear attentive.

"Say we analyze the DNA of the red poppies and it turns out that they all have a mutation in the gene for poppy color that's found *only* in the poppies with red color, not in any of the thousands of white poppies. We can be fairly certain that mutation—that change in the poppy color gene—causes the red color."

Elly nodded. "So, that's how you're able to link mutations with diseases? If people have a certain disease like, say, some kind of muscular dystrophy, and each of them has the same mutation, then you're saying that mutation might be the cause of the disease?"

Rúnar placed the pots back on the windowsill, turned around, and rubbed his hands together. "Yes. You catch on pretty quickly."

"Only because you explained it so well, sir."

"That's my job," Rúnar said with false modesty.

Brynja felt slightly nauseated listening to Rúnar pontificate. Did he really think he was impressing Elly?

She stepped forward. "I'm sorry, we have to get going. I've got a paternity case to look over, Elly's due back at the police station, and I'm sure you're busy as well. Let me know what you find out about the parchment."

Rúnar didn't take his eyes off Elly. "Listen, if your taskmaster ever lets you out from underfoot, I'll take you for a drink and teach you a bit more about what we do here."

They left Rúnar's office and walked down the hall. Brynja gave Elly a little more background on Rúnar and his personal habits. He could be inappropriate but was generally harmless. Nonetheless, after seeing the interest he took in Elly, she advised her intern to think twice before dealing with him directly.

Brynja's cell phone rang, interrupting the conversation.

"Brynja?" Stína's voice blared out from the other end of the line. "I called my guy at the Magnússon Institute. The one who works in manuscripts. Talk about a bird in the hand. We hopped right into bed and picked up where we left off."

"One minute." Brynja covered the speaker and mouthed to Elly that she should return to the station.

Elly nodded and took the stairway to the exit.

Brynja stepped into her office and shut the door. "Sorry, Stína, I'm back."

"So, I'm lying there naked as a jaybird," Stína said, continuing where she left off. "And he's telling me all about the *Möðruvallabók*. It's the largest known collection of Icelandic family sagas and it dates to around 1350 AD. As if we didn't know that, right?"

"Right."

"And no one knows the identity of the medieval scribes who copied the sagas into the *Möðruvallabók,* but they probably lived in some monastery in North Iceland. Yadah yadah…"

"Did you tell him about the poem?"

"Yes. He didn't know what to make of it other than the fact that the *Möðruvallabók* is called the *Book of Möðruvellir* because some guy in the early 1600s named Magnus Björnsson wrote something on one of the pages about being at Möðruvellir."

"I saw his name in the margin," Brynja said. "What else?"

"My guy was a proverbial fountain of knowledge," Stína paused and laughed. "A fountain of more than knowledge, come to think of it."

"Stína?"

"Sorry. Anyway, apparently, in 1684, Magnús's son Björn took the *Möðruvallabók* to Copenhagen. He gave it as a gift to the royal court, to the royal antiquarian. That's why there were so many protests in Denmark about returning the books to Iceland. Many Danes insisted that they'd been given a gift, but, on the other hand, Icelanders insisted they were the rightful owners since the books were written here."

"I still don't know what any of this has to do with the poem and Lúkas. Did your manuscript guy say anything else about it?"

"That lawyer who wrote his name in the *Möðruvallabók*—Magnus Björnsson? He lived on a farm right next to Möðruvellir Church. At a farm called Hof."

Brynja's stomach twisted into a knot. Was that it? Was that the connection?

Did Magnus Björnsson bring the *Möðruvallabók* to his farm at Hof after he signed his name in it at Möðruvellir? Was the poem telling her she would find Lúkas in a root cellar there? Could he have been so close to home all this time?

Chapter 13

The following morning, Brynja grabbed the alarm clock next to Ari's bed, appalled at the time. She must have fallen asleep after he left. They had stayed up late into the night hashing over yesterday's traumatic events: the guard's collapse while delivering the manuscript to her office, the disturbing telephone conversation she'd overheard between Henning and Rúnar, the excuse she'd made about her attempt to access the Paget's file in LinX database, Rúnar's inappropriate fawning over her intern. After Ari had fallen asleep, she had lain awake for hours worrying about Tómas. As much as she wanted to believe obesity had led to his cardiac arrest, she couldn't deny the more logical conclusion he had fallen ill from eating the *kleinur*. Especially since the doctor had thought some of his symptoms resembled poisoning.

She picked up her cell phone from the nightstand to see if the toxicology report was in. Tómas's family had given the doctor permission to relay the results to her as soon as they were available. The screen was blank. No missed calls.

Brynja turned her attention back to the *Möðruvallabók.* Two hours ago, Ari had kissed her goodbye and promised to arrange for security to let her into the Parliament building at nine so she could examine the manuscript more thoroughly. Several of Iceland's precious medieval manuscripts would be on display there for the National Day festivities: the *Íslendingabók*, the *Book of Icelanders,* containing Iceland's history and genealogy through the twelfth century; the *Flateyjarbók*, the *Flat Island Book,* a collection of sagas about the Norse Kings; the *Codex Regius,* or *Poetic Edda,* the thirteenth-century manuscript of Old Norse poetry and mythology; and, of course, the *Möðruvallabók*, the *Book of Möðruvellir*, containing the largest collection of Icelandic family sagas. Her brief look through it yesterday had not shed any light on what the book had to do with Lúkas's disappearance, and after the crisis with Tómas, she'd been unable to concentrate on the poem's riddle.

She got out of bed and pulled on the pair of black slacks and cashmere sweater she'd worn the day before. She drank a quick cup of coffee, then locked the door and hurried the few blocks toward Parliament. At the entrance, she held her ID up to the camera and pressed the intercom.

"Brynja Pálsdóttir. Here to see the manuscripts."

The guard buzzed her through and greeted her warmly. "Prime minister told me you'd be coming, ma'am." He pointed toward the lobby. "If you'll just wait here, I'll get someone to escort you up to the rotunda." He walked behind the glass of the security booth and picked up the phone.

Brynja stepped into the empty silence of the great hall. When in session, Parliament was abuzz with the competing agendas of sixty-three MPs representing political parties ranging from the center-right and right-wing Independents and Progressives to the centrist Bright Future party, the leftist Left-Green party and the rising, anti-establishment, direct-democracy party, the Pirates. But in summer, the politicians returned to their respective districts and would be preparing for National Day festivities.

The guard tapped on the glass, raised his index finger, and mouthed, "One minute."

Brynja nodded and looked about the wood-paneled lobby. She walked over to the immense, brass plaque that had been affixed to the wall in 1930, marking the millennial celebration of Iceland's Parliament. She pulled her glasses from her bag and read the embossed lettering.

Althing
1000 years of Parliament

The Althing embodies the Parliamentary Democracy of Iceland, the oldest extant parliamentary institution in the world. The Althing was founded in 930AD on the open fields of Thingvellir as a general assembly of the Icelandic Commonwealth. The country's most powerful leaders, the *goðar*, met annually each summer at Thingvellir to decide on legislation and dispense justice to the thousands of people converging from all corners of the land. The current parliament building, the Althingishús, was designed by Danish architect Ferdinand Meldahl and was constructed in 1881 from Icelandic basalt.

Below were listed the names of each of Iceland's leaders from the tenth century on. Pride bubbled within her. There, in bold letters for all to see, was the name of her fiancé: 'Ari Ketilsson 2015–'

The guard stepped out of the booth and pointed at the stairs. "You can go on up. They're waiting for you in the rotunda."

Brynja climbed the steps of the grand staircase and was once again struck by the grandeur of the large reception room fanning out over the garden below. The rotunda's circle of arched windows, draped in fine silk, cast dapples of sunlight onto the hardwood floor.

A dozen stony-faced guards stood between tall, stone pillars that held carved busts of Iceland's important historical figures: Erík the Red, explorer; Jón Sigurðsson, leader of the Independence movement; Egil Skallagrímsson, Viking poet; Snorri Sturluson, historian, poet, politician, and author of the *Prose Edda;* and Ari Thorgilsson, priest and author of the *Íslendingabók.*

As Brynja approached the cabinet in the center of the room, her heart sank. The books were displayed in a locked, glass case, each of them opened to a spread of just two facing pages. Even if she could convince the guards to open the case, how would she be able to examine the

Möðruvallabók? Would they allow her to lift the manuscript out?

Disappointment and frustration set in, and she began rationalizing. What was she looking for anyway? She had found nothing useful in her first examination, so why did she think a second look would be any different?

Brynja nodded at the officers and leaned in to peer more closely at the manuscripts. Each of the books rested on a velvet-lined cradle. As she turned to ask the guard if he could open the case, her throat and chest tightened. She could barely breathe. Suddenly, the events of the past few days began to make sense. The warning. The meaning of the threat.

The parchment in the box of *kleinur* wasn't meant as a warning for *her*; it was more ominous than that.

Why hadn't she realized it earlier?

At the Thing...

Althing. Parliament.

There is a throng...

Her skin crawled. There would be a crowd, a throng, at Althing tomorrow for the exhibit.

Past all bounds the crowding comes...

The words tumbled through her brain like dice that flipped upon each other until they rolled to a stop and spelled out disaster.

Hard 'twill be to patch up peace 'twixt the men. This wearies me. Worthier it is for men to bear weapons red with gore.

Someone was planning an attack here—at Parliament.

Ari. He needed to know. Lives were in danger. He had to act now—there was no time to waste.

She flew down the stairs and ran along the corridor to Ari's office. The sharp tap of her heels echoed off the stairs and the floor, sounding to her heightened senses like gunshots. Ari. She had to tell Ari. She reached his office and put her hand on the door that stood ajar, composing herself to speak clearly, ready to push it open.

The sound of muffled laughter stalled her. Holding herself together, she poked her head in and immediately wished she hadn't. Ari stood with his back to the door while a curvaceous blond perched on his desk, one stiletto barely touching the floor, the other grazing his leg.

Ásta.

For a moment, she was stymied. Rush in and sound like a crazed fool, or…

Pivoting, Brynja raced to the security desk and scribbled a note for Ari, being as clear as she could be. She insisted the guard deliver the message immediately to Ari's office.

"I'm going to the police now. Tell the prime minister that also."

Without waiting to see what Ari's response might be, she bolted out of Parliament and ducked through the pelting rain.

Brynja went straight to Ísak's office at the police station. He waved her in while speaking with Henning, who was sitting in a chair opposite his desk. She tried to explain the importance of her visit. The chief misunderstood.

"Yes, we've just been discussing that, haven't we, Henning?" Ísak stood up, his solid frame commanding the room. He pressed both palms firmly on his desk and eyed the detective. "All cases in which forensic evidence is collected are to be reported immediately to Brynja.

Apparently, she hadn't been apprised of the Kjarval case. The file should have been sent to her immediately. Understood?"

Henning was busy inspecting a hangnail on his index finger. He glowered at Ísak but didn't argue. "Understood." His voice was barely audible.

At any other time, Brynja would have been grateful for the commissioner's support, but the threat to Parliament overwhelmed every other thought.

"We've got a problem," she said as calmly as possible. "You know, the guard, Tómas—"

"Doctor doesn't know if he's going to make it," Henning said.

Brynja pursed her lips. "After the guard collapsed yesterday—"

"In your office."

Ísak rapped his knuckles on the desk. "That's enough, Henning. We're aware of the circumstances. Brynja, continue."

"After the paramedics took Tómas to the hospital, Elly and I found a note written on parchment underneath the doughnuts he'd been eating. The passage on the note is from *Njál's Saga*. It's a warning." She pulled her phone from her bag and scrolled to the photo she had taken of the parchment before handing it to Rúnar for analysis. "I'm sure it means Parliament is in imminent danger of an attack."

Ísak stiffened and rounded his desk to get a closer look at the photo.

"Listen." Brynja read the first line. "*At the Thing there is a throng.*" Her voice was clear, professional. "*The Thing.* Althing…Parliament." She thrust the phone toward Ísak so that he could read the words himself. "*Past all bounds the crowding comes.*" She looked up. "There will be a crowd descending on Parliament tomorrow for the manuscript exhibit."

"And?" Ísak said.

Brynja tapped the screen. "*Hard 'twill be to patch up peace,*" she read. "And here. *Worthier it is for men to bear weapons red with gore.* There will be weapons at Parliament tomorrow."

Ísak's brow rose. "And you think this is a description of an impending assault?"

"Yes." Her heart pounded.

Henning lifted his cane off the arm of the chair. "Weapons like what? Swords? Battle axes? Are we expecting some sort of Viking raid?" He pushed himself up. "I'll get the Kjarval file."

Ísak held the phone as he walked to the window. He looked out over the placid harbor for a minute before turning back to her. "*At the Thing...the crowding comes*," he repeated. "I agree this is strange. Not only the parchment, but how you found it. In a box of doughnuts, you say?"

Brynja nodded.

"In your office?"

She nodded again.

"Why would someone send a warning to your office about an attack at Parliament? Why not send a warning directly to someone there?"

"I don't know. That question crossed my mind several times." She hesitated. "Perhaps the reason is my engagement to Ari."

"Oh?" Ísak stood straight as an iron rod. "Ari hasn't mentioned anything to me. He and I are great friends as you know."

"We haven't made an announcement. I didn't want anyone suspecting I was hired at Legacy because of my relationship with the prime minister. I've asked Ari to keep it between us for the moment."

Ísak took in the information. "I understand. But anyone who knows me can be assured I recommended you purely on merit. I had to trust that outsourcing forensics to Legacy was the right decision and I thought you'd be the ideal candidate to oversee the department there. Nevertheless, your secret is safe with me. Congratulations." He rubbed the stubble on his chin. "Still, that doesn't answer my question. Why send the warning to you?"

"I don't know. Maybe whoever sent it thought I'd tell Ari?"

"But you just said your relationship with Ari is a closely guarded secret. It's more likely someone knows you work closely with the police.

They may be upset with our decision to send officers out to Thingvellir to monitor the protests."

"What protests?"

"Henning hasn't told you?" Ísak glared at the door through which the detective had departed. "There's a massive demonstration planned for tomorrow afternoon at Thingvellir to protest the DNA databases. Some actress has gotten everyone riled up about genetic privacy and abuse of personal health information. Damn shame if the databases were to be shut down. It would make our job tougher, that's for sure."

Brynja clenched her fists. If Ásta had organized the demonstration, what was she doing in Ari's office? Did Ari know about the protest out at Thingvellir?

Ísak sat down at his desk. "If you're right about an attack on Parliament, we've got a bigger problem than I thought. We've dispatched valuable personnel out of the city. I'll have to call in what little backup we have. I wonder if the protest is actually a ruse to deflect our resources." He reached for the phone and stopped short after glancing up at Brynja. "My God, you're as white as our body bags. Why don't you go home and get some rest? I'll follow up on the warning."

"No, I can't. I've got to—"

"Yes, you can. Get the Kjarval Museum case file from Henning. You can take a look at it from home. See what you think. Is there anything we've missed?"

Just then, Henning walked in, waving the Kjarval file in the air.

When Brynja reached for the manila folder, her fingers seemed to stretch clear across the hallway. She blinked, took in a deep breath, and willed the aura to disappear. She made two more attempts to grasp the file, but her arm flailed wildly in the distance and she couldn't lay her hand on it.

She quickly pulled back. "Leave the file by my bag, will you?"

No one said a word.

The landline on Ísak's desk punctured the awkward silence.

"That'll be all," he said, picking up the phone.

Chapter 14

In the cottage, Brynja struggled to absorb the consequences of the last few hours. She had just set in motion a government alert based on what could be considered a pretty flimsy warning; she had perhaps stretched her measure of good will with Ísak to the breaking point; and she hadn't been able to focus at all on the casework she'd brought home with her.

She was glad when evening finally arrived, and she could shut the door on the outside world. A bottle of crowberry wine sat in the kitchen cupboard. She grabbed it before climbing the ladder to her attic room. She changed into sweats and poured a hefty drink into an empty glass on the nightstand.

Outside, the wind whipped up the hillside. A heavy rain beat against the roof like a hammer pounding nails into the lid of a coffin. Brynja reached for the glass and took a sip of wine. She took another sip and then drained the glass.

The auras were back in Technicolor and 3D. Now was the time to rest while she could, to gain some control over the migraines. If she didn't, she could lose her job. Even worse, if her colleagues learned about her disorder, they could question her scientific conclusions; after all, so much of forensics depended upon the ability to accurately observe and analyze the details of each case. And if she didn't tell them…well, if she didn't tell her colleagues about the auras, they might think she'd been drinking. Or was mentally unstable. Or both. Grasping for the Kjarval file from Henning with fingers that stretched clear across the hallway and, earlier, stumbling across the rippling floor in Rúnar's office—such actions did not exactly instill confidence in one's co-workers.

Closing her eyes, she focused on the meditative breathing technique her therapist had taught her. Exhale slowly, count one. Steady breath in. And out. Count two. Steady breath in. And out. In. And out.

The heavy, brass knocker on the front door pounded through the silence. Brynja tried to ignore it. She needed to be left alone. But the pounding continued.

She glanced at the clock. Six p.m. Who was banging so incessantly? She peeled herself off the bed and climbed down to the first floor. She opened the door to find Ari standing there, holding a bouquet of roses.

"Brynja, are you okay? I've been trying to call you."

She looked away.

"I got your message about the warning," Ari said. "I agree it's strange. But the passage from *Njál's Saga*? I'm not sure it's warning us about an attack on Parliament. After security gave me your note, I called Ísak directly. He seems to think it has more to do with keeping the peace at a protest up at Thingvellir tomorrow. Just to be sure, though, we've bumped up security for the exhibit. There'll be ten additional guards on duty, twenty-four/seven."

Brynja listened, repeating his words to herself. A strong sensation of relief washed over her; he had taken her seriously.

"Why didn't you just come straight to me?" Ari asked.

She imagined how her reason would sound to him. "I saw you in your office. You looked busy."

"If this is about Ásta—"

"Ásta? Why would I care if Ásta was crawling all over you?" Immediately, Brynja shut her eyes, ashamed of her outburst. "I'm sorry."

"Brynja, let me in. As for Ásta, she's out of line. She barged her way into my office and begged me to support her crusade against the DNA database. She wants the government to fund a public service announcement about the need for genetic privacy."

Brynja felt foolish. Had she been looking at Ásta all wrong? Perhaps she'd been flirting with Ari to gain political favors, not to lure him away from her.

"I tried to talk her out of leading a protest to shut down the database," Ari said. "She's organizing one for tomorrow."

"I know. Ísak told me."

She needed to pull herself together. The loss of the database was the real threat to both of them, and to Iceland.

Ari lifted her chin gently with the curl of his index finger and peered into her eyes.

Brynja wondered if her inner turmoil would ever settle.

"Would I be here if I didn't care so much?" He paused and pulled a small, cherry blossom pink box from behind his back. "I brought your favorite, *loftkökur!*"

Her heart practically melted. Ari must have ordered the light-as-air cookies from Yumi Bakarí knowing it was one of the few sweets she could tolerate—cocoa powder, egg, and sugar icing puffed up by baker's ammonia. No gluten flour to aggravate her allergies.

How could she stay mad at him?

Now she felt ridiculous for being so angry about Ásta. She opened the door and motioned for him to come inside.

Ari put the flowers and box of cookies down on the table by the entry and kissed her on the cheek. "What do you say we get a bite to eat at Nordica? They've got a special *Roots of Iceland* menu for National Day."

She hesitated...and then nodded.

Ari pulled out his cell phone. "I'll call for a table." He paused, looked at her, and smiled. "By the way, you look beautiful, but I'm not sure that baggy sweats fit the dress code."

Brynja went upstairs to change. Even though the evening was cool, she chose a strappy, black, cocktail dress that hugged her well-toned curves. Sitting down at the vanity, she rifled through her make-up drawer, highlighted the green in her eyes with a smoky gray eye shadow, and covered the freckles that dotted her cheeks with concealer and blush. She hated those freckles. Why was she the only one in her family with spots like a ptarmigan's egg splattered across her face?

After brushing out her hair, Brynja applied a coat of berry red lip-gloss and noticed that her bottom lip was swollen. She must have been biting it more than usual lately. She adjusted the locket about her neck, stood up, slipped on a pair of spiky heels, and made her way down the ladder.

On the brisk walk over to Nordica, Ari wrapped his jacket around her bare shoulders.

"Please be careful at Parliament tomorrow," Brynja said. "I need you to be safe." She stopped and looked into his eyes. "I know you think I might be overreacting—and it's true I'm pretty overwhelmed between the poem about Lúkas and then the warning from *Njál's Saga*—but I really believe someone could be planning an attack at the Althing."

Ari put his arm around her. "We'll get to the bottom of it."

"Do you think the poem and the warning are related in some way? I'm sure they weren't written by the same person. Whoever wrote the poem apparently wants to help me find Lúkas by pointing to clues in the *Möðruvallabók*. And the other person seems to be warning me *against* trying to find him."

Ari pulled her closer. "You've been through a lot this week. Try to put it all out of your head, just for a bit."

He kissed the nape of her neck and the warmth of his lips flooded her body with yearning.

"You know I love you," he whispered. "If you have any doubt, just wait until tonight." He took her arm to cross the street. "But first, a taste of some of the best aphrodisiacs in town."

After what seemed like an endless wave of people jumping up to greet Ari inside the restaurant, the maître d' seated them at a corner table.

Two shots of *Brennivín* schnapps later, Brynja reached for Ari's hand. "Thank you for being so understanding."

The server arrived with the first course and she pulled back.

"Hay-smoked beets with roasted pine seed and dandelion root," he announced, putting the plates down with a flourish. "Paired with a taste of *Birkir's* birch wood vodka. Enjoy."

Ari was silent for a moment after the server left. "What do you think about all the vegetation?"

She nodded. "Delicious."

"No, I mean in the poem."

She looked up.

"It's rather curious," he said. "I keep thinking about all the plant allusions in the poem. *Sagas planted seed. Wheat from the chaff.* And, I forget exactly. Something about roots. Finding Lúkas in the roots. What was it?"

Brynja looked about the restaurant and recited the lines in a muted voice.

"That's right," Ari said. "*In the ink of Gloom's root cellar.* What on earth does that mean?"

"I've spent the past few days asking myself the same question."

"Well, the suggestion seems pretty clear that Lúkas is up north if he's anywhere. That's where he disappeared and that's where the *Book of Möðruvellir* was written."

"I don't think so," Brynja said. "At least, he wouldn't be up north if he's still alive. I've checked the DNA fingerprints of everyone living within a hundred kilometers of Akureyri. Thousands of samples. None of them even remotely resemble mine."

"None of them?" Ari looked at her quizzically. "But your father, cousins, grandparents?"

"My parents were both only children and I don't have any other relatives for two generations. My mother died before the database was established and my father refused to provide a sample once it was."

"Lúkas's DNA may not be in the database either," Ari said. "Especially if he—or someone else—wants to keep his whereabouts a secret."

The server arrived back at the table. "Braised puffin, burnt-butter celery root, and caramelized parsnip purée." He set down a bottle of Dom Perignon and two champagne flutes. "And this is from the gentleman over there." He nodded toward a table across the room.

A heavyset man in a rumpled, linen suit raised his glass.

"Uh oh," Ari said under his breath. "Brace yourself. It's Roger Burn, the American film director. Must be in town for the festival next week."

Reluctantly, Ari nodded his thanks.

"You know he'll take that as an invitation," Brynja said.

"Unfortunately. And here he comes."

Roger rose, walked across the restaurant, and patted Ari on the back. "Hey, man, I've just been invited to the screening of *Thor's Hammer*." Red veins spread like Rorschach patterns across his cheeks. "Don't know if you've noticed, but a lot of the actors are here. Heard they wrapped early today." He pointed over at the bar. "Check out that babe. Her name's Ásta. Hot." Roger stopped short and glanced at Brynja as though unsure if he should acknowledge her and thus his gaffe.

Brynja whirled around. There at the bar was Ásta, but even more surprising was the man sitting next to her.

Brynja's boss at Legacy. Rúnar Bragason.

They were deep in conversation. Ásta was scowling and slowly shaking that goddess head of hers.

Brynja had a sinking feeling she could be on the verge of real trouble if Rúnar linked Ásta's private genetic history with her attempted foray into the LinX database. It was just the sort of breach the actress was so riled up about.

Roger rolled his eyes. "I overheard them talking about how he could help her with some documentary about genetics or some such thing. Sounds like a real cliff-hanger."

Brynja hoped Roger had gotten the conversation wrong. As CSO of Legacy, why would Rúnar want anything to do with a film of that sort?

"My buddies and I thought she could do better than that old fossil," Roger added. "But apparently he's her uncle."

Brynja wasn't sure she'd heard him correctly. "That man is her uncle?"

"Yes."

Roger patted Ari on the back again. "Well, gotta schmooze." He gestured to the bottle of Dom Perignon before walking away. "The least I can do for all your support here in Iceland. Enjoy."

Brynja scrambled to put the pieces together. No wonder Rúnar was upset she had an interest in the file on Paget's disease. If he was Ásta's uncle, then Paget's ran in his family. The disease might also affect him. It wasn't unusual for people with a rare disease to want to keep the information private, or secret even from other relatives. There was no telling what the reaction might be from co-workers or superiors. Rúnar might be worried that Brynja or someone else would use that information to jeopardize his position at Legacy.

Ari's phone rang and he looked down at the screen. "Sorry, I've got to get this."

He stood up and walked outside. Brynja barely heard him. She ran through the people at Legacy whose reactions could justify removing Rúnar as CSO, and how easily he could fire her for a breach of protocol.

The server appeared with the third course. "Minke whale sashimi with pickled angelica root." He noticed Ari's empty seat. "Shall I wait?"

Brynja smiled politely. "You can set the plates down, thank you. I'm sure he'll be right back."

Ari soon returned to the table, his face ashen.

"What's wrong?" Brynja asked.

"That was Althing's chief of security."

"And?"

"The Magnússon Institute wants to speak with me. They're threatening to cancel the exhibit."

Brynja's heart stopped. "Cancel the exhibit? Why?"

"Your pal Henning took it upon himself to call them. He told them I had arranged to have you see the *Möðruvallabók* in your office."

"I thought you cleared that with the Institute."

"I did."

"So, what's the issue? Why would they want to cancel the exhibit now at this late date?"

"You're not going to like this." He reached for her hand. "Henning told them Tómas was poisoned in your office. He said the book is a security risk and anyone handling it is in danger of being the next target."

"Oh...God." Brynja felt as if the chair had been pulled out from under her.

"I managed to talk them into leaving the books for now," Ari said. "Assured them additional security measures were in place and that I'd be personally responsible for their safe-keeping. But, Henning. Why is Henning spewing rumors about an attempted homicide in your office?"

Chapter 15

During the occupation of Denmark by Nazi Germany,
Iceland severed ties to the Danish Crown and declared itself a Republic.
Voters were asked whether the Union with Denmark should be abolished.
The measure was approved with more than 98% in favor.

Reykjavik's church bells could be heard throughout the city and beyond, the sound of joy and pride in Iceland's independence seventy-three years ago. Every year, the nation celebrated on June 17th, and every year felt as thrilling as the first for those old enough to remember and those who had heard their stories. No one was immune to the spirit of triumph and delight tapped by the pealing bells. In the kitchen, Brynja lowered her coffee cup for a moment as she listened and enjoyed. She felt a lightness in her chest. Today, she would put Henning out of her mind and celebrate with the rest of the nation.

She glanced at the clock. Ten a.m. In less than an hour, the parade would march into Austurvöllur Square and Ari would address the entire nation from the balcony of Parliament. She loved listening to him talk about the things that mattered to him, and today he would give a speech about Iceland's independence and remarkable history. The citizens would cheer, and this would be a good day for everyone.

She stopped to check her phone. Ari had promised to call the Magnússon Institute and to let her know if they still planned to cancel the exhibit. She was relieved to see no message from him.

Her thoughts turned to Pabbi and Jónas. What would they be doing today?

She dialed Jónas's number and reached him after just one ring.

"*Halló?*" His voice was weak.

"*Hæ hó jibbí jei og jibbí jei!*" Brynja said, repeating the familiar Independence Day greeting.

"Is that you, *litla mín?*"

"Yes. How are you? You sound tired."

"I'm getting some breakfast ready for your father. He's doing better. Able to get up and down the stairs without much help."

Her heart lifted. "I'm so glad. Think you might be able to drive Pabbi into town and watch the parade in Akureyri? It might do him some good."

Jónas was silent for a moment before speaking. "You know he doesn't like crowds, *litla mín.*"

He was right, of course. After the explosion that had injured Mamma, her father had shied away from any gathering of more than a handful of people. "Maybe just take him for a drive up the valley?"

After letting Jónas know she'd set up an appointment for Pabbi at the neurologist and reminding him to take care of himself as well, Brynja said goodbye and hung up. She climbed the ladder to her loft and sorted through the clothes hanging in her closet. She decided to dress for the occasion in a royal blue maxi-skirt, a fitted, white blouse, and a red scarf.

Nothing less than national colors would do for the celebration today. She tossed a beaded shawl over her shoulders, climbed down the ladder from her attic bedroom, and rushed out the door.

The streets were filled with Icelanders celebrating their independence. Clowns tumbled to the tempo of carnival music; children skipped beside them with gas-filled balloons tied to their wrists; parents maneuvered baby strollers through hordes of revelers; rowdy teens blew air horns and tossed confetti; and the old folks watched it all from the comfort of folding chairs set up along the parade route. As she threaded her way toward Parliament, Brynja pushed aside the lingering unease that the threats might be real and might be meant for today.

Inside the Parliament building, she wrote her name in the visitor log and made her way to Ari's office. His secretary Fríða leapt up to greet her. Dressed in a prim, black suit, Fríða was so thin she looked as if she had been pulled through a keyhole.

"Brynja, how nice to see you. Although, I'm afraid you've just missed Ari." She came around her desk. "Can I offer you some coffee and *snúður* rolls?"

"*Takk fyrir*. Maybe a quick cup of coffee, but no pastry."

While Fríða poured the coffee, Brynja felt the familiar sense of well-being that came over her in Ari's wood-paneled office, stocked as it was with the symbols of a proud Iceland: a stuffed gyrfalcon, a vase of flowering, white dryas, and a coat of arms depicting the four protectors of Iceland—the bull, the eagle, the dragon, and the rock giant. On the wall hung photographs of every prime minister since Denmark had granted Iceland home rule, from Hannes Hafstein in 1904 to the world's first openly gay head of government, Jóhanna Sigurðardóttir, in 2009. And there the pictures ended. She smiled. It was just like Ari not to display his own photograph.

"Cream or sugar?" Fríða asked.

Brynja shook her head and picked up the cup. "No coffee for you?"

"I've already poured myself half a pot," the secretary said, flitting about the office like an animated skeleton. "I shouldn't drink so much coffee...high blood pressure and all. But I need to keep fuel in my tank with all that's going on around here."

"I'm sure the day will be a huge success," Brynja reassured her. "I don't know what Ari would do without you, though." She stood up. "Think I could poke my head into the rotunda? I'd love to see the manuscripts again before the public's allowed in."

"I'm afraid you'll find an empty room up there," Fríða said. "The Magnússon Institute called early this morning and canceled the exhibit. Ari tried his best to dissuade them, but they insisted on picking up the books."

Brynja steadied herself against the wall. "The manuscripts aren't here?"

"Didn't you know?"

Brynja shook her head. Why hadn't Ari called her? She'd set out this morning with such expectations. Looking forward to viewing the *Möðruvallabók* on display was part of it, and now the book was gone. Did the institute actually believe the guard had been poisoned in her office? And now how would she get another chance to look through the manuscript?

"Come, sit down," Fríða said. "You're pale as a winter moon."

"I'm okay," Brynja managed to say. "Do you know when Ari will be back?"

"The prime minister's in the chamber preparing his speech. He asked not to be disturbed, but I'm sure he wouldn't mind if it were you."

Brynja glanced toward the door. "No, I'd better not interrupt him. This speech is important." She took one more sip and handed the cup back to Fríða. "Thanks for the coffee. Would you let Ari know I came by?"

On the steps in front of Parliament, she pulled out her phone.

There, on the screen, she saw a message from Ari.

Exhibit's been canceled. So sorry. Will explain later.

Relieved that he had at least tried to reach her, she texted back.

I'll be in the square. Front and center. Under the balcony. Good luck with the speech.

Brynja wandered through the crowd waiting for the parade to start. She looked about for any suspicious activity, feeling both distressed at the thought of the threats, and ridiculous for entertaining the idea that she could spot dangerous activity better than the trained police stationed around Austurvöllur Square. Restless, she bought a bottle of *Egils Appelsín* soda at a nearby booth and signed a petition to prevent drilling for oil in the Arctic Sea. She stopped at a table where children were having their faces painted with the Icelandic flag. On a cordoned off side street, a local farmhand offered pony rides to children. Near the back of the line, a young boy with blond curls and a girl with long, brown braids pleaded with their mother for a ride.

"As long as you watch out for each other," their mother relented, buying them each a ticket. The words crimped Brynja's heart.

A marching band rounded the square, instruments blaring. Nearby, Elly, in leather pants and an electric yellow jacket, waved wildly from behind the sawhorses in front of Parliament. Brynja raced across the street just before the band and a scout troop tromped over the cobblestones.

"This is so exciting," Elly said. "Reminds me of the Changing of the Guard in Copenhagen when they march from Rosenborg Castle to Amalienborg Palace."

Brynja nudged her intern. "Today's not the day to advertise you're Danish, Elly. The only reason we finally established independence from your country is that Denmark had bigger things to worry about during World War II."

"Really? Guess we really weren't told everything in school. Hadn't a clue." Elly looked up at the balcony. "I heard the prime minister's going to give a speech." She leaned in close and whispered. "You'd never get this close to a head of state in Denmark. The guards only let me through to the front because I told them I was with you."

The parade was in full flow now. Icelandic horses pranced down the street, their hooves reverberating off the cobblestones like the rhythmic clapping of wooden boards. The woman riding the lead horse wore an embroidered, woolen jacket and skirt, a silver belt, and a tall, curved headdress with a silk veil.

"That's the Lady of the Mountain, the *Fjallkonan*," Brynja said. "She's wearing Iceland's national costume."

Elly buttoned her jacket. "I thought the national costume here was anything that keeps you from freezing your butt off."

Brynja laughed. "Pretty much."

The *Fjallkonan* approached, waving at the crowd. Dismounting, she stepped up onto a podium in front of Parliament.

"The Lady of the Mountain embodies the beauty and spirit of Iceland," Brynja explained. "She's going to recite the poem *Ancient Iceland*. Just a heads-up, it's a bit of a dig at Denmark for suppressing our independence for so long."

"I never knew there was such an intense rivalry between—" Elly stopped short. "Are you okay?"

Brynja's mouth was hanging open. She closed it and began to seethe.

The woman standing in front of them—the beautiful, independent woman chosen to be this year's *Fjallkonan*—was no Lady of the Mountain. More like a Lady of the Evening. *Ásta.*

Brynja forced a thin smile. "I'm fine."

Could Ari have had anything to do with this?

Ásta fanned her long, blonde curls over her tightly fitted bodice. The crowd roared and a sea of Icelandic flags waved over the square.

Ásta began to recite *Ancient Iceland*. "*From the harbor-fog here...*"

Brynja whispered, "She's talking about Denmark."

"We all desire to go home to see you in your beauty. We are bored by this flat land, this foggy region, as if it were a face without a nose, a face without eyes..."

"Denmark's not *that* bad," Elly said, jutting out her chin in mild offense.

Ásta spread her arms wide and looked up at the sky. Her honey-sweet voice rang out. *"Quite different to see your high white waves reach up to a clear blue sky. Your crystal rivers shine in the sparkling sun..."*

"I've probably seen the sun once since I've been here," Elly hissed.

"And your golden heaths dance beneath snow-white glaciers..."

Ásta caught sight of Brynja and shot her an icy glare before stumbling into the final refrain. Brynja was taken aback. What had brought that on? Had Ari told her he was seeing someone, and Brynja was that someone? But Ásta would already know that after seeing them holding hands in the square a few days ago. She thought back to the dinner at Nordica. Had Rúnar told Ásta that she was looking at the Paget's disease file?

"Old as fire and ice-clad earth, I am your beauty, your spirit, come down from above. Old as fire and ice-clad earth, I am your Lady of the Mountain."

As Ásta finished her recitation, Ari appeared on the balcony to thunderous clapping and whistles. He waved at Ásta and the cheering throngs below.

Hoping to catch his eye, Brynja gazed up at the balcony, but he had turned his attention to the center of the square and was frowning.

A chorus of screams rose from among the crowd as a loud blast echoed overhead, quickly followed by another.

Too stunned to move, Brynja gripped the sawhorse to keep her knees from buckling. Then, instinctively, she grabbed Elly and gave her a small push, urging her to flee with the stream of now-panicked on-lookers rushing from the square.

Seconds later, Ari's voice boomed over the loudspeaker. "Keep calm. The police have the situation under control. There is no need to panic."

Brynja strained to see what was happening. Pinned against the sawhorses by the onslaught of people fleeing the scene, she was trapped in a tight space behind a man with a young child perched on his shoulders and a large woman smelling of hotdogs and sweat.

She pushed the sawhorse aside and tripped over the hem of her maxi-skirt.

Ari's words began to calm the crowd. Many of the spectators stopped running and looked back at the spot where the explosion had occurred. As the center of the square cleared, Brynja could see two policemen grabbing a couple of teenage boys and giving a 'thumbs-up' to Ari.

"Look," said the small boy atop his father's shoulders. "Those kids have firecrackers. Can we get some, too?"

Chapter 16

Brynja arrived at her office early Sunday morning, hoping the return to a place with clear rules and boundaries would help calm her. She was hiding from herself after the firecracker incident yesterday. She had overreacted. Complete loss of control. How could she have let that happen? She was a forensic scientist. Her entire career rested on the ability to remain steady and clear-headed and objective, and go about her work in a thoughtful, methodical manner. All of that had evaporated yesterday. She had assumed the worst before knowing the facts. She felt like she was becoming two different people. One was rational and careful. The other, emotional and volatile.

From the office window, Brynja surveyed the harbor below. Fog settled over a fleet of fishing boats as they bobbed out to sea. Her distress at yesterday's events receded, leaving her with another, more painful question. Had she also been too quick to judge Ari's intentions? After calm had settled in the square, she had left Ari alone to deal with a mountain of questions from the press. She had gone home and fallen asleep to Stína's reruns of *Birdwatching Bonanza*. Why had she not instead made her way to his side?

Brynja turned to her desk. Drawn again to the unequivocal nature of her work, she sat down and refocused her energies. Uncertainty didn't solve cases. She picked up the file on the missing Kjarval painting and read through the entries, satisfied to see that Henning had at least taken the proper steps to collect and analyze evidence from the scene. He had dusted for fingerprints, requested DNA analysis on the duct tape used to constrain the guard, taken photos of footprints outside the first-floor windows, and collected a cigarette and bandana left on the ground where the thieves had broken into the museum.

It was all there, everything she'd expect from a competent investigator.

Maybe she had been unfair to Henning as well.

She closed the file and put in a call to the Selfoss police to see if any of the leads on Inga Grímsdóttir's husband had panned out. They hadn't.

Next, she read through the recent activity log. Aside from the firecracker incident yesterday, there had not been much to report. The usual citations for disorderly conduct fueled by a night of revelry and intoxication had been issued, and a report of domestic abuse had sent two officers out to Vesturbær. The graffiti gang had been back at it, tagging buildings on Laugavegur with their signature *Despicable Me* minions.

She recalled Ásta's icy glare and her growing goodwill dried up. She wondered about Ásta's motives. Was she truly vying for Ari's affections or did she have another goal? Was she attempting to seduce him in order to shut down the database?

After a fleeting doubt, Brynja booted up the computer. She paused, then stood up and peeked into the outer office. Even though it was the weekend, Elly had insisted on reviewing the calendar for the upcoming week. She'd stepped out for a bit but would be back soon.

Reassuring herself that she was alone in the office, Brynja clicked on the icon for LinX. The database had three levels of security, each requiring a different passcode. The first enabled the disease database to offload from the server, the second accessed specific disease files along with barcodes masking the identity of affected individuals, and the third—the level Ásta and others were most concerned with—enabled the user to unmask the barcodes and reveal the identity of individuals harboring DNA mutations underlying that specific disease. As chief of forensics, Brynja had clearance to access the third level of LinX...but only if solving a criminal case necessitated such an action.

She had downloaded the LinX file for Paget's disease two days ago but hadn't accessed the most sensitive level, the level that would reveal whether Ásta had the Paget's mutation.

She knew the risk she was taking. Rúnar would be furious if he found out but Brynja couldn't help but wonder if Ásta's perfectly shaped face would someday skew into the contorted features of a Paget's sufferer. This was a horrible disease.

She typed in 'Paget's disease.'

One hundred and sixty-seven bar-coded samples popped up on the screen, each linked to an Icelander with the Paget's mutation in their DNA. The founder effect had ensured every Icelander carried the same mutation even though, worldwide, there were hundreds of other mutations that could cause Paget's. Since Iceland was founded by a small number of settlers and grew over time as an isolated population, the low level of genetic variation between individuals meant that every Icelander with the disease had the same mutation: the P392L mutation in which a single DNA nucleotide cytosine was changed to a thymidine.

And Ásta's family carried it. Or so she had said.

Brynja stared at the jumble of barcodes on the screen. With one stroke of the keyboard, she could unlock the encrypted database and identify just who these individuals were.

Her fingers hovered over the command 'unmask.'

She sat back, put her hands in her lap. No. It wasn't right. The database had been developed for research into genetic disease. She could justify accessing the information if it pertained to a forensic case, but this was personal. Ásta would be right to consider her privacy violated. The idea of someone revealing the identity of individuals with the Paget's mutation just to satisfy some personal interest or curiosity was precisely the reason behind her crusade to shut down the database.

Brynja shut her eyes. How could she have come so close to crossing that line?

Her silent remorse was broken by a series of metallic taps reverberating off the floor of the outer office and into hers. With a flick of her hand, Brynja exited the database and wheeled around in her chair.

Henning loomed just inside the doorway, a set of keys jiggling in his nicotine-stained fingers.

"What are you doing here?" Brynja asked. "And how did you get in?"

Henning pointed his cane at her. "What the hell do you think you're doing?"

"I'm sitting in my chair in my office on a Sunday following up on the graffiti case from last night. Checking the spray can DNA and fingerprints—"

"Do you really think I'm that stupid? Those results wouldn't be in yet. That's LinX you were looking at. What are you doing snooping around in the disease database? I don't have to tell you that's grounds for dismissal from Legacy. Even I know that."

"Look, Henning, I'll decide when it's appropriate to access the database."

Henning shoved a piece of paper in front of her nose and slapped it down on the desk. "And what's this all about? You've run an ink analysis? On what?"

Brynja looked at the fax and then up at Henning. "Where did you get that?"

"From the fax machine at the police station. The chemistry lab sent us a copy."

Her heart skipped. "I had them analyze the ink on the warning parchment we found in the box of *kleinur*. The one from *Njal's Saga*."

She desperately hoped Henning hadn't read through the entire report and realized she'd had the ink of the poem about Lúkas analyzed as well. He'd want to know why, and all she'd be able to say was that that was her business. He could turn her search for Lúkas against her by informing Ísak she was using professional resources for personal reasons.

"If we can identify the ink used to write the warning," Brynja said, "maybe we'd know the type of pen used and be able to find out where it was purchased. We could zero in on the person who was planning an attack at Parliament."

"Unless I missed it, there was no attack at Parliament." Henning pursed his lips. He tapped his finger on the fax. "Ísak should have been kept in the loop about this."

"We'll go over the case as we always do. In our joint meetings. I'm sure you understand things have been a little chaotic with National Day and—"

"And what? The guard Tómas on the brink of dying?"

Brynja stifled her irritation and forced herself to smile. "I read over the Kjarval file and you did an excellent job collecting evidence from the museum. I haven't had the chance to follow up on whether the lab could identify the burglar from the duct tape."

Henning puffed out his chest. "Seems some of the DNA doesn't come from an Icelander. Maybe someone from Greece or Italy. But I've deduced there must have been an accomplice inside the museum as well since the majority of the DNA is Icelandic. That's why I came over.

Thought I'd get the most recent results from the lab."

"We shouldn't be surprised to find Icelandic DNA. It's most likely from the museum guard, not an accomplice. We can establish that." She lifted her chin. "You do know that's my job, right? DNA identification?"

Henning pressed his lips together as though not sure what he wanted to say before turning on his heel and leaving.

Elly poked her head into the office and sat down. "How did Henning get in? Reception usually rings me first."

"I'm not sure," Brynja said. "I've got to speak with security. He shouldn't have *carte blanche* to barge in here as he does." She looked down at the fax Henning had left on her desk. "Anyway, we've got the report back on the ink analysis."

Elly jumped up. "Can I take a look?"

Before she could answer, Elly rounded her desk and started to read the report out loud.

University of Iceland
TLC Report, Ink Analysis
Case 1032
June 16, 2017

Samples: Three small fragments
               Sample 1: Paper. Red Ink. 8 mm x 30 mm
               Sample 2: Paper. Black Ink. 9 mm x 27 mm
               Sample 3: Parchment. Brown Ink. 8 mm x 31 mm

Solute: $EtOH/H_2O$

TLC: Composition Analysis and
               Comparison to International Ink Library

Results:

Fragment 1   Red ink
                     Plant-based (Alizarin)
                     Non-commercial origin

Fragment 2   Black Ink (Iron-gall)
                     Commercial origin
                     2013. Ren Blæk Inks, LLC

Fragment 3   Brown Ink
                     Plant-based (Willow bark and Bearberry)
                     Non-commercial origin

Brynja felt a sinking disappointment.

Elly turned the paper over, but the reverse side was blank. "That's it?"

"I'm afraid so," Brynja said. "We need more information. This doesn't get us any closer to the person who wrote me that poem, nor to the person who wrote the warning in the doughnut box. It doesn't even tell us *where* they were written. Let me call over to the lab." She dialed the number, put the phone on speaker, and motioned to Elly to sit down.

"Chemical Forensics Lab," a voice on the other end answered. "Theó Friðriksson here."

"Hi, Theó, Brynja Pálsdóttir. Hoping you'd be in on a Sunday."

"Wife's got her entire family in for the weekend. Had to escape for a bit."

Brynja chuckled. "Well, I'm glad you did. Listen, I've just received your ink analysis and was wondering if you could give me some additional information."

"If I can. What is it you'd like to know?"

"I'm curious as to where the inks were manufactured."

"Give me a minute to pull up the report."

Brynja heard Theó shuffle some papers on his desk and punch the keys on his keyboard.

"Here we go. Which sample are you interested in?"

"Actually, all of them. Whatever you can tell me."

"All right, then," Theó said. "Sample one. The red in your ink is from alizarin, an organic compound. Alizarin was used historically to impart a red color, primarily for dyeing textiles, but on occasion it was used for adding color to red inks."

"Where is it made?"

"I couldn't find a match to any companies that make this ink. It may be that whoever used the red ink made it themselves."

"What about sample two? The black ink on that same paper?"

"That's standard iron gall ink. Used for fourteen hundred years until the invention of synthetic inks in the twentieth century."

"I've never heard of iron gall ink."

"It's made from iron vitriol, gum arabic, and gallnuts."

"Gallnuts?"

"Yes. Ink needs some kind of tannic acid to react with the iron in order to produce a pigment. Gallnuts were the most common source of tannic acid in medieval Europe. The acid also makes the ink sink into the parchment. Gum arabic is a tree sap. It's an adhesive, so the ink stays on the quill until it's touched to the parchment."

"I still don't know what gallnuts are."

"They're knobby structures on trees formed by gall wasps laying eggs inside the bark. When the larva develops into a wasp, it bores a hole in the gallnut and flies away. Historically, the finest gallnuts for harvesting tannic acid came from Aleppo in Syria. But you'll find them on any oak tree."

Brynja thought for a moment. "You're saying that the ink was made the old-fashioned way by crushing gallnuts?" She paused. "Since we hardly have any oak trees in Iceland, I'm guessing those companies aren't located here."

"That's right. I searched the International Ink Library and found that the ink from sample two is manufactured by a specialty company called Ren Blæk Inks in Aarborg, Denmark."

Brynja looked at Elly, who mouthed, "Never heard of it."

"Can you buy it here?" Brynja asked Theó.

"No, I'm afraid not. It's sold only in Denmark."

Brynja picked up the glass of water from her desk and swirled it around slowly before taking a sip. So, the black ink used on the poem about Lúkas was sold only in Denmark.

"Is the other ink from Denmark also? The one with the deep brown color?" She flipped to the second page of the report. "Sample three?"

"That's impossible to know. It's not produced by any commercial company. Someone would have had to have made it on their own, much like your red ink in sample one. Since the brown ink is a plant-based ink, it's possible to make it wherever those particular plants are grown." Theó coughed. "Of course, the requisite plants could have been imported."

"Why would someone want to go through all that trouble?"

"For one thing, they might have been trying to copy how the old manuscripts were written." Theó sneezed. "Excuse me. One minute."

Brynja tapped her fingers on the desk. The warning that she and Elly had found in the box of *kleinur* was not only written on parchment similar to that of the old manuscripts, but also using exactly the same type of ink.

"Someone has gone to a lot of trouble to replicate the passage in the *Möðruvallabók*," she said to Elly.

Theó blew his nose and came back on the line. "The brown ink is made from willow bark and bearberry. In medieval times, the bearberry leaves, stems, and berries were boiled down together in an iron pot and then sticks of willow bark were mixed in."

Brynja pursed her lips. It was actually fascinating. "What provides the tannic acid?"

"The willow bark. And the bearberry plant contains some tannic acid as well. As you know, we've got bearberry plants crawling all over the meadows here."

Brynja leaned back in her chair. Was the person who sent the warning parchment so intent on reproducing medieval writing that they went so far as to make the ink in the same way the monks did centuries ago? Who would do something that obsessive?

Theó sneezed again. "It almost seems as though someone cut that parchment right out of one of the old manuscripts."

Brynja gasped. "That can't be."

"Sacrilege," Theo said, articulating her feelings.

She thought back to the time she'd spent reading the text, gently turning the old pages. She had found the passage in the *Möðruvallabók,* but what if she had missed something? Was the passage repeated on another page? A page that might have had the passage removed? Perhaps there were other clues she had missed.

"Anything else I can help you with?"

"Not now. Thanks, Theó. Thanks for your work. Hope things settle back down at home."

As she hung up, Brynja heard a door slam shut. She looked at Elly and leapt up to see who was in the outer office.

The room was empty. Only the slightly mossy scent of Henning's hand-rolled cigarettes lingered in the air.

Chapter 17

The following day, Brynja did her best to set aside her own personal concerns and focus on her work. She'd spent the morning discussing laboratory results from several cases, including a paternity suit brought by the purported daughter of a wealthy banker. Later, she pored over the interview transcripts of museum personnel in the Kjarval file. Apparently, no one had seen the burglary firsthand, but the janitor, a recent immigrant from Italy, had been quite evasive. Brynja called Ísak and requested he ask for a blood sample. The janitor reluctantly agreed, and Henning brought him over to the lab at Legacy to have his blood drawn.

Late in the afternoon, she followed up on an eyewitness report that had come in from Hrísey Island with a description of a man matching Inga Grímsdóttir's husband. The microRNA results on Inga's blood indicated her disappearance—or more likely, death—was a suspicious one, which, in addition to the fact the he hadn't been seen in days, made him a person of interest. Brynja was keen to investigate the lead but would need to have an officer from up north accompany her to Hrísey. The small island was a short ferry ride across Eyjafjörður, not far from Munkathverá. A trip to Hrísey would coincide nicely with her plans to visit the farm and check on Pabbi. His DNA results would be in soon.

She took the last flight up to Akureyri that evening and arrived at Munkathverá by taxi. Seeing that the lights were out, she left her bag on the front step. Knowing that Amma never went to bed before midnight and not feeling tired herself, Brynja walked the short distance south to the old woman's farm. She knocked gently on the door.

Amma soon appeared, wiping her hands on her cross-stitched apron. The nutty aroma of roasted meat simmering in the simple earthiness of thyme and root vegetables wafted through the doorway. "My, my, what a delightful surprise."

"I'll just be a minute, Amma. Stína asked me to pick up one of the cameras she left when we were here last week."

"Nonsense. Come in, dear. I'm just making some stew."

Brynja followed her to the kitchen and stood at the counter while Amma stirred a pot on the stovetop. She glanced down at the recipe book.

HORSEMEAT STEW
Hrossakjöt súpa

5 cups water
3 pounds cubed horsemeat (shoulder or rump)
2 carrots, sliced coarsely
2 rutabagas, cubed
4 potatoes, cubed
3 leeks, soaked and sliced
salt and pepper

Bring the water to boil.
Rinse the horsemeat with cold water and drop into the boiling water.
Lower temperature to medium.
Allow the meat to cook for 2-3 minutes.
Skim off the fat and add salt.
Cook for 30 minutes.
Add carrots, rutabagas, potatoes, and leeks.
Cook for another 20 minutes.
Season to taste with salt and pepper.

Brynja gagged. It had been a long time since she'd eaten horsemeat. No one in Reykjavik ate horse any longer, although just about everyone had been raised on it. Foreigners were appalled at the custom, and any mention of horsemeat had long ago been wiped from the menus of Reykjavik's restaurants popular with tourists. But out here in the country, the old generation of farmers saw no need to bow to such pressure.

"You look famished, dear. Let me ladle you a bowl. I'll have to take a look 'round for the camera. I don't quite remember where I put it."

"Thank you, Amma, but I'm not hungry. I see you're busy. Perhaps I'll come over in the morning for the camera."

"No, no. Stay a while. Sure I can't get you some stew?"

Brynja shook her head and kissed the old woman on the cheek. "Tomorrow, then?"

She said goodbye and headed to Munkathverá. Trying not to wake Jónas and Pabbi, she quietly opened the door, tiptoed to her room, and fell asleep.

Sometime in the early morning hours, the tune of the national anthem, the *Lofsöngur—The Song of Praise—*drifted into her dream.

It was Autumn, 1995. Brynja stood wide-eyed and eager, alongside Lúkas and Stína, on their first day of primary school. Iceland's flag fluttered in the schoolyard breeze. Hand over heart, she proudly sang the patriotic hymn:

> *Inspire us at morn with Thy courage and love,*
> *And lead us through the days of our strife.*
> *At evening send peace from Thy heaven above,*
> *And safeguard our nation through life.*

The hymn over, Lúkas ran across the playing field, chasing the squawking of razorbills. He jumped, trying to catch hold of the birds' wings as they soared above the cliff. Trapping his foot in a craggy wedge of lava, Lúkas stumbled and fell, his legs dangling over the cliff edge. She ran to him and reached for his hand, but she felt only the touch of his fingertips before he tumbled into the gorge below.

Brynja woke with a start and froze for a moment in that deep valley between dream and reality. From the rafters above, tiny bits of turf floated down, and specks of dust drifted in the still light.

Versions of the nightmare had haunted her for years. An icy pond, a fishing boat, and, now, a cliff. The locations were always different, but each dream scene was invariably shattered by her failure to save Lúkas from disaster.

Brynja rubbed her eyes, trying to shake the music of the *Lofsöngur* wafting through the room. It slowly dawned on her that the tune was coming from her iPhone.

Her voice cracked as she picked up the phone. "*Halló?*"

"*Góðan daginn*, my sweet. Good morning! That sure took you a while. Little too much to drink last night?"

"Oh, Ari. *Halló.*" She should have known it was Ari; she had programmed the national anthem as his ringtone.

"I've been trying to reach you," Ari said. "I called your office and Elly told me you've gone up north. Why aren't you returning my calls?"

"Things have been pretty hectic at work. I've got a lead on the Inga Grímsdóttir case up here."

"Anything I can help with?"

"Thanks, but no." She paused. "How did Ásta come to be selected Lady of the Mountain this year?"

"I don't know. Why?"

"No reason. Listen, I can't talk right now. I have to check on Pabbi."

"No, wait—"

"I'll ring you as soon as I'm back."

"I can't wait that long. Let's talk now."

"I've really got to go."

"*Brynja.* Take a look out your window."

"Why?"

"Trust me. Just take a look."

She walked to the front of the room, pulled the linen curtains to the side and squinted into the early morning sunlight. She bit down on a smile. Ari's black Range Rover was snaking along the far end of the dirt road leading up to the farm. As she flung open the sash to get a better view, her throat tightened. Another vehicle followed Ari's: a white, Nissan patrol car with *Lögreglan*—police—painted on its side.

"Ari?"

"Don't worry. I've just got a police escort. Government can't possibly let the PM wander around the country on his own these days, now, can they? Anyway, I don't want to wake Jónas or your father, but I've got a surprise for you. Put on something nice and come out."

"I—I don't think I've got much other than jeans here but give me a minute."

Her heart pounded. She rummaged through the closet and pulled out the tailored blouse and slacks she had worn to her high-school graduation. Pleased that they still fit, she brushed out her hair, twisted it into a side braid, and added a touch of blush to her cheeks. After slipping on a pair of low heels, she checked on Pabbi and, seeing that he was sleeping peacefully, hurried to the car.

Ari stepped out and opened the passenger door for her. Brynja thrummed with excitement. Once inside the car, he pulled her close and caressed the bare skin beneath the open collar of her blouse. His lips met hers and the warmth of his mouth sent a current running through her entire body.

"More of that later, I hope," he said, brushing a strand of hair from her forehead. "But first, we've got an appointment." He started the engine and steered the car toward town.

"Where are we going? I can't believe you drove all the way up here. Don't you have to prepare for the Arctic Council?"

"I've got a last-minute meeting with Blue Bioeconomy folks up here to explore how best to increase the value of marine products. Flights were booked so we had to leave Reykjavik at three this morning. I've texted Fríða to give her the day off. She's been working nonstop." He glanced over at Brynja. "You look frazzled. Everything okay?"

"I don't think I've slept in over a week. I've been so preoccupied."

Ari leaned over to gather her against him. "Tell me, love."

His kindness penetrated her reserve. Tears of relief stung her eyes. "It's been almost too much. Tómas collapsing in my office, that creepy warning note, Henning watching my every move, undermining me." She lowered her head. "And with all the commotion, I didn't get much of a chance to look at the *Möðruvallabók*. Just that first day in my office." She reached for the silver locket and held it tight. "I know it's selfish, but I really need to examine every single page of that book. Somehow, Lúkas is in there. Is there any chance you could arrange to get me into the Magnússon Institute somehow?"

Ari tapped his index finger against the steering wheel.

"I'm sorry, that's too much to ask," Brynja said. "I don't want to get you in any more trouble. Henning's already made a big deal about your sending it over to my office."

She turned her head to stare at the fjord, its dark gray waters rippling beneath a shroud of diaphanous fog. "The worst thing is I think my father's suffering from some kind of dementia. I'd like to bring him down to Reykjavik and make sure he's getting the attention he needs. I need to get Jónas on board. He thinks Pabbi has the flu, but I don't agree. I'm having Pabbi's DNA tested."

"I didn't think dementia was genetic."

"Unfortunately, early-onset Alzheimer's definitely runs in families. Most people affected by it have a mutation that's been inherited from one of their parents."

Ari hugged her tighter. "Whatever happens, we'll sort it out together."

She put a hand on his thigh. "What about you? What's happening with your chief of staff search?"

"I'm not so sure I really need a chief of staff. Fríða handles just about everything in the office and I get all the advice I need from the MPs. I'd rather listen to their concerns directly."

Brynja kissed him on the cheek. "Man of the people." She rested her head on his shoulder.

They drove along a narrow strip of roadway through the town of Akureyri, sheltered from the winds by the Hlíðarfjall mountain range. Several of the old, timber-framed houses hugged the base of the fjord and echoed the influence of Danish merchants who had monopolized the fishery trade centuries earlier.

Ari slowed for a school bus as they approached the Botanical Gardens, its lush greenery defying the frigid reach of the Arctic Circle.

Brynja averted her eyes. "That's where it all started."

Ari looked over. "What?"

"The explosion that injured my mother. It ruined my family before I was even born."

"Must have been devastating," Ari said. "I can't imagine."

"My mother holed up in bed for years and my father was consumed by caring for her. Neither one had much time for Lúkas and me."

"Maybe that's why you're so independent," Ari said, attempting to cheer her up.

They stopped for a cup of coffee at Kristjans Bakari before heading north again. Ten kilometers on, Ari turned off the main road, parked, and unbuckled his seatbelt.

"We're here," he said, smiling.

Brynja stared at the quaint, wooden church nestled in a grove of birch trees. "We have an appointment *here?*"

She looked about for another building but the church, with its simple, rectangular nave of white timber and bright red roof, was the only structure in sight. For a brief moment, she questioned just how well she knew Ari. Was *this* why he wanted her to dress nicely? For a wedding? *Their* wedding?

"I hope you didn't—"

Before she could say more, Ari jumped out and came around. "Come."

She followed him to the rear of the car and watched as he opened the trunk.

Brynja's hand flew to her mouth. A wooden crate lay on the floor. But it wasn't just any crate. It was the same wooden box that Tómas had brought to her office last week. The box that carried the *Möðruvallabók.*

Speechless, she looked up at Ari and grabbed his arm. "Is it—?"

"I don't really like to throw my weight around," he said, pretending to flex his biceps. "But being prime minister has got to be worth something. I talked the Institute into loaning it to the Akureyri Museum. Just our luck—some Norwegian diplomats are touring North Iceland next week and they'd like to see one of the manuscripts. I promised the Institute I would bring the *Möðruvallabók* up myself and they agreed, but on two conditions: The book stays up north for just one week and it remains under police protection at all times." He waved at the two officers in the police car that had escorted them.

"But this is Möðruvellir Church. Not the Akureyri Museum."

"Of course. We're just making a quick stop before the museum. I did some research on the *Möðruvallabók*. Apparently, it was found at this very site in 1628. Maybe they know something more about its history, something not yet published."

For the umpteenth time this morning, Brynja's heart melted. Not only had Ari figured out a way for her to examine the manuscript further, but he'd taken the time to read up on its provenance as well.

Ari signaled to the officers that he'd only be a minute and then lifted the heavy box from the trunk. "Let's go have a chat with the pastor."

A frail, elderly clergyman in a black, ankle-length cassock opened the door. His eyes widened at the sight of Brynja before nodding to Ari. He bowed his head, cleared his throat, and introduced himself in a soft, steady voice. "Pastor Dalmann Ingólfsson. It's an honor to meet you, prime minister. Please, come in."

Beckoning them into the sacristy, he laid his hands on a mahogany credenza. "Thank you for bringing the book. Why don't you rest it here?" He moved a choral sheet from the surface and slid shut several drawers of liturgical vestments.

Ari deposited the heavy crate on the credenza, lifted the manuscript out, and placed it beside the box. He wiped his hands on his slacks. "There."

The pastor rested his palm on the book, his eyes half-closed as though in prayer. He was silent for a moment before crossing his chest. "In the name of the Father, and of the Son, and of the Holy Spirit, Amen." He opened his eyes and turned to Ari. "I cannot tell you how much this means to me."

"The pleasure's all mine." Ari gestured to Brynja. "May I introduce Brynja Pálsdóttir?"

"Yes, of course," the pastor said. "From Munkathverá, right? I've heard your father's taken ill. Word spreads quickly here, as you know. I had our custodian María take some pastries and jam from the kitchen here over to him as soon as we heard. Give him my best, will you?" His smile slipped. "I have not seen you in church, my child. Shame that you young people are moving away from the Lord."

Brynja glanced at the worn carpet. What could she say? For her, God was not a testable hypothesis.

The clergyman cleared his throat and patted her shoulder. The silence didn't seem to bother him. "Well, then, let me ring María for some coffee. You've never tasted anything quite so divine as her *rúgbrauð* with fresh herbs from the garden out back. María's a bit touched but a wonderful cook. I'll be right back."

After a moment, he returned and stood in front of the credenza. His wrinkled hand hovered over the *Möðruvallabók* as if he were christening a newborn child. "Imagine that. Our book coming back home after all these centuries."

He opened the wooden cover. Slowly, he turned the pages of browned vellum. Brynja stood on one side of him, Ari on the other.

"It never should have left here. It belongs to us. The words, the ink..."

Brynja watched him. "The ink?"

Pastor Dalmann pointed at the dark brown script. "See this?"

A stout woman in a worn, cotton dress tied about her ample waist with a frayed apron bustled into the room, porcelain cups rattling on the silver tray in her hands.

"Thank you, María," the pastor said, pointing to a table between two armchairs.

María nearly tripped on the carpet in her haste to lay it down.

"Ask, and it shall be given you," she said between labored breaths. "Seek, and ye shall find. Knock, and it shall be opened unto you. Matthew 7:7."

The pastor gave her a dismissive wave of his hand. "That'll be all, María." He closed the cover of the book and fastened the clasp with a slow, deliberate motion. "This is all we have left. The monks lost nearly everything when the monastery burned down long ago, but the *Möðruvallabók* survived." Awe transformed his face as he turned to Ari. "I'll guard it with my life, prime minister, I promise you. It'll never leave this church again."

Ari's jaw dropped. "But—"

Brynja started at the sound of her cell phone.

"I'm so sorry," she said, reaching into her purse to turn it off. She looked at the screen and saw that the call was from the lab at Legacy. "Will you forgive me? I need to answer this."

"In that case, it must be a call from 'upstairs.'" Pastor Dalmann's eyes gleamed with an odd humor.

Brynja stepped outside and answered the phone. "*Halló?*"

"*Halló*, Brynja. It's Stefán. I've got the DNA results from the sample you sent me. That silver spoon."

Brynja held her breath.

"Do you want the good news or bad news first?" he asked.

Her heart sank. Bad news could only mean one thing. Her father must have one of the Alzheimer's mutations. And that meant she had a fifty-fifty chance of having inherited the same fate.

"The good news, I suppose," she said.

"Well, first of all, I was able to extract enough DNA from the saliva."

Great. That was the good news?

"And the bad news?" Brynja asked.

"Actually, there's more good news," Stefán said. "I've analyzed the DNA, as well as the sample you banked of your own DNA a while ago. Neither of you has any of the mutations we know about for early-onset Alzheimer's disease or any other type of dementia."

Brynja closed her eyes and lifted her face to the sky and the sun breaking through the morning fog. Perhaps this was a call from above after all.

"Thank God," she said. "Thank you, Stefán. That's all good news. No bad news."

Stefán paused for a moment and then let out a deep breath. "It's just that, well, genetically speaking, Páll Björnsson can't possibly be your father."

Chapter 18

Thence come the maidens mighty in wisdom,
Three from the dwelling down 'neath the tree;
Urður is one named, Verðandi the next, and Skuld the third.
On the wood they scored
Laws they made there, and life allotted
To the sons of men, and set their fates.

-Völuspá, The Prophecy of the Seeress
Poetic Edda, 13th Century

From the driver's seat of Ari's Range Rover, Brynja peered through the windshield and watched Air Iceland flight #102 hurtle down the narrow strip of runway and take off over the fjord.

Ari had planned to present the *Möðruvallabók* to the Akureyri Museum immediately after their visit to Möðruvellir Church, but, not five minutes after she'd spoken with Stefán, Ari had been called back to Parliament for an urgent special session to discuss the escalating conflict over fishing rights in the East Fjords. Brynja had pleaded with him to leave the manuscript at the church until he could fly back to present the book to the museum. After arranging for the book to be guarded by the local police and gaining approval from the Magnússon Institute, Ari had agreed.

The plane disappeared behind a cloud, taking Ari away. How could she ever have doubted his love for her? Why was she not able to unfreeze her heart? Had the loss that followed her—the tragic twists and turns of her past—made her too guarded? She started the car and her thoughts went to another problem.

Stefán's words still thundered in her ear. Pabbi not her father? Her parents had been so devoted to one another. Her mother would never have had an affair; she was sure of it. Brynja caught sight of herself in the rear-view mirror. She even looked like her father. Same wavy, brown hair. Same oval face. Same almond-shaped eyes.

Had the lab at Legacy made a mistake? Was there a break in the chain, an error distributing DNA samples from the liquid nitrogen tanks to the lab? Or did the mix-up occur in the lab itself? Somehow, her father's sample must have been inadvertently switched with another. But this explanation only made matters worse. If Legacy couldn't even get the small request to analyze her father's DNA right, how could she have confidence in the results from the forensic evidence? She resolved to conduct a thorough review of procedures at the lab. In the meantime, she would have to send Stefán another sample of Pabbi's DNA—she still had the hair from his brush if she couldn't get her hands on more saliva—and insist the lab take more care with the analysis.

The clock on the dashboard read twelve-thirty p.m. Jónas would be worried. In her rush this morning, she had forgotten to leave him a note, and he would be wondering where she had gone. She shifted into gear and left the airport.

As she sped eastward toward her childhood home, she went over everything she hoped to accomplish during her visit north. She wanted to take Jónas back to Möðruvellir with her but that wouldn't be easy. Jónas had always refused to attend church. In fact, except for driving the pickup into town for the occasional errand, he pretty much kept to himself, content to tend to his duties within the confines of Munkathverá farm. She would have to insist he go with her to examine the book. Maybe then they could solve the riddle of Lúkas's whereabouts.

She thought it ironic that the long-sought answers might come from within the walls of a church; she had never been particularly religious. At the same time, she couldn't deny that fate—whatever that was—shaped everything in its path. Her knowledge of genetics made her all too aware of the often-cruel twists that fate could deliver. A tiny addition or deletion of just one nucleotide in the three billion bits of DNA within each cell could spell disaster. Muscular dystrophy, cystic fibrosis, neurofibromatosis...the list was endless. A single glitch in the birth of a cell could burden a lifetime.

Centuries before the science of genetics was born, Norse mythology spelled out its own version of fate. The *Norns*, the Goddesses of Fate—*Urður*, the Past; *Verðandi*, the Present; and *Skuld*, the Future—were present at a baby's birth. They stood beneath the roots of the World Tree *Yggdrasil* weaving the child's future into the tapestry of life. Each person's life was a string in their loom. *Urður* spun the threads, *Verðandi* wove them together, and *Skuld* cut them short.

Brynja loved these stories. Ari's name was Old Norse for 'eagle.' King of the skies. Powerful and strong. She had to wonder whether the *Norns* had been present at her own birth, and whether her name had sealed her fate. The name Brynja meant 'coat of mail' or 'armor.' Had the Goddesses of Fate known that she would need a shield against a lifetime of pain?

Brynja parked the car on the grassy patch at the end of Munkathverá's dirt road. Eager to share the news with Jónas that the

Möðruvallabók was at the church, she grabbed her bag, burst open the front door, and ran to the kitchen.

Jónas was once again hunched over his typewriter, tapping away at the keys.

"*Litla mín,*" he said, turning around at the sound of her clattering into the kitchen. "Please don't run off again without telling me where you're going. I—I worry about you."

Looking at the thinning hairs on Jónas's head, Brynja's heart softened. She leaned down and gently kissed his cheek.

"You're not going to believe this," she said. "Remember the poem? About Lúkas?" She reached into her bag for the poem and set it on the table. She sat down, pulled her chair close to his, and tapped a finger on the third line. "Look here. *The Book of Möðruvellir.* I'm sure if we take a close look at the *Möðruvallabók,* we'll be able to find some clue as to where Lúkas is." She smiled broadly. "And guess what? Ari drove up from Reykjavik with the book this morning!"

Jónas pushed his chair back. "Really?"

Brynja nodded. "Ari managed to have the Magnússon Institute loan it to the Akureyri Museum. Isn't that great?"

Jónas scanned the floor near her bag. "Where is it? Let's take a look."

"It's at Möðruvellir Church. Ari and I went to talk with the pastor. Dalmann Ingólfsson. Ari thought he might be able to give us more information on the *Möðruvallabók* since Möðruvellir was where it was found hundreds of years ago. Maybe the pastor can help us figure out the poem. I showed it to—"

Jónas interrupted. "You do know Pastor Dalmann is no friend of the family, don't you?"

Brynja gave him a blank stare.

"Dalmann certainly plays the part of the pious priest, but he's lacking a commandment or two," Jónas said. "I'm sure the pastor's age has slowed his libido some, but years ago, he was quite a ladies' man, even though he had a wife at the time. He apparently thought 'Thou shalt not commit adultery' didn't apply to him. Dalmann managed to get the blacksmith's wife pregnant and had an affair with a young student over at the schoolhouse." Jónas paused. "Even your own mother seemed much too friendly with him."

Brynja tensed. "What are you saying?"

"Nothing other than I don't trust that man. And neither does your father. He forbad your mother from attending services at Möðruvellir and it caused quite a rift between them."

Jónas stood to stir the pot of oats on the stove. "Perhaps you could get the book from the church and bring it here? I'll get your father some breakfast. Then he needs a bath." His voice trailed off and he leaned against the counter.

Brynja's gaze settled on the droop of his shoulders. Shoulders that had borne the weight of caring for the farm and their household all these years. Her father's illness had clearly taken a toll on Jónas.

"We don't need to tell Pabbi the *Möðruvallabók* is at the church. But we've got to find out more. Think how happy he would be to finally know what happened to his son. Maybe Lúkas is alive after all."

Jónas turned off the stove and slowly put the ladle in the spoon-rest. "I hope you're right, *litla mín*. I've never given up thinking we might find him."

"I really think whoever sent me the poem knows where he is. I haven't figured out the riddle yet, but I will. *We* will."

Jónas retrieved a paper from a drawer in the sideboard and sat back down. "I copied down the words when you were here last and typed them up. I've had a lot of time to mull them over." He pulled a pair of wire-frame glasses from a drawer and sat down. "I did have one thought."

Brynja pulled her chair closer.

"See here?" Jónas said. *"Tear the wheat from the chaff and you will find your other half..."*

"Yes?"

"That line struck me. I always thought Axel and Rúnar Bragason's sister Thorunn might have had something to do with Lúkas's disappearance. They lived just up the road and she was a strange woman, always weaseling her way into picnics and playgrounds and whatever games children were playing. Never could have children of her own, apparently." Jónas stopped talking and wiped his hands on his overalls.

"And?"

"Thorunn was at the carnival that day. She left for the Westfjords soon afterwards and never came back."

"You never told me that."

"I told the detectives about it. The police scoured up and down the coast there for months after Lúkas went missing."

Brynja's brow crinkled. "Why do you think Thorunn had anything to do with Lúkas? Being strange and childless isn't a crime, is it?"

Jónas shook his head and tapped the poem. "*Tear the wheat from the chaff.* Do you know who the only wheat farmer in Eyjafjörður was back then?"

"I'm guessing Thorunn?"

Jónas drummed his fingers on the table. "That's right. Thorunn was a wheat farmer over at Hof."

"Hof?" Brynja could barely get the word out. "The farm next to Möðruvellir?"

"Yes."

Brynja leapt out of her chair. "Jónas! You may be right. Let me think. The man who first found the *Möðruvallabók* at Möðruvellir back in the 1600s lived at Hof. Maybe he brought the book to Hof from the monastery. Maybe that's why the poem mentions the *Book of Möðruvellir* and finding Lúkas in a root cellar. Maybe there's a root cellar at Hof. I thought of that before but now it makes even more sense."

The excitement that coursed through her veins rapidly disintegrated into despair.

If Lúkas is in a root cellar, he's probably buried there. And all this time I assumed he was alive, waiting for me. Suppose he isn't? Suppose I've been deluding myself?

Brynja sat back down and traced her finger over the last line of the poem. She swallowed and looked up at Jónas. "I've been searching for so long, and now I have something concrete. Please, you have to help." She studied the lines of the poem again. "What do you think about the last line? *In the ink of Gloom's root cellar.*"

He lifted his shoulder in a half shrug and shook his head.

"It's all so confusing," she said. "At the church, the pastor started to say something about the ink, but I had to step outside for a phone call. When I went back inside, he and Ari were having a heated discussion over whether the book could be left at Möðruvellir. The upshot is it'll stay at the church for now. I can't bring it here, but we could go back to the church together. Amma can come over and stay with Pabbi."

"No, Amma's done too much already," Jónas said. "Just yesterday, she brought over some fresh-baked *skonsur* for your father." He fumbled with the pages of a calendar on the table. "Anyway, I can't go to the church with you. Your father has an appointment with the doctor today." Jónas pointed to the calendar. "See? Four p.m. With the neurologist."

"Jónas, that appointment is on Friday the twenty-third. Today is Tuesday the twentieth."

Was Jónas losing his mind as well?

Jónas seemed not to hear her and continued tapping the calendar.

"Pabbi's appointment isn't until Friday," she repeated. "You can come to the church with me. I'm sure the answer lies in the ink somehow. Besides, it'll do you good to get out for a while. I can ask Amma to come over just for an hour or so."

Jónas stood up and walked to the stove. "I'm afraid Pastor Dalmann wouldn't welcome me there. Too much bad blood between your father and him." He lifted the lid off the pot. "But you go. I'll be curious to know what you find out. We can talk about it when you get back." He picked up a spoon from the counter and tasted the oats.

Brynja froze. *Of course. That's it.*

She'd switched the spoons. That's why her DNA had not come up as a match for Pabbi's. She had grabbed the spoon that Jónas had eaten *skyr* with instead of the one her father had used.

Such a simple explanation. She kicked herself for her carelessness.

Science was always right. All her training in the scientific method had taught her to favor the hypothesis requiring the fewest assumptions. It was always a case of Occam's razor. The simplest explanation was usually the correct one.

Chapter 19

Brynja went up to her father's bedroom and sat quietly, watching his chest rise and fall. His color had returned, and he seemed less agitated. Maybe this wasn't dementia after all; Pabbi had fallen ill quite suddenly and his weakened physical state was unusual for the early stages of the disease. There must be something else, some other explanation for his condition. Perhaps it had been some sort of viral or bacterial infection. Encephalitis or meningitis.

When she reached for her phone to see if they could move up the appointment with the neurologist, she noticed a text from Ísak.

Call me when you get a chance.

She stepped outside her father's room and dialed his number.

"Brynja? I spoke with the police station up in Akureyri. They're shorthanded because of the officers stationed at Möðruvellir Church. So, even though you're not technically a member of law enforcement, they've given you permission to investigate the report regarding Inga's husband out at Hrísey. I let them know how impressed I am with your handling of the case."

"Thank you. I'll get out to Hrísey this afternoon. Anything else while I'm up north?"

"No, but apparently we're both wrong about the meaning of the parchment you found in the box of *kleinur*. The protest against the DNA database was a peaceful one. Only fifty people or so showed up. And, aside from the firecracker incident on National Day, Parliament's been quiet."

Brynja heard a door shut on the other end of the line.

"I've got to go," Ísak said. "I'll expect a report from Hrísey then?"

"Absolutely." Brynja paused. "And thanks for your support."

She hung up and checked on Pabbi. He was still asleep. Looking about the room, she spotted his brush and tucked a few hairs in a tissue. She would have the lab rerun his analysis using DNA derived from the hair follicles. After kissing her father gently on the forehead, she went downstairs.

In the kitchen, Jónas was hunched over his typewriter. He jerked back. "Oh! I thought you'd left for the church."

"No, not yet. I was hoping Pabbi would wake so I could get a better idea of how he's doing. He seems calmer, not so fitful."

Jónas leaned forward, shielding the typewriter from view.

"Doing some accounting? Inventory on the sheep?" Brynja asked, peering over his shoulder. "Oh." She winced. "Sorry, I didn't mean to interrupt."

Jónas was writing a letter to his sister Hanne, his only living relative. Hanne was a painful topic for Jónas, and he didn't often like to talk about her. Their mother had died giving birth to Hanne, a disabled but happy child. With their father out at sea fishing for cod, the responsibility of caring for Hanne had been left to Jónas. But when a violent storm took their father's life and, along with it, the family's livelihood, Jónas had had no choice but to place his sister in a home for the disabled. He had enrolled in the Hólar Agricultural College, hoping to develop an organic foods business in order to earn sufficient income to bring her back home. But those hopes were dashed when Hanne developed epilepsy; she required constant medical supervision.

Beyond that, Brynja didn't know much about Jónas's past. From time to time, after Lúkas had disappeared, when she was old enough to manage without him for a few days, he had taken leave of Munkathverá to visit Hanne. Jónas had always returned somewhat sullen; he hated to leave her in the care of strangers. The letters seemed to soothe his guilt somewhat.

Brynja put her hand on his shoulder. She knew better than to ask him how Hanne was doing. He simply did not want to talk about her.

Jónas stood up. "Hungry, *litla mín*?"

"No, thank you. I'm actually headed out to Hrísey to question a witness about a case I'm working on. I'll stop by the church on my way back. Sure you don't want to come?"

Jónas shook his head. "Your father needs me. I'll be curious to know what you find out, though."

Brynja kissed him on the cheek, grabbed her fleece from the rack, and headed out the door. If she hurried, she could catch the two o'clock ferry to Hrísey Island. On the short drive to the dock at Árskógssandur, she dialed the neurologist again. After several rings, she reached the doctor's voicemail, but learned only that he was out of the office and would respond as soon as he returned.

At the boat dock, Brynja parked the car and boarded the ferry. Just two hundred people resided on Hrísey, but the small vessel was kept busy in the summer shuttling tourists back and forth to the island. Today, the ferry was full to capacity with a large tour group interested in the island's history. In the 19th century, Norwegians and Swedes had established a salting factory for herring on the island. Over time, it had developed into a thriving, locally-owned business until, in the 1960s, overfishing in Icelandic waters put an end to the industry.

A friendly, slightly overweight American couple wedged themselves onto the bench next to Brynja and chatted non-stop for the duration of the twenty-minute crossing. They were particularly excited to stop at the 19th century house of Shark-Jorundur to view the exhibition on shark hunting in Iceland. The profession had been a highly profitable one, as shark liver oil had been used for street lighting until being replaced by petrol. The conversation led to the woman's recent experience tasting fermented shark, and she insisted on showing Brynja her Rotten Shark Club certificate.

After disembarking on Hrísey, Brynja waved goodbye to the couple and headed straight to the lighthouse where the keeper claimed she'd seen Inga's husband. She walked along the coastline path through meadows of angelica, wooly willow, and common juniper. Just past a grove of dwarf birch, a swarm of Arctic terns swooped down on her, engulfing her in a flurry of white-feathered wings and pointed, black beaks that pecked her head. Brynja grabbed a stick and waved it in the air, warding off the attack; she must have wandered too close to the nesting birds.

She hurried toward the bright orange lighthouse and climbed the stairs to the balcony. A young woman of twenty or so with a windburned face was polishing the huge lens.

Startled, the lightkeeper dropped the rag and jumped back. "Whoa. *Halló.* What the—?"

"I didn't mean to frighten you," Brynja said. "It's Lilja, right?"

The young woman nodded, then picked up the rag and rubbed it back and forth on the lens as if she were cleaning the entire glass façade of the Harpa Concert Hall.

Brynja showed the lightkeeper her ID. "Didn't the Akureyri police inform you I'd be coming out this afternoon to talk with you?"

"No. No, they didn't. But wait, what? What do you mean the police? Am I in trouble?"

The girl paced along the narrow ledge, restless as the sea below.

"You're not in the least bit of trouble," Brynja said. "I'm just here to ask a couple of questions about the other day." She explained she was working on a case involving a missing person. "We got a call that someone in the lighthouse here had spotted a suspect in the case."

The lightkeeper averted her eyes. "I didn't call. That wasn't me."

Brynja flipped to a page in her notepad. "Has anyone else been in the lighthouse with you?"

"I'm allowed, you know. I'm just doing this for the summer. They said I could—"

"It's okay," Brynja reassured the young woman. "That's not what I'm concerned with. Can you tell me who might have made that call if it wasn't you?"

"Must've been my friend Katrín. She's from Selfoss but she spends every summer up here. Katrín was kind of freaked out cuz when she looked down from the lighthouse, she said she saw a man on a boat that looked like someone in a photo from the Selfoss newspaper. She's kind of dramatic so I didn't pay too much attention to it."

Brynja jotted down the name. "Can you tell me where I might find Katrín?"

"Sure, she's working at the café on Sjávargata. You can't miss it. It's the only restaurant on the island."

"Thank you." Brynja wrote down the name of the restaurant and handed the young woman her card. "I'll let you get back to your work. Sorry I frightened you."

She turned to descend the circular staircase.

"Ma'am?" the girl called after her.

"Yes?"

"My friend. Katrín. I don't want to get her in trouble."

"Neither of you are in any trouble," Brynja said. "I assure you."

"But…Katrín was *djamma* when she was up here."

"*Djamma?*"

"Partying. Drunk. She probably just imagined seeing that guy you're interested in. She was so out of it I had to help her down the stairs so she wouldn't fall. Please don't tell anyone. Her mom would be so mad."

After tracking Katrín down at the café, the girl admitted that she'd been drunk and had been playing a prank on both her friend and the police by pretending she'd spotted Inga's husband.

Brynja admonished the young woman and immediately called Ísak to let him know the sighting of their main suspect had evaporated like alcohol from a shallow glass.

Ísak cut her short. "I've just had a call from the Westman Islands," he said. "They found him."

"Inga's husband?"

"Yes. He'd dyed his hair red and pasted on some ridiculous mustache, but a passenger on the car ferry thought he resembled the police sketch in the paper. The ferry captain insisted on seeing his driver's license and they got into a bit of a fist fight."

"Have they brought him in for questioning?"

"He's behind bars. The police on the island forced open the trunk of his car. They found a woman's body stuffed in a duffle bag. I'm assuming it's Inga, but we'll know for sure soon."

Brynja stomach dropped. "Oh. God. Horrible."

"You're to be commended for the clever RNA analysis of her blood. That'll go a long way toward putting this guy away for life."

Brynja sat down on the bench overlooking the fjord. Ísak's words were scant consolation. If the body was Inga's, a young girl had lost her mother.

Chapter 20

On the ferry from Hrísey back to the mainland, Brynja turned her thoughts once again to the *Möðruvallabók*. She looked at her watch. Although it was late afternoon, the church was just a few kilometers south of the ferry dock and she hoped the pastor wouldn't mind another visit to follow up on their previous conversation.

She was relieved when he welcomed her with a broad smile and asked her to wait in the sacristy while he went to the kitchen for some refreshments.

María's voice reverberated down the hallway, first a low rumble and then an outburst. A door slammed shut and heavy footsteps tromped along the path outside.

Brynja stood on her toes to peer through the arched windowpane. Although the glass was crazed and distorted with swirls, she could see María kneeling in front of the garden, her generous backside wobbling as she tore turnips, carrots, and herbs from the soil and threw the vegetables into a basket. The woman stood up, brushed her hands on her apron, and lumbered back inside. Passing the window, she looked up at Brynja, her eyes flickering with contempt.

Soon afterwards, Pastor Dalmann came back into the sacristy. He lit the wall sconces and turned on a floor heater.

"Well, then," he said, blowing into his hands and rubbing them together. "Where did we leave off?" He motioned for Brynja to join him at the credenza. "I'm sure you know the *Möðruvallabók* is one of the most valuable Icelandic manuscripts. It contains the only complete versions of several of the sagas. The entire book was penned by a single scribe in the fourteenth century. Such dedication."

He lifted the cover of the book and ran his hand over the wheat-brown pages. "It was written on vellum—"

"Calfskin."

"That's right. The book has more than two hundred vellum leaves made from the skins of more than a hundred calves. Centuries ago, even one cow could mean the difference between life and death, so you can only imagine just how important and valuable these manuscripts were."

Brynja nodded. "And still are."

"In most of medieval Europe, the hides were scraped with a sharp tool and then dipped in a lime bath to remove the hairs and soften the skin prior to stretching it on a rack. Since there's no limestone in Iceland, though, the poor monks had to use urine as an alkali."

The pastor pulled two old books from a nearby shelf and laid them on the credenza. "See here. The vellum in the *Möðruvallabók* is much darker than in these English texts. The urine used for the Icelandic manuscripts stained the hides to a dark yellow-brown."

"You seem to know a lot about the way the books were made," Brynja said. "What can you tell me about the actual stories, the sagas?"

Pastor Dalmann stood up straight as the back of a wooden pew and smiled. "Before I became a pastor, my child, I studied liturgical poetry. Not that the sagas are sacerdotal. On the contrary, they're about the lives of ordinary men. Nonetheless, there's a lot of beautiful poetry in the sagas."

"Can you tell me anything about the way it was written? Such as the style of poetry or the ink that was used?" Brynja hesitated. "The truth is, I'm hoping you can help me figure something out." She reached into her backpack and showed him the poem. "I received this a while ago. It's a riddle poem and it mentions the *Möðruvallabók*. I'm convinced it has something to do with my brother, Lúkas."

The pastor took a step back. "Oh?"

"My brother disappeared when we were seven years old."

The pastor crossed himself and muttered a prayer. "Yes, I remember. May his dear little soul rest in heaven."

"Lúkas has never been found. I'm holding out hope that he's still alive. I think whoever sent me this poem knows where my brother is."

The pastor retrieved a pair of spectacles from the pocket of his cassock and leaned over the poem. He read the words slowly.

Upon the madder mead
Where the sagas planted seed
Arose the Book of Möðruvellir.
Tear the wheat from the chaff
And you will find your other half
In the ink of Gloom's root cellar.

"Very strange," he said, stroking his chin. "It clearly references the *Möðruvallabók*." He looked closer. "But I'm afraid your poet has never read the sagas. Or at least doesn't understand the type of poetry in the sagas. The style's all wrong." He pointed to the first three lines. "Look here. Your poem is a tail-rhymed stanza with a simple rhyming structure. Icelandic saga poetry is much more complex. More sophisticated. It's composed primarily in *dróttkvætt* verse."

"*Dróttkvætt?*"

"Yes. *Dróttkvætt* is poetry comprised of eight lines with two stanzas. Not six lines, as you have here. Furthermore, alliteration ties the lines into pairs, and assonance appears within each line."

"I'm sorry…assonance?"

"Repetition of a vowel sound in non-rhyming syllables."

Brynja nodded slowly, trying to absorb every word.

"The poetry in the sagas is called skaldic poetry. A *skáld* was an Old Norse poet who composed poetry during the Middle Ages at the courts of Scandinavia and Iceland. Skaldic poetry is known for its use of kennings."

"I think I remember learning about kennings. Something about word play."

"Kennings are an intricate system of metaphors. Two or more nouns joined in a phrase, forming a whole new meaning. Such as mind-reader for a person who knows what you are thinking." He clasped his hands together and looked at Brynja. "Or gumshoe for detective." He chuckled.

Brynja smiled. Ari had proudly told the pastor she was a forensic scientist and worked closely with the police. "So, you're saying that the poem I received is not skaldic. It's not in *dróttkvætt* and it doesn't have kennings."

"That's right. But there are some similarities. Your poem has riddles in it, as does skaldic poetry. Here, let me look for an example." He gently turned the parchment pages of the *Möðruvallabók* until he found what he was looking for. "Here's one from *Kormák's Saga.* Kormák was a *skald*, one of the warrior-poets. This is what he wrote upon first seeing his beloved."

The pastor read each line, followed by its translation.

Brámáni skein brúna   *The* *moon of her eyelash*, *that valkyrie*
brims und ljósum himni   *of* *herb-surf*, *adorned with linen -*
Hristar hǫrvi glæstrar   *shone hawk-sharp upon me*
haukfránn á mik lauka;   *beneath her* *brows' bright sky;*
en sá geisli sýslir   *but that* *beam from the eyelid-moon*
síðan gullmens Fríðar   *of the* *goddess of the golden torque*
hvarmatungls ok hringa   *will later bring trouble to me*
Hlínar óþurft mína.   *and to the* *ring goddess herself.*

"The lines are alliterative pairs. *Brámáni brúna...brims.* And each of the lines contains an internal rhyme. *Hristar glæstrar; haukfránn lauka.* See that?"

Brynja squinted to read the gothic script.

"And there are quite a few kennings, especially when describing the woman. *The moon of her eyelash,* meaning her eye. And the *brows' bright sky,* meaning her forehead."

This was indeed remarkable and interesting, but she needed to steer him back to the poem about Lúkas. "What do you think about the riddles in the poem I received? Do you think those are kennings? Like my *other half,* meaning Lúkas? And *wheat from the chaff? Gloom's root cellar?* What do you think of those?"

Pastor Dalmann leaned over to read the poem again. "Well, we don't have to read much further than *upon the madder mead* to know—"

A loud rap on the door cut him short. María burst into the room, dripping with sweat.

"María!" The pastor pursed his lips. "I didn't call for you."

María pushed him aside and stormed toward Brynja, her chest heaving with deep, labored breaths.

Pastor Dalmann jumped forward. "Now, now." He grabbed the custodian's arms. "You've just had a spell. Calm down. All is well. All is well. Calm down, now."

He turned to Brynja with the frantic look of a man wrestling a two-ton polar bear.

"You'd best leave."

"But—"

"Leave us!"

Early the next morning, after bidding goodbye to Jónas and reminding him she'd be back on Friday for Pabbi's appointment with the neurologist, Brynja returned to the church. She had to know what the pastor had been about to say before María interrupted them.

She parked Ari's car by the main road and walked down the dirt path, trying her best to ignore the conspiracy of ravens circling above.

Two of the guards greeted her, looking as if they could use some coffee. She knocked softly on the door and breathed a sigh of relief when Pastor Dalmann appeared, and not María.

He put a finger to his lips. "This is not a good time, my child. We've got a memorial service starting in just an hour."

"I only need a minute. I'd be so grateful."

The pastor looked over his shoulder toward the kitchen. "María's baking for the congregation. I've only got a little while before she's finished."

"I'll be quick," Brynja said, sliding past him into the sacristy.

The pastor followed her in but kept his eye on the passageway.

Brynja looked into his pale, gray eyes. "I'm just curious what you meant about the *madder mead*. Isn't mead what they used to call wine? The wine the Vikings drank before battle? The wine that made them go totally berserk?"

"My heavens, dear child," the pastor said. "Calm down. It's true the Vikings drank mead, but they whipped themselves into frenzy by wearing bearskins, *ber-serkrs*, and eating hallucinogenic mushrooms. I'm sure your poem refers not to *mead* from the Old English word *medu*, meaning honey or sweet drink, but to *mæd*, which means meadow or field."

"When I googled it, I did see that mead can mean meadow. But the more common definition is that fermented drink they made with honey."

The aging clergyman led the way to a small window overlooking the pasture. He put his hand to the glass. "Aside from the patch of land that María uses to grow herbs and plants for her cooking, these fields are covered by grasses and dicots like buttercup, angelica, and lady's mantle in the summer."

Yes, she knew all that.

"But back when Iceland was settled," the pastor continued, "the climate was much warmer. These fields were covered with a plant called madder." He spread his arms wide. "In fact, that's how our monastery got its name, Möðruvellir. *Moðru* comes from the Old Norse *maðra*, meaning madder. And *vellir* means fields. So, I would guess your *madder mead* refers to these fields around Möðruvellir."

He walked to the door of the sacristy and poked his head out into the hallway before stepping back in and hovering over the manuscript. "I believe the answer to finding Lúkas lies right here in Möðruvellir."

Brynja drew in a quick breath.

"This book," he continued, "is the *Möðru-valla-bók*. The Madder-fields-book." He ran his finger over the pages. "And you can rest assured it'll never leave these fields again."

Brynja said nothing. Ari was going to have to remind the pastor that the manuscript was going to the Akureyri Museum in a few days and then back to Reykjavik.

Pastor Dalmann motioned toward the door. "You'll have to leave soon, I'm afraid. María will be…the service will be starting soon."

"I will. But are you saying that Lúkas can be found here? In Möðruvellir Church?"

"Heavens, no. I would know if Lúkas were in the church. I'm sure your poem refers not to the church, but to the fields of Möðruvellir valley. Beyond that, I don't think I can help you."

Brynja's heart sank and the despair of earlier years returned. She was sure if Lúkas was alive, he wasn't in the Möðruvellir valley. She had lived here until she'd left for university at age eighteen and she'd been back many times since. Either she would have seen Lúkas, or someone else would have. Obviously, her brother had aged since his disappearance, but someone surely would have recognized him. The pastor was a sweet, old man, and definitely a knowledgeable one, but he was no sleuth. His guess as to Lúkas's whereabouts seemed just about as good as hers.

Basically, he had no idea.

Although…if Lúkas *wasn't* alive, he *could* still be in Möðruvellir valley.

She took a deep breath and asked the next question. "Do you know anything about the people that live at Hof? The farm adjacent to the church?"

"A woman named Thorunn Bragadóttir lived there but moved away quite some time ago. The property's been in her family at least since the 1600s. I'm not sure anyone lives there now."

"Would you know if there's a root cellar on the farm?"

"There used to be one, yes. But they filled it in more than forty years ago, after refrigeration came in." He motioned to Brynja to join him at the window. "You can see where it was." He pointed to the plot of land she'd seen María kneeling at. "Guess the soil was quite fertile there. María's been able to grow a plentiful garden in that spot."

So, that's not the answer. There was no root cellar at Hof. And, likely, no Lúkas.

"Just one more thing, Pastor. What were you going to say about the ink in the *Möðruvallabók*? You said something about the ink when we brought the manuscript here yesterday."

"Yes, I did. The monks used a dark brown ink made from bearberries and willow."

A chill ran down her spine. Dark brown ink was used on both warnings in the box of *kleinur*. And Theó Friðriksson in the chemistry lab had said the ink on the warning was the same as the ink in the *Möðruvallabók*. But the warnings didn't make sense.

Pastor Dalmann continued, oblivious to the change in Brynja. "The ink in the *Möðruvallabók* is obviously quite different from the red ink used to write your poem, though."

"Yes, it looks very different—bright red compared to dark brown. I had the ink analyzed. It contains a red dye called alizarin."

"Oh? Yes, so interesting. Do you know where alizarin comes from?"

"No, I don't."

"In medieval times, they made alizarin by crushing the roots of a plant called *Rubia tinctorum*. In fact, the English translation of *Rubia tinctorum* is 'Red of the Dyers.'" He again walked to the window. "And do you know the common name of *Rubia tinctorum*?"

Brynja shook her head.

With a triumphant smile, the pastor said, "Madder. *Maðra. Moðru* if we're talking about the possessive. Madder is the name of the plant that used to cover the fields here. The red dye came from the root of the madder plant."

Brynja turned to stare out the window.

In the ink of Gloom's root cellar.

Ink. Root. The red ink on the poem was made from the root of the madder plant. And madder used to cover the fields surrounding Möðruvellir. And…and what? Her mind went blank. If she had all the pieces, why weren't they fitting into place?

The rope tying her to Lúkas slipped from her hands, and she was adrift again. She tried to pull the threads together, but it still didn't make sense.

The pastor's gaze shifted to the open door of the sacristy. "You'll forgive me. María will be in any minute."

"Yes, thanks for taking the time—" Brynja's phone rang.

"Shut that off," Pastor Dalmann hissed. "You've got to go. Now." He took hold of Brynja's arm and hurried her down the front steps of the church. "María's been quite agitated since visiting her sister in Reykjavik last week. I don't want to upset her any further by bringing in strangers or delaying the service in any way."

Brynja crossed the churchyard, opened the car door and waved goodbye to the pastor. He had proven a thoroughly unexpected fount of information. She now had so much information that she was unsure how to assimilate it all. The poem and the warnings were written in different types of ink: The red ink of the poem was alizarin ink and the brown ink of the warning was the same type the medieval scribes used for the *Möðruvallabók*. The poem and warning were of different styles: The poem a basic rhyming pattern and the warning a sophisticated, highly structured *Dróttkvætt*, drawn directly from the sagas. Whoever had penned the warning knew the saga manuscripts extremely well. But the person who had written the poem must also have some knowledge of medieval writing since the phrase *madder mead* was taken from the Old Norse *moðru-vellir* and the red ink was traditionally made by crushing the roots of the madder plant.

Brynja had started the engine and turned south when she remembered the earlier phone call. She pulled to the side of the road and dug through her bag for the cell phone.

Two missed calls. Both from Ari. She was about to dial his number when his ringtone played again.

"Ari?"

"Brynja. Thank God I caught you."

"What's wrong?"

"Fríða, she—"

"Fríða? What's happened?"

"Someone mailed a rhubarb cake to my office yesterday. You know I hate rhubarb, so I gave the cake to Fríða to take home."

"And?"

"Fríða ate a slice of it last night. Or two slices, I'm not sure. All I know is, after dinner, she complained of a headache and went to bed."

"Ari, I'm sure Fríða will be fine."

"No, Brynja, she won't be fine. She's dead. Fríða's dead."

Chapter 21

The drive back to Reykjavik was hair-raising, and only got worse once Brynja entered the city. After weaving through the crowds celebrating the Summer Solstice Festival, she parked Ari's car and stepped out to the pounding pulse of drumbeats filling the air over Austurvöllur Square.

At the visitor entrance to the Parliament building, she buzzed the intercom, showed her ID, and proceeded to the lobby. It was empty save for a couple of guards who stood in the shadows; the MPs were not in session over the summer. She spotted Ari across the room, hunched over on a low, birchwood bench, his hands clasped in front of him. She hurried over.

"I'm so sorry about Fríða." She sat down and took his hand. "You look exhausted. Have you been here all night?"

He lowered his head. "She was a good woman, Fríða. She was my support, my friend. I gave her that cake."

"You don't know the cake made her sick. Fríða had high blood pressure. Maybe she had a stroke."

"No, it was the cake. Henning called me."

Henning?

"Henning said Fríða was poisoned. Something about the rhubarb cake containing poison. He wants to speak with me."

Brynja tensed. She squeezed Ari's hand, wishing she could assure him it just wasn't possible Fríða had been poisoned. But Occam's razor was sparkling in the light. Tómas had fallen ill immediately after eating *kleinur* and now Ari's secretary was dead after eating rhubarb cake. The simplest explanation requiring the fewest assumptions was that they had both been poisoned. Still, Tómas was overweight and Fríða suffered from high blood pressure. Maybe it was all just a terrible coincidence.

But she didn't think so.

Ari ran his fingers through the locks of hair that fell across his forehead. "At least Henning agreed to talk here instead of at the station. The media would've had a field day. I can hear it now. *Prime Minister: Prime Suspect.*"

A series of loud, metallic clicks resounded through the lobby and the security door slid open. Henning nodded at the guard and limped along the parquet-wood floor, the determined tap of his cane echoing in the hollow chamber. Ari and Brynja stood to greet him.

Henning extended his hand to Ari. "My condolences. I'm sure this is quite difficult for you." He glared at Brynja and turned back to Ari. "I thought we'd decided to talk in private."

"I'd like Brynja to stay," Ari said. "That is, if you don't mind." Not waiting for Henning's response, he turned to leave. "Let's talk in my office."

Brynja avoided looking at Henning; out the corner of her eye, she could see him trying to get her attention, and she had no interest in explaining to him why she was here at Ari's side.

Ari unlocked the office door, hesitated at Fríða's desk, and then passed on. He waved them through to the conference room and motioned to Henning and Brynja to take a seat at the mahogany table overlooking a quiet garden with white and peach and yellow rose bushes. The setting was purposeful—intended to put visiting diplomats and other dignitaries at ease.

Brynja felt anything but.

Henning dangled his cane on the edge of the table and cleared his throat. "Perhaps we could start with Fríða's last supper, so to speak." He retrieved a notepad from his bag. "According to her husband, they ate a very simple meal at home. Mashed fish and brown bread. For dessert, Fríða brought out the rhubarb cake you baked for her. Apparently, she was quite touched."

Ari folded his arms across his chest. "I didn't bake that cake. It was delivered in the mail to my office Friday."

"Oh?" Henning said. "By whom?"

"The mail clerk."

Henning balled his fist. Brynja knew he would have snapped at anyone else, but Ari was the prime minister.

"With all due respect, I mean, who mailed you the cake?"

"I've no idea. Fríða receives my mail." Ari leaned forward. "Why do you suspect her death had to do with the cake?"

"It's fairly straightforward. Immediately after eating two large slices, Fríða complained of a headache—"

"Fríða's been under a lot of stress," Ari interrupted. "She had dangerously high blood pressure."

"Oh? I didn't know that." Henning scribbled in his notepad. "After she complained of a headache, Fríða's husband put her to bed. At two in the morning, she woke him up, saying she had an intense burning in her throat."

"Did her husband eat any of the cake?" Brynja asked.

Henning's nostrils flared. "Not that I know of."

Brynja shook her head. "Probably should find that out."

Henning ignored her comment. "As I was saying, Fríða had a burning in her throat. After her husband brought her some water to drink, she seemed to feel better and fell back asleep for a while. When she woke a few hours later, her mouth was covered with open sores and she was hot as hell. Her husband rushed her to the ER."

"Poor Fríða," Ari said.

"The doctors gave her fluids and did some lab tests on her blood and urine, but the diagnosis came too late. Fríða fell into a coma and died."

A coma. Tómas fell into a coma, too.

Chilled by the parallel, Brynja reached for a pitcher of water. Her throat was dry. As she grabbed the handle, the pitcher shrank in size and morphed into a tiny, glass teacup. She blinked. *Not now, please. Not now.* She shut her eyes, then opened them again. The teacup swiveled, round and round and burst into a kaleidoscope of a thousand tiny teacups. Splinters of glass. Fiery shards of white-hot, blinding light.

She gasped and jerked her hands back to shield her face, knocking the pitcher over.

"Brynja?" A look of puzzlement crossed Ari's face.

She jumped up and hit her foot on the table leg. "It's nothing. Just nerves."

She left the room.

A minute later, she returned with a cloth and fresh pitcher of water. After wiping the table dry, she poured them each a glass and handed one to Ari.

She set the pitcher down and turned to Henning. "You were saying? Fríða's diagnosis?"

"Well, uh, yes." Henning's eyes ping-ponged between Ari and Brynja. "Are you—?"

"I'm fine. This is about Fríða. What was the diagnosis?"

Henning coughed. "Okay, then. Well. The lab tests on her urine showed crystallization. After hearing what Fríða had eaten, an intern put two and two together and said he'd seen rhubarb poisoning in sheepdogs many times. Seems we have so many animals in Iceland that doctors recognize these poisons." He flashed his eyes at Brynja. "I'm sure you remember Tómas's doctor connected the guard's symptoms to those he saw of poisoning in horses."

Brynja stewed. "We don't know the cause of Tómas's illness. His toxicology results haven't been reported."

Henning turned back to Ari. "Anyway, the doctor's family bred sheepdogs. On occasion, some of the young pups would come back from the fields after munching on rhubarb leaves sick as a dog." He cleared his throat again. "No pun intended. At any rate, the veterinarian warned them to keep all animals away from rhubarb plants."

"But people eat rhubarb all the time," Ari said.

"The doctor ordered some additional tests." Henning flipped to a page in his notebook. "Fríða's blood results showed excessively high levels of oxalic acid. The lethal dose is 375 micrograms per kilogram, and her levels were well above that."

"If the cake had high levels of oxalic acid," Brynja said, "then it might have been an accident, a cake made by someone who doesn't know how dangerous the leaves are."

"Except a genuine gift would have a card or note attached," Ari said. "This had nothing. And how many gardeners don't know about rhubarb? Every garden and greenhouse across the country grows rhubarb."

"It's true that rhubarb is one of the few vegetables we can grow here," Henning said. "Probably why it's so popular. But the leaves are poisonous. Who wouldn't know that? The leaves contain much higher levels of oxalic acid than the stalks. I think the doctor said they contain something like 0.5 percent oxalic acid."

"That sounds right," Brynja said. She did a quick calculation in her head. "Say, for argument's sake, that Fríða weighed sixty-five kilograms. She'd have to have eaten about twenty-five grams of pure oxalic acid. That's five kilos, almost eleven pounds of leaves. You can't tell me there were eleven pounds of leaves in that cake, Henning."

Henning flipped through his notebook again. "I spoke to Poison Control. Apparently, when the leaves are cooked down with soda, the oxalic acid leaches out into a viscous liquid. It might well be whoever baked that cake intentionally boiled the leaves and added the toxic concentrate to the batter."

Ari blew out his cheeks. He looked exhausted. "I'm always getting baked goods from sweet, old ladies thanking me for attending some knitting contest or pastry bake-off." He paused. "I never considered how dangerous that particular cake could be. Why would I? In fact, I opened the box, took the cake out, and sliced off a piece since I was so hungry. I was disappointed to see it was a rhubarb cake, but I thought Fríða might enjoy it. So, I gave it to her."

Henning scribbled in his notepad. "Can you describe the cake for me?"

"If I remember correctly, it was a two-layer cake with rhubarb jam filling. There were chunks of cooked rhubarb stems and the frosting was topped with poppy seeds. I'd never seen rhubarb cake made that way."

"And the name of the person who sent it to you?" Henning asked.

"I've said I don't know. Fríða unwrapped the package and put the box on my desk."

"Perhaps the wrapping is still here," Brynja said.

She jumped up and hurried out of the conference room to Fríða's desk, Henning at her heels.

She spotted a wad of moss green paper in the trashcan.

The same paper the box of kleinur was wrapped in.

Brynja reached for the paper and lifted it out of the wastebasket with the edge of her scarf.

"I'll take that," Henning said, snatching the paper from her and laying it on top of Fríða's desk.

"Now your DNA will be all over the packaging," Brynja said.

Henning shot back. "Whoever is doing this wouldn't be so careless as to leave fingerprints, and this is my investigation."

"You'd still do well to remember who's in charge of forensics." She retrieved a tissue, flattened the paper on the desktop, and leaned over to inspect it. "There's a return address," she said. "32 Kjarrholt, 400 Ísafjörður, Westfjords."

Henning grabbed hold of the wrapping paper and slid it into his bag. "I'll have to take this to the station as evidence." He tapped his cane on the hardwood floor and stared at Brynja. "Two poisonings in one week. Tómas Gylfason and now Fríða. You seem to be in the middle of both."

Ari stood at the doorway. "I expect a complete and professional investigation, Henning. If you are not prepared to do that, I'll ask that someone else be assigned."

"I was just making an observation."

"As far as Tómas goes," Brynja said, "all we know at the moment is that his symptoms possibly resemble those of poisoning. And in horses, nonetheless. That's it. Nothing more. Let's remember Tómas is morbidly overweight. He could well be diabetic. Insulin shock could also account for his coma."

Who was she trying to convince? The parallel was all too obvious.

"Speculation," Henning said. "One last thing. We searched Fríða's home and took the cake box in as evidence. We found this tucked beneath what was left over."

He reached into his bag and pulled out a slip of parchment, placing it on the table before them.

The words were written in dark brown ink.

The horse of the necklace sways,
My bald head bangs when I fall.
My piece's soft and clammy
And I can't hear when they call.
                                        -Egil's Saga

Brynja stiffened.

Egil's Saga. The second saga in the *Möðruvallabók*. There was a progression to the warnings. And, quite possibly, to the poisonings.

As much as she didn't want to believe it, Henning could be right.

The detective hobbled past her to the door.

"Ten o'clock tomorrow," she called after him.

Henning craned around, derision once more flattening his gaze. "What about ten o'clock?"

"Meeting. My office. Ten o'clock."

After a glance at Ari, he turned away without answering, and left.

Brynja released a long breath and looked down at the table.

He had left the parchment behind.

Chapter 22

I know where Odin's eye is hidden,
Deep in the wide-famed well of Mimir;
Mead from the pledge of Odin each morn
Does Mimir drink: would you know yet more?

-Völuspá, The Prophecy of the Seeress
Poetic Edda, 13th Century

Fueled by anxiety, Brynja had been unable to sleep. At five a.m., she'd pulled herself out of bed and gone to the one place she could think clearly: her office. The siren song of the midsummer solstice had drawn many of her colleagues at Legacy downtown last night to celebrate with shots of *Brennivín* and liters of *Einstök* ale and they wouldn't be in for a few hours. She had the building to herself.

Brynja placed the evidence bag containing the parchment from the rhubarb cake on her desk. As soon as Stefán arrived, she would take it to the lab and instruct him to analyze the DNA on it. Next, she booted up the computer and checked the National Registry for the return address on the wrapping paper. No one was listed at 32 Kjarrholt in Ísafjörður. She searched the digital phone directory, ja.is, but no one was registered there either. Remembering Jónas had said Thorunn moved to the Westfjords shortly after Lúkas disappeared, she typed Thorunn's name into both directories. Nothing. She sat back and tapped her fingers on the desk. Rúnar surely knew where his sister Thorunn lived, but how could she ask him?

Frustrated, Brynja pulled a pad of Post-its from the drawer. She laid out a matrix of the note cards on her desk. On the left, she scribbled phrases from the poem about Lúkas. On the right, ingredients in the cake that had poisoned Fríða. She stared at the Post-its, searching for the thread that could tie the events of the past week together.

Plants, seeds, roots, ink. Pieces of the puzzle.

She shuffled the small slips of paper into a pattern.

madder mead	in the ink
planted seed	poppy seeds
root cellar	rhubarb
batter	poison
wheat from the chaff	???

According to the pastor, the red ink of the poem was alizarin, crushed madder root.

Ari had said that poppy seeds had been sprinkled on the cake.

Rhubarb could be forced to grow in a root cellar.

Oxalic acid in the cake batter had poisoned Fríða.

What was she missing? What matched with wheat from the chaff?

Brynja stood up and peered out at the tombstone gray clouds

hovering over the harbor. The answer was out there. If only she knew where. Her favorite of the Old Norse stories had always been that of one-eyed Odin, the god of wisdom and poetry. Odin was so thirsty for knowledge that he sacrificed an eye to Mímir, the god of memory, in exchange for wisdom. When he threw his eye into Mímir's well, a fountain of water sprang forth with the knowledge Odin sought.

I would sacrifice an eye to know where Lúkas is, she thought, pressing her forehead against the cold glass. *The eye that lost sight of him twenty years ago.*

She turned and noticed of the scuffmarks Tómas's boots had made as he writhed on the floor. His vomit had left a stain in the wood. She realized, to her shame, that she hadn't checked on his recovery. Landspítali wouldn't give her an update over the phone, but Henning likely knew of his current condition. She dialed his number.

"Do you know what time it is?" Henning croaked on the other end of the line.

Brynja glanced at the clock. "I'm sorry. I really am. I lost track of time. I—I'll call back later."

"Who the hell is this?"

"It's Brynja."

"Well, now that you've already ruined what little sleep I was getting, what is it?"

"I thought you might know how Tómas is doing. I haven't had a chance to get back to see him at the hospital and—"

"Tómas is no longer in the hospital."

Brynja felt enormous relief. "I'm so glad to hear that. I'll visit him at home tomorrow, then. Sorry again for calling so early."

She hung up, turned to the computer, and typed 'Tómas Gylfason' into the National Registry.

The ring of her phone interrupted the search.

"*Halló?*"

"Henning here. Listen, Brynja, Tómas is not in the hospital."

"Yes. You just told me that."

"Tómas is not in the hospital because he's dead. He died of ergot toxicity yesterday afternoon. The doctor was right. *I* was right. Tómas was poisoned."

Brynja hung up, raced down the hall to the restroom, and vomited. She washed her face, wiped her hands, and returned to the office. Henning was a bastard. He'd known about Tómas's demise yesterday, in Ari's conference room, and not said a word about it.

She eased herself into her chair, drank a sip of water, and stared at the computer screen. So, Tómas really had been poisoned. She wracked her brain to recall what she had learned about ergot poisoning in medical school.

She opened the search engine, typed in *ergot* and *poison*, and read the excerpt.

> Ergot refers to a group of fungi of the genus *Claviceps*. One species, *Claviceps purpurea,* produces alkaloids that can cause ergotism in humans and other mammals that consume grains contaminated with its fruiting structure. Symptoms of ergotism include convulsions, seizures, nausea, and vomiting. Periodic outbursts of ergot toxicity have occurred throughout history—such as the dancing plague of the Middle Ages and the 'bewitching' of Salem, Massachusetts—presumably from the growth of the fungus on rotting rye, barley or wheat.

Wheat.
Wheat from the chaff.

The main ingredient in *kleinur* was wheat flour. Henning was right. The *kleinur* must have been laced with ergot.

Jónas's words echoed in her mind: *Do you know who the only wheat farmer in Eyjafjörður was back then?* Maybe he was right to suspect Axel and Rúnar's sister Thorunn. She had lived at Hof, next to Möðruvellir Church. Had she harmed Lúkas, buried him there, and sent the warning to scare Brynja off from searching for him? But, then, how would she know about the poem with clues to Lúkas's whereabouts?

Brynja sat up straight. She would have to get over to Hof and survey the property. Maybe there was another root cellar on the farm, one that Pastor Dalmann was unaware of. And, somehow, she'd have to track Thorunn down in the Westfjords. If the woman still lived there.

She had to think now, not react, just think. If the *kleinur* had been meant for her, it had to have been sent by someone who didn't know her very well, someone who didn't know she was allergic to wheat. But that note—*Be warned by another's woe*—had come with the *kleinur*. A deadly gift and a warning together. Did someone know that Tómas—who had probably never refused an offer of food in his entire life—would be delivering the *Möðruvallabók* to her office? The rhubarb cake had been sent to Ari. Did they know that Ari hated rhubarb? Did they guess rightly that he would give it away? Were she and Ari both being framed?

Chilled and confused and scared, Brynja wrapped herself in a cashmere shawl and lay down on the couch. The tick of the wall clock grew louder and louder, until the entire room pulsated. She pulled the shawl up over her head and shut her eyes.

The clap of footsteps darting across the outer office startled her. Had she fallen asleep? She glanced at the time: six a.m. *Who could possibly be here so early?*

The hurried footsteps gave way to an impatient whoosh of drawers and the frantic rustle of papers. Someone was searching through Elly's desk. Brynja crept toward the door and peeked through the crack.

"Elly!" Brynja let out a sigh of relief.

"Oh! Brynja!" Elly jumped, tripping over the leather fringe of her maxi-skirt. "You scared me. I—I didn't think you were back yet. I—uh—okay then."

"Is everything all right?"

Brynja stared at the disarray on the desk. Elly was not simply shuffling papers. She was piling them into a box along with pens, her iPad, a framed photo of her Jack Russell terrier, and her *I'm Danish, What's Your Superpower?* coffee cup.

"I don't think I'm cut out for this job," Elly stammered.

Brynja hurried over to Elly. "Are you quitting? No, Elly, please. Put your desk back together. You're doing an amazing job. You've been so helpful."

"I'm sorry, I just don't think I'm going to be able to deal with Rúnar. I know that's part of the job but I—I just can't."

Brynja put her arm around Elly's shoulder. "Come, sit in my office." She poured Elly a glass of water and sat next to her on the couch. "Tell me what's going on."

Elly's lip trembled as she spoke. "Rúnar texted me yesterday. He asked me to come to his office. He said he had the DNA results from the warning parchment we found with the *kleinur*. I thought it was strange that he asked me to come over without you, but you were up north, and I knew you'd want to know the results, so I went."

Brynja's heart sank. Rúnar, the cad.

"When I got to his office, Rúnar insisted on giving me a cup of this weird-tasting tea. He said it was a special tea made from poppies." Elly rubbed her hands down her maxi-skirt. "At first he bored me half to death with all this mumbo-jumbo about poppy genes, and dominant versus recessive traits, and allelic something-or-other, and I don't know what else."

"Elly—"

"No, it's—" Elly's voice cracked. "I didn't have a clue what he was talking about, but I pretended to be interested. Maybe I shouldn't have been so attentive. Maybe it's all my fault." Her hands flew up to wipe the tears from her eyes.

"What happened?"

"I don't know what happened."

Brynja squeezed her eyes shut for a second. She felt sick. "What do you mean?"

"I was there but I wasn't there." Elly pressed her hands over her face and elbows to her side as she bent over.

"It's okay," Brynja said softly. "You're here now, with me."

Elly sniffled and took a sip of water. "All I remember is that I started to feel dizzy and I swear I could see the flower buds on those poppy plants burst open and all those colors swirling together like a giant lollipop at a carnival." She swallowed. "Rúnar started saying something about how I was a delicate bloom, a fragrant flower…"

"Do you remember how much of the tea you drank?"

"I was nervous. I think I drank the whole cup."

Brynja cringed. The Iceland poppy, like all poppies, was basically a narcotic. Although less potent than the opium found in the seedpod, the leaves contained enough chelidonine alkaloid to create a sense of euphoria when steeped in tea.

She hesitated, then looked Elly in the eye. "Did Rúnar touch you?"

Elly lowered her head and spoke so quietly that Brynja had to lean in to hear what she was saying.

"I tried to leave, Brynja. I really did. But Rúnar grabbed my arm and told me to lie down on the couch until I felt better. I must have blacked out for a minute because the next thing I knew he was hovering over me with his disgusting breath steaming all over my face and I don't know what came over me, but I slapped him and that's when he grabbed my arm again. I thought his eyes were going to burn right through me." She fidgeted with the stack of metal bracelets on her wrist. "Then I must've fainted again."

Brynja placed her hand on Elly's.

After a moment, her intern looked up. "When I came to, Henning was there."

"Henning?"

"Yes. They were talking about you."

"About me?"

"I didn't catch everything but Rúnar was saying you had no right to download the Paget's file. He was furious. He said those files are confidential and they would jeopardize his family if people found out about them. He said you should be fired."

Brynja held herself still and let Elly talk.

"Henning said you should be investigating your own DNA instead of sticking your nose into other people's business."

"Are you sure that's what he said?"

"Yes, I'm sure," Elly said. "But they must've made a mistake."

"What do you mean they must've made a mistake?"

"Rúnar said the results from that parchment, you know, that warning with the doughnuts about *weapons red with gore*—"

Brynja's heart skipped. "Yes?"

"Rúnar said the DNA on the parchment is yours. He said the closest match in the database is to your DNA. It's all over the warning."

"But that's not possible. I was careful to put on evidence gloves before picking the parchment out of the box."

"It gets worse." Elly's voice cracked. "Henning said you must've written the warning to intimidate Tómas into leaving the *Möðruvallabók* with you. And when he didn't, you poisoned him."

"What? That's absurd. Just think about it. That would mean I came to work prepared for murder. That I'm even capable of murder. It's too insane to even think about." She stood up. "What I'm really concerned about is you. Did Rúnar touch you?"

Elly shook her head.

"But he frightened you and violated you by giving you a drug without your knowledge or permission. That's harassment and a crime."

"What's going to happen now?"

"I'm going to file a complaint immediately." Brynja softened her tone. "I hope you'll stay. And we'll make sure Rúnar leaves you alone."

Brynja shot Elly a tight smile and picked up the phone.

And then I'll have to deal with Rúnar and Henning and the DNA report.

Chapter 23

An hour later, Brynja found Elly sitting still as a brooding dove in the outer office.

"Rúnar won't give you any more trouble," she said. "I spoke with HR. He's on notice. Considering the kind of tea he gave you, he's on thin ice and he knows it."

"Really?" Elly straightened up, her expression flitting from a stunned blankness to sudden awareness.

"Even so, if you do still decide to leave, I think you should see a lawyer and consider filing charges. I'll go with you."

"No," Elly said quickly. "Not yet, anyway. I'll think about it."

"If you're sure."

"I am. And I'm not going to leave. I've decided to stay."

"Well, I'm glad, very glad."

"I have something to tell you. But you should eat something first.

You look pale. Here." She handed Brynja a bowl. "Stefán from the lab brought some berries by yesterday."

Brynja smiled weakly. Elly was right. She hadn't eaten anything, and her stomach was tight as the knot she used to tie her braids with.

Brynja led the way into her office. "What did you want to tell me?"

Elly plunked down in the chair opposite Brynja's desk. "I've been thinking. After you told me about the parchment in the box of rhubarb cake, I did a little research. Those words were taken from *Egil's Saga*, right?"

"That's right."

"Well, I looked up *Egil's Saga* online and found out Egil Skallagrímsson was a pretty complicated Viking dude. He was part poet, part warrior, part farmer."

Brynja nodded absently. She was more concerned with the warning from *Njál's Saga* in the box of *kleinur*. How could her DNA be on that parchment? That made no sense. Either Legacy had screwed up, or someone had planted it there.

When she had called Ísak to reiterate her concerns about Henning, he had agreed some action was needed. He would put the detective under increased supervision and, at the end of each shift, require Henning submit a written report detailing each of his activities.

Brynja was so caught up in her thoughts that she was startled when Elly put her hands on the desk.

"Get this," the girl said, only inches from Brynja's face. "Some scholars think that Egil had Paget's disease. That disease you were looking up in the LinX Disease Database."

"Paget's?"

Brynja tried to remember if Egil was the Viking settler Ásta had said she was descended from.

"In my research," Elly said, "I found an article online in an old issue of *Scientific American* by this professor in California. He suggests that the poetry in *Egil's Saga* means Egil had Paget's!" Elly opened her iPad and pointed at the screen. "This is the passage, right? The words on the parchment under the rhubarb cake?"

Brynja scrutinized the lines.

> *The horse of the necklace sways,*
> *My bald head bangs when I fall.*
> *My piece's soft and clammy*
> *And I can't hear when they call.*

She shuddered. "Yes, that's it."

Did Ásta have something to do with the warning notes? And with the killings? At first glance, the passage didn't seem too ominous. But the parchment had been tucked into the box of poisoned cake. *That's warning enough.*

Elly fidgeted with the bangles on her wrist, oblivious to the jarring, metallic clank each time they ratcheted up and down. "What do you think?"

Brynja felt increasingly uneasy. She tried to remember how much she'd told Elly about LinX and why she had downloaded the Paget's file. She took a sip of water to calm her nerves.

Elly tapped the iPad screen. "Do you think it makes sense what that scholar says about Egil? That he had Paget's? Maybe the warning has something to do with that case you're working on involving Paget's."

Brynja let out a slow breath. Elly had not gleaned that her download of the Paget's file from LinX was for personal reasons.

"I can see why that professor might think Egil had Paget's," Brynja said. "The second line says: *My bald head bangs when I fall.* People with Paget's do get dizzy spells. And maybe..." She hesitated. "Maybe *my piece's soft and clammy* refers to peripheral nerve damage. I remember reading that the skin of people with Paget's gets hot over areas where the bone's growing." She paused again. "Of course, *my piece* might also refer to his penis, and—if he's writing it's soft—maybe he's saying he's impotent. It could be that Egil was just an old man when he wrote that passage."

Elly frowned.

"And if he's old," Brynja added, "the last line would make sense, too. *I can't hear when they call.*"

"Deafness?" Elly asked, standing up.

Brynja nodded. "Could be. As I said, he may just have been an old man. On the other hand, people with Paget's do often have deafness—caused by either compression of cranial nerve VIII or defects in the ossicles."

"Ossicles?"

"Small bones in the inner ear."

"That's exactly what the article says, that one of the symptoms of Paget's is deafness. But what I don't really get is that first line. *The horse of the necklace sways.* The professor wrote that it's a kenning for neck." Elly brushed the bangs from her face. "What's a kenning?"

"It's a word puzzle. Old Norse poetry in the sagas was full of them. Like *hawk's plain* for hand and *skull forest* for hair." She pointed to Elly's wrist. "*Arm serpent* for bracelet."

Elly twirled the bangles. "Arm serpent, I like that."

Brynja looked back down at the passage. "*The horse of the necklace sways.* The neck sways. I can imagine the skull of someone with Paget's could get so heavy with so much extra bone growth that they have trouble keeping their heads from bobbing. Or swaying."

She drummed her fingers on her desk. Why on earth was there a passage about Paget's disease in the box of poisoned cake?

"Give me a moment, Elly? I need to think."

"Sure thing, boss."

Elly left the room and closed the door. Brynja got out a piece of paper and scribbled some notes, trying to tie together everything she knew.

Ásta was worried about having inherited Paget's. Rúnar is Ásta's uncle and might have the mutation as well. Years ago, Rúnar's brother

Axel had a falling out with Pabbi and basically stole a tract of farmland from Munkathverá. Magnus Björnsson, the lawyer who wrote his name in the Möðruvallabók in the 1600s, lived at Hof, the farm of Axel and Rúnar's sister Thorunn. Thorunn was a wheat farmer and moved to the Westfjords just after Lúkas disappeared.

Ásta said she was descended from a Viking settler. Was that Egil Skallagrímsson? The parchment mailed with the cake that poisoned Fríða quotes a passage from Egil's Saga. Egil likely had Paget's disease. Ásta may have inherited Paget's disease.

She put down the pencil. *This is leading nowhere.*

Turning to her computer, the icon for LinX flickered on the screen as if calling out to her.

She hesitated, then pulled her chair closer. This was now a criminal case. Two deaths from eating poisoned foods. One package sent to her office and the other to Ari's. And the latest had come with a warning referencing Paget's disease.

Now she would be justified in searching through the LinX Paget's file. Each of those individuals would need to be questioned.

She hovered over the icon, and then clicked, opening the file for Paget's disease. The same barcodes she had seen a few days ago populated the screen. Another stroke on the keyboard would reveal the identity of those individuals.

She tapped the mouse again and the barcodes came alive, transformed from a series of vertical lines to the names of living, breathing people—and their ancestors with Paget's. Her pulse quickened.

She scrolled down and searched for Ásta.

Just like the phone book, the database listed individuals by their first names. The screen flickered with an array of Ástas.

She sat back, realizing she didn't actually know Ásta's last name. Why hadn't she thought of that? Ásta was one of those mononymous celebrities who went by one name, like Björk or Beyoncé.

Her eyes bounced from one Ásta to another: *Ásta Ármannsdóttir; Ásta Axelsdóttir; Ásta Gíslasdóttir; Ásta Sigurðarsdóttir; Ásta Viðarsdóttir.*

She had to narrow down the list and pick the actress out of the lineup. But how?

Ásta was Rúnar's niece, and Rúnar had never married, so Ásta had to be a blood relative of his. Was she the daughter of Rúnar's brother Axel—the neighbor who had laid claim to their land at Munkathverá decades ago? Or Rúnar's sister, Thorunn?

She could ask Rúnar what Ásta's last name was but that would raise a red flag. He was already furious she had downloaded the Paget's file from the LinX database, although at the time she hadn't unmasked the names of specific individuals. His anger made more sense now that she knew Rúnar was Ásta's uncle.

She typed in Rúnar Bragason. At the very least, she would be able to locate Ásta within his pedigree. The pedigree that popped up had three generations, the oldest being that of Rúnar's parents, who had had three children. Two of them were sons of less-than-stellar character: Axel Bragason was a conniving, cruel man who had stolen some of Pabbi's land at Munkathverá, and Rúnar had all but sexually harassed Elly. The family tree confirmed Brynja's understanding that neither Rúnar nor Axel had children. Axel could not be Ásta's father. Her name would not be Ásta Axelsdóttir. But Axel and Rúnar had a sister, Thorunn. The wheat farmer at Hof who had left Eyjafjörður right after Lúkas disappeared.

Brynja's eyes darted down to the circle in the pedigree that denoted Thorunn. Below her, a square and a circle; a boy and a girl. Leif and Ásta. *That was it.* Ásta was Thorunn's daughter.

But hadn't Jónas told her Thorunn could not have children? And, yet, there they were, two children. Brynja looked at their date of birth. 1997. Twins. Leif and Ásta must have been born after Thorunn moved away.

Not sure of her next step, she overlay the 'disease' filter on top of the family pedigree. Any circles or squares corresponding to individuals with the mutation for Paget's in Ásta's family tree would now be shrouded in black.

Only one shape was filled in with solid black. Axel. He had the P392L mutation for Paget's.

Rúnar and Thorunn did not have the mutation. And since Thorunn did not have the mutation, she could not have passed it on to her daughter.

Ásta doesn't have the mutation for Paget's disease. And neither does Rúnar.

This was starting to make less sense. If Rúnar didn't have the mutation, then why was he so worried about having it known that his relatives carried the mutation? Brynja distinctly recalled hearing him talk about his concerns that the information not get out. But it was Ásta who was so openly worried and opposed to the database.

How could she let Ásta know she had nothing to fear? Her mother didn't carry the mutation, so she was in the clear.

If she told Ari, he might inform Ásta she was free of the disease and convince her to back off her crusade to shut down the database. But then he would have to explain how he knew and that would ignite a firestorm about Brynja's access to the LinX database.

She looked back at the screen, to the black square that indicated Axel Bragason had the Paget mutation in his DNA.

The hair on the back of her neck prickled as she recalled the man.

As a child, she had tried to avoid Axel, but the farming community was a small one. Several times, Axel had gone out of his way to bully her and Stína. He had always left Lúkas alone, but she and Stína had been terrified. Axel had been a grown man, thirty years older than they were, but he had often acted like a deranged teenager. One year, at *réttir*, Axel had pulled on her braids, yanking the red ribbons from her hair. He'd tripped Stína so that she'd fallen into the muddied mess kicked up by the sheep. At *Thorrablót*, Axel had thrown back several shots of *Brennivín* and forced them to eat so many mouthfuls of *blóðmör* that they had felt sick. Axel had known they wouldn't dare complain; the sausage made of sheep blood and chunks of fat was a traditional part of the celebration and everyone was expected to eat it.

Brynja clutched the silver locket about her neck. The database search was not bringing her any closer to finding Lúkas. Or the psychopath who had apparently poisoned both Tómas and Fríða. Unless Thorunn actually had something to do with Lukas's disappearance and was killing people in a desperate attempt to stop anyone from finding out the truth? But how would Thorunn have known about the poem Brynja had been sent?

There were simply too many connections for it all to be coincidence, however. Thorunn had lived at Hof, where her ancestor Magnus Bjornson had taken the *Möðruvallabók*. Thorunn had farmed wheat, the grain mentioned in the poem about Lúkas. Tómas had died from ergot poisoning, which could result from infected wheat. Paget's disease—seemingly referred to in the latest warning— ran in Thorunn's family. Thorunn had moved to the Westfjords shortly after Lúkas disappeared.

Brynja had to know more. She shut down the computer, collected her belongings, and marched into the outer office.

"Elly, I've got to get up to the Westfjords. The cake had a return address in Ísafjörður, and I need to track down the person who sent it. Just why someone would mail a package laced with poison and postmark it with a return address, I have no idea. In this business, you come across some pretty strange people. Sometimes criminals actually want to be caught and it's possible that's the case here."

Elly looked up from filling out Brynja's meeting calendar. "Didn't you say Ísak already contacted the Ísafjörður police and asked them to check it out?"

"Yes, he called the station up there and they paid a visit to the post office. The clerk couldn't remember anything about the package or what the person looked like. The police are waiting for a search warrant before they investigate the address." Brynja picked up her satchel. "Sometimes, when you need something done, you've got to do it yourself."

"I can handle the office while you're gone."

"That would be great." Brynja rested her bag on Elly's desk and looked her intern in the eye. "Be sure to inform Ísak immediately if Rúnar dares to approach you. He's been warned and he can't pretend otherwise."

"Thank you."

"And I'd appreciate your following up on a couple items."

"Sure thing. Shoot."

"Let the lab know I'll be out of the office just for the day. See if Stefán's completed the DNA analysis on the duct tape from the Kjarval heist. And when you're over at the police station, ask Ísak or Henning if they've identified the members of the graffiti gang. The spray paint cans they're using just aren't giving us enough material to go on."

"Got it. Good luck. Call me if you need anything else."

Brynja hurried from the office, relieved to be able to take some action. The solution to each case was in the details, and she was eager to gather them and pull them together into a single, coherent picture.

And, perhaps find Lúkas in the process.

Brynja boarded the Brjanslaekur ferry from Stykkisholmur early the next morning and parked her car below deck. After checking travel conditions yesterday, she'd learned a mud slide had blocked a portion of the road to the Westfjords. Since flights in and out of Ísafjörður were cancelled due to high winds, her only option was to take the ferry and circumvent the road closure. Although Brynja had explained she had work to do, Stína had insisted on coming along.

As the boat steamed toward the jagged cliffs of the Westfjords, Brynja stood on the open deck, breathing in the salt air. She braced herself against the pitch of the churning waves in Breidafjördur Bay and the peril of the journey ahead. The gusty winds and pelting rain did nothing to dampen her resolve.

She felt a tug on her arm.

"Are you crazy?" Stína shouted through the storm. She yanked her inside. "Good thing I came with you—otherwise, you would've been swept overboard."

Ducking into the cabin, Brynja peeled off her windbreaker and sat down at one of the long, metal tables bolted to the floor. The smell of wet wool rose from a group of teenagers drinking beer and playing with a deck of cards.

The line for the snack bar snaked around their table.

"I'll get us a hot drink," Stína said, squeezing into line in front of a man zipping his bomber jacket. "Did you invite all these people?" she asked, batting her eyelids. "I thought it was just gonna be the two of us."

He looked up in surprise. "Do I know you?"

"No, not yet." Stína smiled. "But, hey, do you believe in love at first sight or should I walk by again?"

The man's face slowly melted into a grin. "You're very—"

"I'm Stína," she said. "Can I buy you a drink?"

Brynja shook her head. She worried about her friend. Stína's flirtations had always been harmless, a way of breaking the ice with strangers. But she couldn't seem to move beyond casual relationships with any of the men she met. Stína had never had a constant male presence in her life—her father had left the family when she was just four—and Brynja wondered whether Stína was truly the free spirit she presented herself as, or whether her flirtations were a way of keeping men at a distance.

Regardless, Stína was a loyal friend, and had been for as long as Brynja could remember.

Growing up on adjacent farms, they had been inseparable as youngsters and the pain of losing Lúkas had brought them even closer. As children, Stína had insisted Lúkas sit next to her for hours on end as she made up stories from her *Birds of Iceland* picture book. Lúkas had always complied, but only if she waited for him to draw the birds before turning the page. They were both so stubborn.

And now, after Brynja had told her about the poem, the warnings, and the poisonings, she had dropped everything to come along and be by her side.

Stína handed a cup of hot chocolate to Brynja and opened a bag of potato chips for herself. "So, let's go over our game plan." She pulled a pencil and notebook from her backpack and threw her legs over the bench. "Let's sketch out what we need to do when. I love detective work."

Brynja folded her hands on the table. "It's not that complicated. We've basically got one item on our agenda."

Stína picked up the pencil. "Okay, then. Duck soup. Shoot."

"We need to track down whoever mailed the rhubarb cake from the post office in Ísafjörður." Brynja took a sip of hot chocolate, keeping her fingers around the cup to warm them. "We have to stop the killer from poisoning anyone else. I just hope we're not too late. The post office closes at three."

The man from the queue at the snack bar walked past. Stína winked and moistened her lips.

"Stína!" Brynja waved her hand in front of her friend's face. "Get a hold of yourself."

"Right." Stína turned back to the open notebook on the table. "Do you think it's the same person who sent both packages? You said the box with *kleinur* didn't have a return address."

"They were wrapped in the same green paper, and they both contained poison."

"Why don't we just go right to the address on Kjarrholt instead of the post office?"

"The police are working on a search warrant, but they need more proof that the package was actually mailed from someone at that address. They haven't even gotten an answer as to who lives there. No one seems to know. That's why I want to go to the post office and show them a photo of the green paper and the box. Maybe that will jog their memory.

If we can get the name of the person, that'll help police issue a search warrant."

"Okay, then." Stína picked up the pen and scribbled a note.

"I'm also convinced that whoever mailed those packages knows what happened to Lúkas."

Stína reached over and took a gulp of Brynja's drink. "What makes you think that?"

"The poem. Remember all those words about plants in the poem? I suspect the person who wrote the poem knows the killer is capable of harming people with plant toxins. Ergot-infested wheat poisoned Tómas. And oxalic acid from rhubarb poisoned Fríða."

Brynja folded her arms and stared out over the choppy sea.

"It's all connected," she said. "I'm sure of it."

Chapter 24

Stína unfolded a map and laid it out on the table. The two women leaned over to study it.

"Okay, then, we're gonna kill two birds with one stone," Stína said. "We'll find the person who mailed the packages and that person will lead us to Lúkas. At least, that's the plan, even if it does sound too easy."

"This will work," Brynja insisted.

"How much time do we have?" Stína tapped the pencil on her notepad. "I have to be at Látrabjarg tomorrow evening." She pointed at the far western edge of the Westfjords on the map. "My boss says I've got to take the Brooklyn Birders on a tour of the bird cliffs." She rolled her eyes. "I'm not sure who's going to be squawking louder, the terns or the New Yorkers."

"We should be able to get to Ísafjörður by three—"

The ferry swayed violently from side to side, spilling the cup of hot chocolate across the map. Brynja grabbed the edge of the table and looked about the cabin.

"I'll get some paper towels," Stína said, standing up just as the boat lurched to starboard, throwing her to the floor. "Never mind."

She grimaced and climbed back onto the bench. After brushing off her jeans, Stína picked up the map and funneled the chocolate river back into the cup. She picked up the pencil and added a couple of exclamation points to her note.

Brynja looked at the notepad. "That's quite a list."

Stína brushed off the sarcasm. "Maybe if we get the information you need from the post office by midafternoon, we can squeeze in a visit to the old folks. I'd really like to check on Amma, and you've gotta be worried about your father."

"I am. Let's try. That'll also give me a chance to get another sample of Pabbi's DNA. I screwed up with the spoons. I gave Legacy Jónas's instead of Pabbi's. I was hoping they could get enough DNA from the hair I plucked from Pabbi's brush, but they couldn't."

"So, you're not perfect after all," Stína said, smiling brightly and finishing off the bag of chips. "It's understandable you mixed up the spoons. We left in such a rush."

"When Ari called about Fríða, the last thing on my mind was going back to the farm. I left straight from the church and drove down to Reykjavik." Brynja thought for a moment. "I'd also like to meet with Pastor Dalmann again. Maybe we could drive to the farms this afternoon, stay for the night. Then, tomorrow morning, you take the car to Látrabjarg and I'll go see the pastor. I'll fly back to Reykjavik. One of the guards can drive me to the airport. They're stationed at the church until Ari is able to present the *Möðruvallabók* to the Akureyri Museum."

Stína looked at her phone. "I think we've got enough time to do all that. At any rate, we don't have to worry about driving in the dark. Sun doesn't set until just after midnight tonight."

"Actually," Brynja said. "On second thought, let's try to get over to Möðruvellir Church this afternoon before we go to the farms. I'm desperate to find out what else the pastor knows. I've called him a couple of times but can't get through—"

A loud boom reverberated throughout the cabin. The ferry shuddered to a stop. Except for the wail of an infant at the other end of it, a stunned silence filled the room. The comforting sound of the engine was absent. The passengers eyed one another and began to fumble for the life jackets tucked beneath the benches.

A crackling sound warned of an imminent announcement over the loudspeaker. "This is your captain speaking. There is no cause for alarm. We seem to have bumped up against an undersea lava scarp. This happens from time to time. A minor scrape, I'm sure." He coughed. "We're just off the coast of Flatey Island. We'll be towed in and can dock there and have a mechanic inspect the propellers. All passengers disembarking at Flatey, please collect your belongings. Those ticketed to the Westfjords, please stay on board."

"No way in hell are we staying on board," Stína said. "Good luck finding a mechanic on this tiny island that can fix a boat this size in the next hour. We're screwed."

Brynja buried her head in her hands.

"Look," said Stína. "Worst-case scenario, they'll send a second ferry and we'll make it to Ísafjörður tomorrow."

"I don't think the post office is open Saturday," Brynja mumbled.

"Well, at least we're on dry land at Flatey, not twenty leagues under the sea. Or is it twenty thousand?" Stína stood up. "Anyway, I'm gonna track down that guy from the snack bar and see if I can get some horizontal refreshment."

Brynja gave her friend a bemused smile. "You go ahead. I'll try to reach Pastor Dalmann again." She pulled out her phone, waved Stína off, and scrolled to the number for the church.

"*Halló?*" sobbed a woman on the other end. "God bless us one and all."

Brynja recognized the custodian's voice. "María?"

"My tears have been my food day and night whilst they say unto me: *Where is thy God?*"

"María, it's Brynja Pálsdóttir. Everything okay?"

"Ye know not what shall be on the morrow. *For what is life?* It is a vapor that appeareth for a time and then vanisheth away."

Brynja exhaled slowly. "María, would you be so kind as to put Pastor Dalmann on the line?"

The custodian sniffled and then blew her nose with a force that nearly ruptured Brynja's eardrum. "The blessed one...the blessed one hath left us. Two turns of the heavens above hath passed."

What? The woman must have misunderstood. Brynja repeated her question. Maria repeated her reply, such as it was. She had to be confused. Pastor Dalmann would never have left the *Möðruvallabók* unattended.

"María?"

"The Lord is his shepherd; He shall not want. He maketh him to lie down in green pastures: He leadeth him beside the still waters." She began to wail. "The blessed one hath been stricken down upon the pasture of almighty God. Upon the fields of goodness and grace."

Brynja's heart pumped in her chest. "I'm not sure I understand. Is the pastor ill? Are you saying Pastor Dalmann passed away?"

"No, no. He hath not yet entered the Kingdom of Heaven. He still walketh amongst us, though I know not where."

Brynja remembered the pastor's concerns about María and modulated her voice to sound serene and calm. "Are you saying Pastor Dalmann left Möðruvellir? Did he take the *Möðruvallabók* with him?"

"I know not what you say."

"The old manuscript," Brynja said, trying desperately to muffle her growing panic. "The book we brought to the church on Saturday. Did he take it with him?"

"I knoweth not. If the Lord forgiveth, I shall go forth and search the house of God." María sniffled and put down the phone.

Brynja could hear the portly woman's footsteps shuffle down the hall. The door to the sacristy creaked. After several minutes, she came back on the line.

"Mine eyes behold it not," Maria said, breathing loudly. She raised her voice. "Oh, ye of lowly faith, ye whose sins bring evil upon us all. Salvation springeth not from the books of mortals but from the Book of the Lord. All who call on Him shall be saved."

This was a lost cause. "I've got to go, Maria. Take care. God bless."

Brynja hung up. She had to call Akureyri PD and have them direct the guards to check on Pastor Dalmann and the book. But, first, she had to inform Ari. She dialed his number.

"*Halló?*"

"Ari, I don't know what's going on, but I just called the church and I don't think Pastor Dalmann's been there for a couple of days." She hesitated, knowing Ari would be furious with what came next. "I have no idea if the *Möðruvallabók's* still there or if he took it with him."

Instead of the violent windstorm she expected, there was a strange silence on the other end of the line.

"Ari?"

"Please find out if the book is still there. Have the guards check on it immediately. This is all very strange. Especially in light of the fact that I've just had a call from Rúnar—about the parchment note found with the poisoned cake. He says they've identified your DNA on it."

Brynja's heart pounded. Elly had just informed her that her DNA had come up as a match to the *kleinur* parchment, and now she was being framed for the second time. "That's impossible. Henning was the one who found the warning with the rhubarb cake. I never touched it. You know that. You were there when he showed it to us. If anyone's DNA is on that parchment, it's Henning's." She paused. "And, of course, the DNA of whoever wrote the warning."

"That's what Rúnar is implying."

Her stomach seized. "What are you saying? That you believe I wrote the note?"

"The report clearly states that besides some traces of Henning's DNA, a large portion of the DNA matches yours. The closest match in the database is to your DNA."

"Ari, you've got to—"

"I said it had to be a mistake. But Rúnar told me your DNA was on the other warning, too. The one in the box of *kleinur* that poisoned Tómas."

He paused, waiting. The news had been delivered in a monotone voice, a businesslike conveyance of information with a touch of professional concern. He hadn't made an accusation, but she felt the implicit assumption.

"It's not true. You know I couldn't hurt Tómas or Fríða. Why would I mail the warnings to myself, and target you as well? Why would I do that? Right now, I'm trying to determine who mailed the packages. I'm going up to the post office in—"

"Listen, we probably shouldn't even be talking." Ari paused and she wondered if someone was addressing him out of earshot. "I believe you, Brynja, but the reality is you're implicated in the investigation now. I'm under a lot of pressure from the press, the police."

Her mind reeled. "Ari, what does that mean?"

"I don't think we should see each other until this is cleared up." He paused, swallowed, and began again, his voice soft, the diplomat who made everyone feel better. "It's important to keep the lines of investigation professional and clear, to maintain confidence in the authorities involved. I'm sure it will work out, Brynja. The police will get to the truth. We'll talk in a few days once they've corrected the mistake. I'm sorry. For now, I've got to go. I hope you understand. Goodbye."

He hung up.

Brynja punched off and sat stunned. All around her, passengers were moving about, pulling out luggage, hoisting up backpacks, counting jackets and books and cameras, engaged in the staccato conversation that preceded departure. She had no idea where to turn or what to do, but she knew one thing—the report was totally wrong.

She dialed Rúnar's office and laced into him as soon as he picked up. "What the hell are you doing? You can't be serious. That parchment can't possibly have my DNA on it. I didn't touch it. I want to see the analysis. Email it to me."

"I can't do that."

"Of course, you can. It's my department. I'm in charge of forensics."

She could hear his chair screech back on the tiled floor as he stood up.

"Not any longer." Rúnar's voice was measured. "You've been put on leave for the time being."

"*What?*" Her mind reeled. "Put on leave? I'm telling you, Rúnar, I had nothing to do with writing those warnings. That's just absurd. Do you really think I would do such a thing?
Oh, and I guess you think I whipped up that poisoned cake and sent it to Ari's office? I'm sure you've heard by now that we're engaged. I suppose you think I was trying to kill my fiancé?" She took a deep breath. "Seriously, the lab must have made a mistake. Have them reanalyze the parchment and—"

"I can do that, Brynja. And I will. But it's not just the DNA we're worried about, although that is our main concern. You've also been...well, you've been acting a bit strangely and the higher-ups are concerned."

"What are you talking about?"

"If it'd been just one incident, we could chalk it up to anxiety, or stress, or what have you."

"Incident?"

"Brynja, I'm sorry to have to ask you this, but have you been drinking on the job? Or taking drugs?"

"What? Of course not. Why would you think that?"

"When you came to my office with Elly, you stumbled for no apparent reason. I mentioned it to Henning, and he said you had some bizarre reaction to a pitcher of water in the prime minister's office and then tripped on the table leg. We checked with Ari and he confirmed that was the case. Henning also said that when he was handing you some file in Ísak's office, you misjudged the distance and aimlessly clutched the air instead of the folder. Ísak saw it, too. Truthfully, we're all a little concerned."

"No, Rúnar, I'm—" She was about to tell him about the migraines and the visual auras when he cut her off.

"The decision's been made, Brynja. We can talk again in a couple of weeks. In the meantime, get some professional help."

Chapter 25

According to Icelandic folklore, travelers who sit at a crossroads on Midsummer will be offered food and gifts from the Huldufólk, the Hidden People, who live amongst them in nearby hills, cliffs, and boulders.
Those who break down and succumb to the temptation will disappear into the world of the Huldufólk, never to be seen again.

Throughout the night, Brynja had paced up and down the deck while the mechanic fixed the propeller. Unable to sleep, she had struggled to comprehend all she had learned: She was being investigated for the murders because her DNA had been identified on the warning parchments; her visual auras had caused a clumsiness that made it appear to her colleagues as if she'd been drinking or taking drugs; she'd been put on leave from Legacy; Ari had put their relationship on hold; Pastor Dalmann seemed to have gone missing along with the *Möðruvallabók*.

Early in the morning, the captain had given the all-clear and the ferry had made its way from Flatey Island to the Westfjords. Brynja and Stína went below deck and started the car. Brynja tapped the steering wheel and craned her neck to see if the cars in front were moving. She'd managed to learn that the post office in Ísafjörður was open, but they had to hurry before it closed at noon. Even though she'd been put on leave, she was determined to ascertain who had mailed the poisoned rhubarb cake to Ari's office. This was more than a professional case; it was personal.

As she eased her car off the ferry ramp, Brynja's thoughts kept circling back to the conversation with Rúnar. How could her DNA be on both warnings, both parchments? It was impossible. She hadn't touched either of them. There must be an explanation. Either she was being framed, or…

She shivered. Maybe the DNA wasn't hers, but from someone closely related to her.

She had to think, not react. A child or a parent would share half her DNA. But she didn't have any children. As for parents, Mamma was dead, and Pabbi couldn't have mailed the packages; he was too weak, too demented, to even get out of bed. But, what if…? The thought nearly paralyzed her, and she pulled to the side of the road.

That left only one person. The only other person so closely related to her that the DNA on the parchments could possibly be mistaken for hers. Lúkas.

Siblings shared anywhere between zero and one hundred percent of their DNA. Parents passed on half of their DNA to each of their children. If, by some astronomically improbable sorting of the genes during fertilization, she and Lúkas had inherited completely different halves from both Mamma and Pabbi, they would have no DNA in common. If they had been identical twins, they would have inherited exactly the same set of genes. One hundred percent. But she and Lúkas weren't identical twins; they were fraternal. In reality, as was the usual case with siblings, she and Lúkas likely shared somewhere around fifty percent—half their DNA.

But a fifty-percent match to DNA on the parchment would be enough to point the arrow of accusation her way.

She felt sick to her stomach. Rolling down the window, she gulped in the fresh air.

Did Lúkas not want her to search for him? Was he so traumatized by what had happened to him that he had grown into a person capable of murder?

That just didn't make sense.

Someone must have planted her DNA on the pieces of parchment.

Henning? Rúnar? Who else would have the access or the motive? Ásta? That second parchment—the one from *Egil's Saga*—seemed to refer to Paget's disease. And Ásta definitely wanted the database shut down.

As they approached the roadway, Stína stripped off her parka and pointed at a jumble of yellow arrows. "There!"

Brynja slowed to read the signs. Each pointed in a different direction: Ísafjörður 114 kilometers north, Látrabjarg 94 kilometers west, Akureyri 250 kilometers east.

"I hardly know which direction to go. Obviously, the most important thing is to find whoever is mailing the poisons. But Pastor Dalmann may be missing. María seemed to say as much when I phoned the church. But when I contacted the Akureyri police and they had the guards knock on the door, María seemed calm, not her usual bible-babbling self. She wouldn't let the officers in, but she assured them that everything was fine, that Pastor Dalmann was asleep and shouldn't be disturbed."

"And they believed that maniac? Fuck a duck," Stína said, rummaging through her backpack.

"We've got to get over to Möðruvellir," Brynja said. "Make sure the pastor's okay and that the *Möðruvallabók* is still there."

"Well, you can't be two places at once," Stína said. "You should have cloned yourself while you had the chance." She propped her feet on the dash and leaned back. "You know as well as I do, we don't have a choice. We have to go to the post office first. You'll never forgive yourself if someone else is poisoned."

"I know." Brynja exhaled. "I know." She crossed the intersection and headed north toward Ísafjörður.

In front of her lay an expanse of white snow, broken only by the winding strip of black asphalt that she hoped would lead to the serial killer. In a strange way, she felt soothed by the rugged landscape, by a world shaped by forces greater than the chaos created by mankind. In fact, the Westfjords seemed blissfully unaware that summer had arrived. The remote peninsula hugged the outer reaches of the Greenland Sea and, for most of the year, arctic storms made its rural roads impassable. Even today, nearly the longest day of the year, icy threads in the morning mist swept down from the snow-capped mountains and settled on the pavement with a crisp sheen that crackled beneath the tires.

Stína looked out over the frigid landscape. "Ever wonder why Icelanders celebrate *Sumardagurinn fyrsti* in April when the first day of summer is actually in June? And then call today Midsummer?"

Brynja fingered the locket around her neck. For her, *Sumardagurinn fyrsti* was never a day for celebration. It was a day of mourning, the day Lúkas had disappeared.

"Really," Stína said, not letting up. "Can we not get with the program? Four seasons like everyone else in the world?" She ripped opened a bag of *Kúlur* chocolate balls and offered some to Brynja. "Apparently not. We still have two seasons. Cold and colder. Jeez."

Stína tossed her beanie onto the back seat and shook out her short bob. "So, what's up with María anyway? She's as mad as a wet hen. I bet she knows more than she's letting on. If his holiness left the church, it's probably because he couldn't stand being around all that crazy talk. What was it she said to you? *All who call on Him shall be saved? Really?"*

"I'm sure María's just upset. She seemed to be saying Pastor Dalmann left without a word and she hasn't seen him for days. But then she told the officers that he's fine and sound asleep in the sacristy. The poor woman is not quite right; she's obviously confused. María's looking to God for answers. To each his own."

"Well, it's not for me," Stína said, munching loudly. "Might as well believe in the Hidden People." She pulled a brochure from her backpack and flapped it in the air. "Check this out. I got it at the library on Flatey." She swallowed the candy and then started to read.

"The Flateyjarbók, the Book of Flat Island, is the largest medieval Icelandic manuscript. Written in 1387, the Sagas of the Norse kings come to life on two hundred and thirteen vellum leaves. The codex also contains The Saga of the Greenlanders and the Saga of Erik the Red, father of Leif Erikson, the first European to discover North America—"

"Stína, I appreciate everything you're doing for me. I really do. But my plate is full thinking about the *Möðruvallabók*. I still can't figure out how it's going to help us find Lúkas. Does the brochure say anything about the *Möðruvallabók?"*

"I think so. Yes, here it is. *In 1651, King Frederick III of Denmark ordered all medieval Icelandic manuscripts be turned over to Denmark."* Stína looked over at Brynja. "It says *all* manuscripts. That must mean the *Möðruvallabók*, too."

She flipped the page. "It seems like Iceland wasn't too happy about handing the books over to Denmark. Listen to this. *The owner of the Flateyjarbók, Jón Finnsson, refused to give it up until Bishop Brynjólfur Sveinsson forced him to do so. In 1656, the manuscript was placed in the Royal Library of Copenhagen."*

Brynja looked at the clock on the dash. "We should be able to get to Ísafjörður by eleven. Just in time before the post office closes."

"Brynja, you're not listening. Here," Stína continued. *"Following Iceland's independence, the Flateyjarbók was the first of Iceland's treasures to be returned from Denmark. Other manuscripts soon followed, including the Möðruvallabók, which had been held for centuries by a wealthy Danish family.*"

Brynja briefly took her eyes off the road and glanced at Stína. "Does it say anything more about the Danish family that kept the books all that time?"

Stína scanned the rest of the brochure. "Only that they were the descendants of the royal antiquarian."

"Can you ask your connection at the Magnússon Institute if he knows anything about them?"

"I'll try, but I think I pissed him off last night. I told him I needed a little space. That I just need to spread my wings."

"Do me a favor and call him anyway?"

Stína nodded, then popped open a can of soda, gulped some down, and belched. "Sorry."

She balled up her sweater, propped her head against the window, and promptly fell asleep.

Brynja reached over to the dash and pressed her office number on the Bluetooth controls. Stína could sleep through anything.

After one ring, she heard Elly's voice. "Legacy Forensics."

Does she know I've been put on leave?

"*Halló*, Elly. It's Brynja. I'm not sure you've heard, but there's been a misunderstanding. I won't be in for a few days."

"You okay?"

"Yes, I'm fine." Brynja paused. Elly deserved to know the truth. And it would be best she heard it from her. "There's been a mistake. Remember you overheard Rúnar and Henning say my DNA was found on the parchment we had Rúnar analyze? That warning we found in the box of *kleinur*?"

"*Ja?*"

"Apparently that wasn't just a rumor. The lab analysis confirmed the parchment came back with a close match to my DNA."

"That's not possible," Elly said. "I was there. I know you didn't touch it."

"That's right. The lab's made a mistake. Not the first time, I'm afraid. At any rate, until they rerun the analysis, I'll be out of the office."

"That's just crazy. I can vouch for you. Want me to talk with Rúnar?"

"No! Maybe you could approach Ísak, but please, please don't have anything to do with Rúnar. At least not until I return."

"Just a minute," Elly said.

Brynja heard the office door close before Elly came back on the line. "I've got a meeting with Ísak this afternoon, so I'll let him know I was with you when we found the warning. And, actually, Rúnar hasn't been around so there's no chance of bumping into him. No one seems to know where he is, not even Henning. That reminds me. The painting's turned up. The Kjarval painting. The janitor at Hallgrímskirkja found it stashed in the church's basement. Chief Ísak called Rúnar yesterday to get an update on the duct tape DNA, but Rúnar's been out, like I said. He hasn't returned the chief's call."

"Strange."

"Should I continue coming over to Legacy while you're gone?" Elly asked.

"No, I don't see much point in that. Maybe we could keep in touch via cell. I've got your number and you have mine."

"Sounds good. Call me anytime if you need anything."

"I will. Thanks, Elly. I'm sure the lab will be able to correct the error after repeating the analysis. In the meantime, it's probably best to keep our communications confidential for now."

"Will do. Take care."

Brynja hung up. She hadn't told Elly about the other reasons she'd been put on leave. That the lab had determined her DNA was a close match to that on the second warning as well, the one found with the cake that poisoned Fríða. And that her auras appeared to Ísak, Henning, and Rúnar as though she was under the influence.

She would have to come clean and tell her colleagues about her disorder. She would have to explain that the incidents were a result of migraines and temporary auras and not due to drinking or drugs. She hoped they would believe her. Aside from one episode of the television show *House* in which a patient experienced the same symptoms, AIWS wasn't exactly on the public's radar. The disorder was extremely rare. First identified in the 1950s by the British psychiatrist Dr. John Todd, AIWS was believed to be caused by abnormal electrical activity in the brain causing tempory bouts of abnormal blood flow to the areas of the brain that process visual perception.

She would have explain all that to Ísak, Henning, and Rúnar.

And then she could only hope Legacy would reinstate her as chief of forensics. That was, once the question of her DNA on the parchment samples was cleared up.

For now, she would focus her energy on who had mailed the package from the post office in Ísafjörður. She drove the next hour along the narrow road, its shoulders piled high with the still-frozen snow of winter, listening to the wind howl and Stína snore.

Thetta reddast, as her friend would say. *It will all work out in the end.*

If only she could believe it.

Ten kilometers out, Brynja spotted the sign for Ísafjörður and nudged Stína. "Hey, wake up. We're almost there."

Stína jerked her head and rubbed her eyes.

Brynja looked over. "I think I remember where the post office is, but I may need your help."

Stína grumbled, reaching into her pocket for her phone. "Hold on." She opened Maps.me. "It's on Hafnarstræti. Second right off the rotary."

"Thanks."

A few minutes later, Brynja parked the car in front of the post office. Ísafjörður Pósturinn was nothing more than a room on the bottom floor of a red slat and corrugated steel, commercial building. Brynja stood outside for a moment to clear her head in the brisk morning air. Shivering, she rubbed her hands together and motioned to Stína that she'd be right back.

She pushed open the door and approached the lanky, young postal clerk at the counter.

He smiled. "Just in time. We close in ten minutes. What can I do for you?"

Brynja showed her ID, explained she was working on a forensics case for the police, and asked to speak with the supervisor.

Soon, a disheveled man in his mid-forties or so, with matted streaks of oily hair and a body like a stack of lumpy pillows, waddled out of the stockroom. He held a chunk of *harðfiskur* in one hand and wiped a dusting of dried fish flakes off his chin with the other.

"Supervisor Eiríksson here." He leaned forward on the counter, his breath reeking of stale fish.

"I'm hoping you can help me determine who sent a certain package a week ago. Perhaps you might remember who mailed it?"

The supervisor sneered. "We get a lot of packages in and out of here, young lady, especially this time of year with the roads finally cleared and tourists mailing Icelandic sweaters and stuffed puffins to their kids back home."

Charmer. "It was wrapped with an unusual, green paper." Brynja opened the photo on her phone. "Does this ring a bell?"'

"Doesn't ring any bells of mine," the supervisor said, tearing off a bite of *harðfiskur*. "What's all this commotion over some package, anyway? I already told the police that I don't have a clue who mailed it." He slapped the counter and was turning to leave when he apparently changed his mind. "Listen, lady, ever hear of a return address?" He raised a bushy eyebrow. "Hate to tell ya, but that's usually the best way to know who mailed it."

Brynja clenched her jaw. "Yes, of course. Maybe you can tell me who lives at this address?" She wrote down *32 Kjarrholt, 400 Ísafjörður* on the back of an envelope and showed it to him. "I'm afraid there wasn't a name."

"Can't help ya there. But Kjarrholt's out of town up against the mountains. I suggest ya get over there and check it out for yourself."

Across the room, a young postal clerk was hoisting boxes onto a dolly.

"You know better than that, boss," he shouted. "She's not going to find anyone living on Kjarrholt anymore." The clerk turned to Brynja and smiled apologetically. "Not for some time now, sorry to say. Avalanche back in 'ninety-nine."

Not as sorry as I am, Brynja thought. After coming all this way, she had arrived at a dead end.

"A darn shame," the clerk added. "Thorunn Bragadóttir used to grow wheat out that way. The house and farm were buried under a mountain of snow. Good thing they weren't home at the time. Not sure where Thorunn went after that but her daughter Ásta's made it big in the movies. I know that much."

He was whistling when Brynja exited the post office.

Chapter 26

Brynja stood on the post office steps, head bowed, wondering what to do next. She'd had such high hopes for tracking down the sender of the packages, and now she had nothing.

"It's gorgeous out here," Stína said, focusing her camera on a covey of rock ptarmigans feeding on a grassy patch below a willow tree.

Brynja headed toward the car. "Let's get over to the church. I'm worried about Pastor Dalmann. And I need to see if *Möðruvallabók* is still there."

They left the post office and started along the ragged coastline toward Möðruvellir. Brynja glanced at the roiling waves of the sea below. More convinced than ever Thorunn was involved, she mulled over all that she knew about the woman. Jónas said Thorunn moved to the Westfjords shortly after Lúkas disappeared. Apparently, she'd raised two children there, one of whom was Ásta. Thorunn had lived on Kjarrholt, the street listed as the return address on the package, but her home had been buried by an avalanche. Before moving to the Westfjords, Thorunn had grown wheat at Hof, the farm next to Möðruvellir Church. The poem mentioned wheat, *wheat from the chaff*. Thorunn's ancestor, Magnus Björnsson, had signed his name in the *Möðruvallabók* and had lived at Hof in the 1600s, when a root cellar would have been a common fixture. *In the ink of Gloom's root cellar.*

There were just too many coincidences.

She turned to Stína. "Could you get my phone and dial Ísak's number?"

Stína reached into the backpack and then hesitated. "But you said Legacy's put you on leave. I assume that means you're also not doing forensics for the police at the moment? Won't Ísak be upset that you're still working on the case?"

"Maybe. But there are more important things than how he feels about me at the moment."

Stína dialed and put the phone on speaker. After several rings, Ísak's secretary answered and informed Brynja that the chief was out of the office but would return her call as soon as he returned.

Hours later, Brynja still hadn't received a call back.

As they entered Akureyri, Stína insisted they stop to get a bite to eat before going to the church at Möðruvellir. Brynja agreed and parked the car outside Akureyri Café. They dashed through the pelting rain toward the entrance.

"Lovely weather for ducks," Stína shouted.

The restaurant was a restored fishing hut that sat on the edge of town and looked out onto the harbor where, for centuries, fishermen had hauled in laps of Atlantic cod from the frigid depths of the Greenland Sea. Every part of the cod had been destined for consumption by a people often on the brink of starvation: The roe was smoked in fiery kilns; the milt—the sperm—was stirred into whey; stomach linings were stuffed with clumps of liver and boiled until tender; the brown, freckled skin was roasted and eaten as bread in a climate too hostile for growing much grain; the sound—the air bladders—were fried; whole heads were simmered into soup; bones were softened in sour milk; and flesh was either dried into slabs of *harðfiskur* or salted for export to Spanish and Portuguese markets. Today, the menus were much less exotic.

Brynja read down the offerings.

Once they'd ordered from the chalkboard menu, Stína jostled her way through the crowded room, found a spot on the wooden benches at the community table, and waved Brynja over. They were chatting with an aging couple seated opposite them when a waiter with muscles bulging beneath his too-tight shirt slid a sizzling, iron pan in front of them.

"Cod fillet in a béchamel sauce with mashed potatoes and purple cabbage," he said. "Careful, it's hot."

"Oh, I can handle hot," Stína said, cocking her head and winking at the waiter.

"Jeez, Stína, could you be any more obvious?"

"Sure, I could. I could wind up, whistle like a great crested grebe, and sprint sixty-six feet across the surface of a lake in a mating dance that even Baryshnikov would be proud of. Now *that* would be obvious." She smiled and took a sip of water. "But I'm too subtle for that."

Despite having eaten handfuls of licorice and two bags of bacon-flavored potato chips on the drive from Ísafjörður, Stína devoured her food. Not for the first time, Brynja wondered how her friend stayed as thin as a fence post.

After cleaning up the last of the mashed potatoes, Stína wiped her mouth on the rough, paper napkin. "Listen, it's only four o'clock. We ought to get over to the church and find out what's up with Pastor Dalmann and the *Möðruvallabók*. You're eating like a bird anyway." She took a few bites off Brynja's plate.

They paid the check and drove the ten minutes north to Möðruvellir Church.

The police cars were no longer outside, and the church parking lot was empty. Brynja's heart sank. She parked and turned off the engine.

"I'm not letting you face that Loony Tune alone," Stína said.

She slammed the car door, marched up the steps to the church, and motioned for Brynja to follow.

Stína rapped loudly on the door. No answer. She banged louder, then tried to open the door herself, but it was locked.

"C'mon," she said. "Let's look around. Someone's gotta be here."

They followed the dirt path to the back of the church. A lingering scent of smoke hung in the air over blackened logs scattered across the yard. Brynja ducked under the charred branches of a birch tree and wiped a thin layer of ash from the lead-glass window of the refectory's small kitchen. María was stirring something in a large pot on the cast-iron stove.

She knocked gently on the window. María seemed oblivious to the tapping on the glass, taking a sip of liquid from the ladle and reaching up for a bottle on the shelf. She shook it over the pot and continued stirring.

"Guess she only hears the voice of God," Stína said.

The phone in the kitchen rang. María wiped her hands on her apron and lifted the receiver off the wall.

"*Halló?*"

Brynja put her finger to her lips.

María lowered her voice. "Please don't call here. The pastor will be angry. He's told me I can't sell any more vegetables from my garden. He won't have it. Says it's holy ground and not to be used for profit."

Brynja's jaw dropped.

María paused, listened to the voice on the other end of the line and then said, "I know, I know. But the only reason he lets me stay here is because he feels sorry for me. I've convinced him I'm crazy and can't survive out there in the world. If the pastor finds out what I'm doing, I won't have a place to live."

"Okay," Stína said. "That's more than I need to know about María's secret garden, and her secret life." She rapped loudly on the glass.

María jumped, muttered a hurried farewell into the phone, and hung up. She bustled over to open the door.

"Not a word," Brynja whispered to Stína.

"Ye are welcome into the house of the Lord," María said, leading them into the kitchen.

As she looked down into the custodian's puffy, bloodshot eyes, Brynja reminded herself that Maria was now performing, hiding her real personality. She considered her options and decided to continue with the charade.

She laid a hand on the woman's fleshy arm. "How are you? Has the pastor returned?"

María wiped her brow and spoke in a voice so shaky that Brynja had trouble making out the words. "I knoweth not where he hath gone."

"Perhaps he's gone to visit a member of his congregation?"

María sniffled and shook her head.

Brynja narrowed her eyes, wondering if now was the time to confront her. She wasn't feeling inclined to be patient with the custodian.

"Let's take a look in the sacristy. Perhaps there's some clue there as to why he left."

She hoped beyond hope that the *Möðruvallabók* was still on the credenza.

María nodded, turned off the stove, and led them down the hallway into the sacristy.

"If I be guilty," she wailed. "If I be guilty, oh heavenly Father, woe unto me. And if I be innocent in thine eyes, even so, I shall not lift my head. For I am full of shame and drowned in my affliction."

Brynja glanced at the credenza. The *Möðruvallabók* was no longer there. *Perhaps he simply put it out of harm's way. Or...perhaps Ari called and asked the officers to take it to the Akureyri museum.* She shuddered. *Or could María have taken the book? Sold it for profit like the vegetables in her garden?*

Hoping to find the manuscript hidden away with others, Brynja played along with María a little longer. She walked toward the cabinet where Pastor Dalmann kept his other manuscripts.

María bustled over and grabbed Brynja's arm before she had a chance to open the cabinet door.

"Ye shall not touch," she hissed. "Put down thy reach. Given it be to Satan for the destruction of the flesh, so that his spirit may be saved on the day of the Lord."

But Brynja needed the manuscript. And she was concerned about Pastor Dalmann.

Softening her tone, she tried a different tack. "This must be dreadful for you, María. We're your friends. Let us help." She guided the custodian to the settee and sat down beside her. "Why don't you tell me what happened?"

María looked upwards and raised her arms as if she could touch the heavens. "Oh, holy one, your sun will never set again, and your moon will wane no more. The Lord will be your everlasting light and your days of sorrow will end."

Behind María's back, Stína raised her eyebrows and shook her head.

Brynja shot her a look and turned back to María. "Don't worry, we're going to find Pastor Dalmann." She patted the woman's hand. "He may have simply paid a visit to someone in need. Perhaps a member of the congregation is sick?"

María stopped wailing and turned to Brynja. She shook her head. "Darkness had fallen and a blazing torch appeareth in the night. A lowly one came bearing fruit with seed. And God saw that it was good."

"Are you saying that someone came to the church with some sort of fruit basket?"

María reached for a handkerchief in the folds of her apron and blew her nose. "A tart." She nodded. "A berry tart." She pointed at the table next to Pastor Dalmann's chair where a half-eaten tart lay next to a crumpled napkin holding the remains of a crust. "The good pastor partook of the gift brought forth to him in the darkness of the night."

Brynja's mind raced. "Can you describe the person who delivered the tart?"

María shook her head. "Mine eyes grace not mere mortals in the night; they lift but to serve the good Lord."

"Did you inform the police officers?"

"I shan't defile this house with the sins of mortal men. How canst we keep our way pure? By guarding it according to the Lord's word. Psalm 119:9-10."

"Oh, for fuck's sake," Stína muttered under her breath.

Brynja leaned in close to the custodian. "You're saying you didn't let the guards in?"

María nodded, then let out an explosive sneeze that startled both Brynja and Stína.

Brynja covered her mouth, and turned to look at the tart, its swirl of red berries winding inward on its surface.

"Did the person who brought over that tart eat a slice as well?"

"I knoweth not." María sniffled. "I bade the pastor a good night. And a great fire descended upon the land—" María stopped short and looked closely at Brynja. She began to breathe loudly, and shouted, "You!"

Brynja jumped up.

Stína rushed over, grabbed Brynja's arm and pulled her in the direction of the sacristy door.

María erupted off the settee in a crescendo of fury. "It's you!" she spewed. "It is your book which hath brought forth evil upon this house, the house of the Lord."

Brynja wrestled free from Stína's grip and moved quickly to pick up the tart. She turned toward the cabinet. Maria could pretend to be as crazy as she liked, but Brynja had to find out if the *Möðruvallabók* was in there.

"Like a muddied spring be the righteous who give way to the wicked." Beads of sweat dripped from the custodian's forehead. "The righteous pastor hath given way to the wicked."

Or maybe not. Maybe María was covering something up.

"Out!" María screamed. "The Lord shall cast you out to wallow in the barren fields of eternal damnation."

"We heard you on the phone, María," Brynja said.

Before she could challenge her further, María pulled a large kitchen knife from her apron pocket and lunged forward, her eyes blazing. "Out!"

Brynja and Stína bolted for the door.

Jumping into the car, they locked all the doors. Brynja tossed the berry tart onto the back seat and shifted the car into gear.

"Can you believe it?" Stína said. "We drove all the way here to talk with that batshit-crazy churchwoman and we *still* have no idea what happened to Pastor Dalmann."

Brynja flipped on the windshield wipers. The sky was gun-barrel black, its underbelly swollen with dark clouds. Twisted veins of lightning crackled in the distance and a restless roll of thunder rumbled across the valley ahead.

"I think I know where he is." She pulled out of the parking lot and headed south along the winding road hugging the fjord.

"Really? I must have missed the class in Crazy-as-a-Loon Bible-Speak. I couldn't understand a word María said. She sounded normal when we overheard her on the phone and insane when we were in the sacristy." Stína turned and reached for the tart.

"No!" Brynja flung out a hand and grabbed Stína's arm. "It's yew."

"Me? What? Look, Brynja, if you think—"

"No, no. Not you. *Yew*. Yew berries. I think that tart was made with yew berries."

Stína nodded her head slowly. "Okay…yew berries. And that's bad because…?"

"That's bad because they're poisonous."

"No, they're not. Amma used to make a jelly out of them when I was a kid. Tasted like crap, for sure, but hardly poisonous."

"For cooking, you have to carefully pluck the seed out of each yew berry using tweezers. The fruit of the berry isn't poisonous. but the seed is incredibly toxic. The Latin name is *Taxus baccata*. *Taxus* is from the same root as toxic, and *baccata* means 'bearing red berries.'"

"Okay, smarty-pants."

"Roman soldiers used to commit suicide by eating yew berries to avoid being taken as slaves. That's how poisonous they are."

"Are you sure they were yew berries in that tart?"

"I'm sure. Pabbi once took Lúkas and me out to a grove of yew trees at Munkathverá. He wanted to make sure we knew what they looked like since they're so rare in Iceland. He picked some of the berries and told us never to eat them whole. Said they'd kill a horse or a sheep in minutes." Brynja gripped the wheel. "Either someone didn't know enough to take the seeds out before making that tart, or they were left in on purpose."

Stína swiveled back in her seat, facing forward, and looked out of the car window. "Are you thinking what I'm thinking?"

Brynja didn't know if she *ever* thought what Stína was thinking. "Are you suggesting María baked that tart for Pastor Dalmann in order to get her hands on the *Möðruvallabók*?"

"Um-hmm."

Brynja let out a deep breath. "We need to get an officer back to the church right away. Dial the Akureyri police department for me?" She turned off the main road and pulled up to the Akureyri Hospital. "If Pastor Dalmann ate any of that tart, this is where he would've ended up. I just hope I'm wrong,"

Chapter 27

The waiting room of the hospital ER was a study in chaos. A swarm of hyperkinetic boys raced Hot Wheels across the linoleum floor while their mother rocked a wailing infant in her arms; a crusty, old woman scowled at the boys as she pushed her walker past; two weather-beaten fishermen in yellow bib pants consoled a young deckhand clutching a bloodied rag wrapped about his leg; and a stocky woman dripping with sweat thought nothing of sharing her misery.

Brynja and Stína hurried to the reception window.

"Can I help you?" a wiry woman asked without looking up.

"Yes, please." Brynja showed the receptionist her ID and pointed to the police department stamp on it. "We're here to see Dalmann Ingólfsson. Pastor Dalmann Ingólfsson."

The receptionist smiled politely. "Chaplains aren't on site round the clock, I'm afraid. They're only called in when a patient's ready to set sail, if you catch my drift."

An image of a Viking funeral ship engulfed in flames and bobbing upon ocean waves flashed across Brynja's mind. She shook the phantom loose, hoping the pastor was still alive.

"I understand," she said. "But I'm not looking for a chaplain. I'm looking for a patient named Dalmann Ingólfsson. He's a pastor."

"Oh, sorry, dear. Let me check." The receptionist put on her reading glasses and scrolled through an intake list on the computer. "No...I'm not seeing a Dalmann Ingólfsson." She squinted at the screen. "Oh, wait, here he is. Yes."

Stína leaned over the counter. "Well? Which room is he in?"

The receptionist tucked a loose strand of gray hair into her bun and shifted in her seat. "Perhaps it's best I page his doctor." She picked up the phone. "Have a seat, ladies."

Brynja nodded and looked around the waiting room. She nudged Stína and jerked her chin toward a man in a woolen sweater with tousled, sandy hair, five-o'clock shadow, and dark, soulful eyes; he looked exhausted. "He seems familiar, doesn't he? Was he on the ferry?"

Stína raised her shoulders and, with her usual *don't-know-but-I'll-sure-as-hell-find-out* determination, made a beeline for the ruggedly handsome stranger. She plunked herself down next to him on one of the folding chairs lining the room.

When Brynja approached, the man bolted out of his seat, the chair legs screeching against the linoleum floor. "Dr. Pálsdóttir?"

Brynja tried to place him. The ferry captain? The clerk from the post office? The waiter at Akureyri Cafe?

"My God, it *is* you," he stammered. "I'm so sorry. It's just awful." He shook like a massive boulder teetering on a shifting fault line. "I was stationed at the church. You asked if I'd like some coffee."

The guard. One of the local policemen stationed outside Möðruvellir Church to protect the manuscript. Brynja extended her hand.

"Officer Óliver Pétursson. Please, sit," he said, moving a hospital bag marked 'Personal Belongings' from the seat next to him onto the floor. "I'm not sure if you know what's happened."

Brynja shook her head. "Tell me."

"Two days ago, in the middle of the night, a shed outside the church went up in flames. I hurried to wake the pastor. He…it was dark. The flames. I rushed toward the flames."

Brynja sat down. "Flames?"

"Yes. Near the kitchen at the back of the church. I went to put it out. It all happened so quickly. We found a hose but then that custodian flew out of the church in her nightgown and ran around in circles shouting prayers. Damned if she didn't try to grab the hose from me. We were able to douse the fire, but then…" He paused to take a breath.

"Then what?"

"That scream. I'll never forget it. It came from the front of the church. By the time I got to the front, the pastor was stumbling down the steps. He was twitching and tearing at his robe like his soul was possessed."

Brynja felt faint. The waiting room spun like a centrifuge off its axis and she gripped the seat of the folding chair to steady herself.

"I yelled at the other officers to call 112, but I knew it would take too long for an ambulance to get to the church. So, I picked up the pastor, put him in the back seat of the patrol car, and drove him to the ER."

"You were right to bring him straight to the hospital," Brynja said. She thought for a minute. "So, then, if you're still here…the pastor's alive?"

"Barely. He's been in a coma for the past couple days. Doctor thinks he had a heart attack. Abnormal heart rhythm. He said he'd have an update soon."

Óliver might find her heartless, but she had to ask the question weighing heavily on her. "And the *Möðruvallabók*?"

"After they wheeled the pastor into the ER, I rushed back to the church." He shook his head. "I couldn't find the book. That crazy woman was bustling about cleaning up soot from the fire. When I asked her where the *Möðruvallabók* was, she seemed to have no idea what I was talking about. I told her the pastor was in the hospital and seriously ill. She acted as if she couldn't even hear me."

Brynja thought back on all she'd learned over the last several hours—Maria's duplicity and the poisonous tart. There had to be more to this fire and the disappearance of the manuscript.

She took a notepad and pen from her bag. "Do you remember any visitors coming by the church the day before? Or that night? Any parishioners or deliveries?"

Óliver shook his head. "There were four of us stationed round the clock. After you and the prime minister visited on Tuesday, the only activity was when you came back early the next morning before the small group of mourners attending the funeral service. It was a quiet night— until the fire broke out, that is."

"Tell me more about the fire. What sparked it?"

"Not sure. We wondered if some coals weren't entirely extinguished before being removed from the stove and piled on the ash heap out back."

Brynja tapped the pen on her notebook. "Did you see María leave at any point? Could she have taken the book from the church without your noticing? I'm wondering if you've seen any indication that María might not be as crazed as she lets on."

Before he could respond, a tall, slender doctor with hair the color of his starched, white coat appeared and approached Óliver. "I understand you were the one who brought the pastor in. It's a bit unusual to be giving you the medical report, but, apparently, the pastor has no family. Given the circumstances, I think you can know."

Óliver nodded. "How is he?"

"He's critical but stabilized for the moment."

Brynja stood and reached to shake the doctor's hand. "Brynja Pálsdóttir, chief of forensics at Legacy in Reykjavik. We work alongside the police investigating criminal cases."

"Oh?" The doctor raised his eyebrows but otherwise appeared unfazed. "Jón Árnason," he said, extending his hand.

Brynja jotted down the name.

The doctor took the stethoscope from around his neck and tucked it into the pocket of his coat. "Let me ask you both something. Do you know if the pastor had cancer? Was he undergoing chemotherapy for prostate cancer? Or perhaps lung cancer?"

Brynja spoke up. "I didn't know him well, but I've had the pleasure of meeting with him a couple of times recently. I doubt he had cancer. In fact, at one point, he mentioned that he hadn't been sick a day in his life."

"Then I can't explain it," the doctor said. "It's very strange. First, I thought it might be a heart attack—that wouldn't be unusual at his age— but all his tests were negative. We couldn't easily diagnose his problem. The more we looked, the more concerned I became that it was medication related."

"What are the symptoms that concerned you?" Brynja asked.

"He's suffering some of the side effects of chemotherapy I often see in patients. Dry skin, sores on his tongue, brittle nails. We did a toxicology screen and found an exorbitant level of a compound called taxine. It's related to taxol, a mitotic inhibitor, er, a substance that prevents cells from dividing. Kills cancer cells."

"I think I know where the taxine in his system came from," Brynja said. "It wasn't from chemotherapy. It was from ingesting yew berries. *Taxus baccata.*"

The doctor pulled a small, electronic pad from his pocket and scribbled some notes. "We don't have yew berries in Iceland. The trees don't grow here."

"Actually, we've got a couple of groves out near Munkathverá and Litlihamar." Brynja pointed to Stína. "My friend's grandmother brought some saplings over with her from Denmark."

The doctor nodded. "How do you know about taxine and yew— ?" He broke off when his beeper sounded.

Reading the message, his face crumbled. "I'm so sorry." He looked up. "The pastor's just now passed away."

Brynja slumped back down in the chair. Three. Three deaths. This had to stop. She had to phone Reykjavik immediately and alert Ísak. A massive manhunt was called for—now.

"We did everything we could to save him," the doctor said. "Let me send for our chaplain."

Brynja glanced at Óliver. He shook his head and looked at the floor.

"No, that's not necessary," she said. "Doctor, this death could be linked to two others. I'd like to ask an officer from the police station to come by to interview you. We appreciate your efforts. Thank you."

Dr. Árnason's beeper went off again. He nodded and excused himself.

Óliver whispered, "My God. How awful."

Brynja flipped a page in her notebook. "Óliver, it's important I ask you a few questions now. I'm sorry about the timing. You say you didn't see anyone come to the church that night?"

"That's right."

Brynja pointed to Stína. "We paid a visit to the church an hour ago and the custodian told us someone had come to the church a couple of nights ago. She referred to the person as 'a lowly one bearing fruit with seed'. But you say none of the four officers saw anyone. Correct?"

Óliver nodded.

"I have reason to doubt Maria's veracity," Brynja said. "I think she knows more than she's letting on. It's possible she even baked that tart herself." She tapped the pen. "You ran to the back of the church to put out a fire. What time was that?"

"Just before midnight."

Brynja made a note. "Could María have set it? Or, if someone *did* bring that tart to the church, perhaps they ignited the fire?"

Óliver rubbed the stubble on his chin. "We were stationed in front of the church. I suppose someone could have walked across the meadow and snuck around back. I was the only one on duty at the time; the other officers were asleep. I woke them up and ran to put out the fire."

Stína put her hand on his arm. "You did everything you could. Why don't you get some rest? Brynja can handle everything here."

"I have to make a report first." Óliver ran his fingers through his hair. "And I don't know what I'm going to tell the prime minister. The note's definitely going to upset him—"

Brynja jerked her head up. "What note?"

"I found a note in the cabinet where the pastor kept the *Möðruvallabók*." He reached into his pocket for his phone. "As I said, after they wheeled the pastor into the ER, I drove back to the church for the book. All I found when I unlocked the cabinet was this."

He showed Brynja a photo on the phone. "It was strange. Really stiff paper with some words that don't make sense. Never seen anything like it. I handed the note over to the station. With the pastor collapsing and the book missing, I thought it might be needed as evidence."

Brynja read the lines.

Asks the ash-tree goddess
All news of my doings.
Mutter naught of murder
Matters then long ended.
Let ashes lie, woman,
Lie low. Else this crow-feeder
Comes to kill once more.

The walls of the waiting room collapsed in on her.
Let ashes lie, woman.
Another warning.

And this time, there was no doubt it was meant for her. If she didn't stop, she would be the next to die.

Chapter 28

Brynja stumbled to the car, the lights of the hospital fading behind her. Buffeted by three deaths and three warnings from an unknown killer, she could think of only one place where she would feel safe, her childhood home at Munkathverá. She drove through town and turned onto the rain-soaked causeway linking Akureyri to the fertile farmland that lay to the east. The sky was heavy and leaden; thick bands of fog hovered over the valley floor.

"Watch it!" Stína shrieked from the passenger seat.

Brynja swerved to avoid a pair of young lambs skittering across the road and up the embankment on the other side. A flock of sheep emerged from the haze, their beady eyes beaming like flashlights.

Brynja slammed on the brakes. "Damn it." She pounded the steering wheel. "Damn it, damn it, damn it."

"You've gotta calm down," Stína said. "*Thetta reddast.*" She picked up her phone from the floor mat. "Hate to say it, but you're getting a little paranoid. Maybe the pastor actually did overdose from chemo meds like the doctor first said. Maybe he wasn't actually poisoned by that yew berry tart."

"Really? You're not rattled by three deaths in less than two weeks? In a country with just about the lowest homicide rate in the entire world?" Brynja pressed on the gas and maneuvered around the last of the sheep. "Sometimes, you can be a little—"

"A little what? A little loyal? A little willing to drop everything at work at the busiest time of the year to help my best friend track down some killer?" She cracked her knuckles and ripped open a bag of *Gúmmíbangsi* candy. "Maybe you could just drop me at Amma's."

Brynja winced. "Sorry. I'm just so overwhelmed. I almost forgot to call the Akureyri police and have them rope off Möðruvellir Church; it's a crime scene now. I did remember to hand Óliver the tart and he's going to send it down to Reykjavik for analysis." She veered right onto the strip of road leading to Amma's farm and looked sheepishly at her friend. "Forgive me?"

"Sure, but it'll cost ya." Stína popped a couple of the chocolate-covered gummy bears into her mouth. "Arrange for that hunky policeman Óliver to execute some *undercover* work with me and I'll think about it."

Despite herself, Brynja smiled.

"Just kidding," Stína said. "But you should say a quick *halló* to Amma before going home. She'll be hurt if you don't."

"Think she's still up?"

At her grandmother's farm, Stína got out of the car and pulled her pack from the seat. "Of course, she's up. Have you forgotten Amma's quite the night owl?"

Leaving their muddied boots on the front mat, they made their way through the herb-scented hallway to the kitchen.

Well into her eighties, Amma bustled about the tiny room with an energy that belied her age. She picked up two logs and threw them onto the fire, then stood up to stir a pot of *Kjötsúpa* on the stove. When she turned around, her cheeks were rosy from the steam.

"Well, *halló!*" she cried, hugging them both. "Will you look what the wind blew in? Sit down. The both of you look famished." She reached into the cabinet and pulled two pewter bowls from the shelf. She set the table, then walked to the door, and put on her woolen overcoat.

"I'll be just a moment," she said. "I've got to feed some hay to the sheep. The young ones will be headed out soon, but the snow still hasn't cleared from the mountaintops. It was a stormy winter, this last one."

"Okay if I fetch some ale from the storage room, Amma?" Stína said.

"Whatever you like, dear. I'll be back in a whipstitch."

Alone in the kitchen, Brynja stood at the sink and looked out the garden window. The sill held an array of bird eggs and feathers Stína had collected over the years. On the pasture, a herd of horses grazed on the fresh, green shoots of summer. Slowly twisting her hair into a braid, Brynja felt calmer, calm enough to wonder once again just how everything fit together.

Lúkas, the poem, the poisonings, the warnings.

She desperately wanted to believe the whole horrific nightmare wasn't entirely her fault. Her hand went to the silver locket around her neck. It felt like an albatross.

If only she hadn't insisted on riding the carousel instead of keeping an eye on Lúkas. She had never forgotten that day, never let the hope of finding him fade or hide under other parts of her life. After two decades of searching, she had failed to find him. And now, all of a sudden, her life was filled with clues to his whereabouts, but also warnings to stop looking for him and threats if she didn't. Why was this happening now? Why not last year? Why not ten years ago?

If she hadn't pleaded with Ari to leave the *Möðruvallabók* at the church, would Pastor Dalmann still be alive?

She took a deep, pained breath.

Why had she agreed to have Ari send the book to her office in the first place? If she hadn't, Tómas would not have found and eaten the *kleinur*. He would not have died from ergot poisoning. Perhaps then Ari wouldn't have been targeted as well, and Fríða spared from being poisoned with the rhubarb cake sent to his office.

Perhaps her relationship with Ari wouldn't be in jeopardy.

Before Brynja's thoughts could go any further, Stína clambered up from the storage room beneath the kitchen and corked open a bottle of home-brewed ale. "Feeling better?"

She shrugged.

Stína indicated for Brynja to sit down and slid the bottle across the table. "So, tell me, what's the deal with the note that Óliver found at the church?"

Brynja took a small sip of ale. "I'm sure it's another warning. He said it was written on stiff paper. Parchment, I suspect. And the gothic script looks the same as on those other warnings. It can't be a coincidence that Óliver found the note where Pastor Dalmann kept the *Möðruvallabók*. Someone is obviously warning me to back off searching for Lúkas." She folded her arms tightly across her chest. "Otherwise, I'm next."

Stína's eyes grew round. "Why do you think that?"

The kitchen door slammed shut behind Amma. She removed her coat, hung it by the door, and scuttled over to the sink to wash her hands. "There. How about we feed you little lambs now?"

"Amma—" Brynja considered launching into the details of all that had happened these past two weeks, then thought better of it. "Amma, would you take a look at this?"

She reached into her bag and pulled out her phone. Óliver had texted her the photo of the warning.

Amma began to read. "*Asks the ash-tree goddess—*"

"Okay. I'm already lost. *Ash-tree goddess?*" Stína said.

Amma shot her granddaughter a stern look.

"The ash-tree is the mythical tree *Yggdrasil*," Brynja said. "It connects the nine worlds in Norse mythology. It's the tree of life that connects us all. The branches reach far into the heavens, and its roots extend deep into the earth."

Amma sat down. "How lovely. That must be about you, Brynja. You're always saying how genealogy is like a huge tree that connects us all through our shared DNA. Did that handsome fiancé of yours write this about you? The ash-tree goddess, the goddess of the tree of life. You are the female geneticist, after all."

Brynja shivered. "No, Ari didn't write it. But I knew it was directed at me. You've just confirmed my worst fears."

Stína read the read of the note aloud and raised her brows. "Okay, genius. Crow-feeder?"

"It's a kenning," Brynja said.

"Oh, that explains it. Sure, a kenning. I think I dated a Ken Ning once."

Brynja opened her mouth to explain the word puzzles to Stína, but Amma interrupted.

"Kennings are descriptive terms, like four-eyes for someone wearing glasses, or bean-counters for accountants. Bible-thumpers, book-worms—"

"Got it," Stína said. "Eye-candy. Chick-magnet. Stone-cold-fox." She finished off the bottle of ale and turned to Brynja. "Speaking of eye-candy, could you call Óliver? I'm gonna need your car to get to the bird cliffs. Maybe he or one of the officers can drive you down to Reykjavik? Óliver said they're always going down there for one reason or another."

"He said he'd stop by Munkathverá in the morning and brief me on what's going on over at Möðruvellir. I can ask."

"Anyway, crow-feeder," Stína said. "What's a crow-feeder?"

"Oh, my." Amma's chair scraped the floorboards as she stood up. "A crow-feeder is a warrior. A murderer. Someone who leaves a dead body for the crows to feed on."

Brynja pressed her fingers to her temples to keep the veins from exploding.

Amma took a step back and laid a hand to her heart. When she spoke, her voice was high-pitched. "Where did you get this? I'm fairly certain it's from one of the sagas."

"The sagas? Do you remember which one?" Brynja asked.

"I'm not sure. Let me think. Back when I was young, the schoolmasters demanded we children read all forty-two sagas. Better shoeless than bookless, they used to say." Amma went to the living room and returned with a dusty edition of *The Icelandic Family Sagas* and a pair of reading glasses. "Yes, yes. Here it is." She flipped to a page in the middle of the book. "Those words are taken from one of the skaldic poems." She wrinkled her nose. "But…just a minute now, the first line in the saga says *ale-horn goddess*, not *ash-tree goddess*. No matter. They both can simply mean 'woman.'"

But Brynja quietly disagreed with the old woman. It *did* matter. Whoever wrote the warning wanted to make sure she knew that she—the *ash-tree goddess*—would be the next victim. "Which saga is that from?"

Amma looked up. "*The Saga of Viga-Glúm.*"

"Viga-Glúm?" Stína asked. "Is that a kenning?"

"No, dear, that's his name. Viga-Glúm." Amma put the book down on the table and cocked her head. "Actually, in a sense, maybe it is a kenning. *Viga* means 'of the killings.' And *Glúm* comes from the same root as gloom or gloomy. So, his name means 'Killer Gloom.'"

Brynja softly repeated the name and its meaning.

"A nasty character, that one." Amma shook her head. "'Killer Gloom.' Imagine that."

Brynja's mind raced back to the poem about Lúkas. *And you will find your other half…In the ink of Gloom's root cellar.*

Amma motioned to the hills surrounding her farm. "Viga-Glúm was a powerful chieftain who lived right here in Eyjafjörður valley. According to legend, his grandfather gave him three family heirlooms: a black cloak, a gold-inlaid spear, and a sword. He was told his family's good fortune was imbued in the heirlooms and that he would prosper if he honored them."

Amma stared into the distance as she recalled the tales she'd read in childhood. "Viga-Glúm murdered many people with that sword. He was crazy—laughed like a hyena during his killing sprees." Amma clucked her tongue. "He got away with it for a while, but his fortune ran out when he used the cloak and spear as bribes during his trial at Thingvellir." She turned around, blinking rapidly. "Oh my. What was the rest of that verse? *Else this crow-feeder comes to kill once more?*"

"Creepy," Stína said.

"I don't like all this talk of murder," Amma said, turning to Brynja. "Was that sent to you? I do hope you're not in any danger,"

Brynja could feel the puzzle falling into place. She was getting closer.

She only hoped she could solve the riddle before the crows came to feed.

Chapter 29

Brynja left Stína and Amma feeling clearer in mind than she had in days. The reference to Gloom in her poem must be a reference to Viga-Glúm, who had lived here in the Eyjafjörður Valley. He would have had a root cellar. But where? Amma didn't seem to know which farm had belonged to his family. Maybe Jónas would know. Or Ari—he had read all the sagas. But Ari had said not to call. Someone in the history department at the university was sure to know. When it was time to leave Amma's farm, she turned toward home and a new perspective.

She reached Munkathverá late in the evening. Jónas and Pabbi were sleeping soundly. The sun would not set for another few hours, and a ride was just what she needed. She headed to the barn and saddled up her mare.

Brynja cantered across the field, breathing in the crisp, cool air. She paused to take in the beauty around her and heard water trickling over twigs in the meandering stream. She gave in to the fact that, at least for the moment, she was not in control. Poisoned food, death threats, three murders. Óliver was handling the pastor's case with the Akureyri police and the other two poisonings were being investigated by the Reykjavik police. After rerunning the DNA analysis on the parchments, perhaps the lab would realize they'd made a mistake and have a fresh lead on the suspect. It was time for her to step back and stay on the sidelines. Let the police track down the killer.

Her new resolve brought an unexpected peace.

She rode on to an old fishing shed, dismounted, and patted her mare on the neck. Inside the weathered shack, she found a woolen blanket and spread it out on a wide bench overlooking the river. Here she could savor her happy memories.

She closed her eyes, remembering the times in late spring when she and Lúkas had played alongside the shed while Jónas prepared the fishing lines. Jónas would step foot in the shallow waters and whisk the fly into the air, then back over his shoulder until the line was nearly straight. Then he would pull it forward, bringing the line to land atop the stream with a single, smooth motion of his forearm. A jerk, a reel, a thrash, and a quick toss into a metal bucket sealed the fate of a spotted brown trout. The evening's dinner.

Lúkas had preferred to sit on the raised bank of the river where he could draw all that he saw. His early sketches of gulls and kittiwakes flying above the fjord still hung in their bedroom.

She fell asleep, a child again.

A distant crackle of thunder woke Brynja two hours later. She shook the sleep from her eyes, called to Drífa, and started back toward the turf house.

Without warning, Drífa reared her head, turned, and bolted toward the sheep corral. Brynja laid the reins on her neck and gave her mare a firm kick to steer her back toward the house but Drífa insisted on heading for the ruins of the old, stone paddock.

Loosening the reins, Brynja let her go. Perhaps her mare missed *réttir*, the sheep round-up, as much as she did. Every year, the young lambs were let loose to graze upon the summer's grass. In the fall, after gaining five times their weight, they were herded back from the mountains. The bucking and bleating sheep resisted, kicking up clods of muddied earth as they were funneled into the pie-shaped corral. Leaning on the outer rails, rowdy spectators in yellow and green raincoats cheered and belted out folk songs as the farmhands grabbed the rams' horns, flung themselves atop the ewes' wooly backs, and sorted the sheep into each farmer's slice of the stone pie.

As Drífa passed the sheep hold, she slowed to a walk. Brynja smiled. Yes, Drífa did remember. After a few turns around the corral, Brynja managed to coax her mare back to the barn and rub her down.

Brynja quietly opened the front door of the house and slipped inside. In her bedroom, she stripped off her jeans and curled up in the small, wooden bed Pabbi had carved for her so long ago. She looked at the matching bed where Lúkas had slept as a child, then lowered the wick of the oil lamp by her bedside. In the darkness, her eyes roamed the old turf walls for the answers to his disappearance, answers that now seemed buried in the past.

She remembered Amma's words.

Viga-Glúm. Killer Gloom.

The ink in Gloom's root cellar.

Was the ink a metaphor for the saga? Or could it possibly refer to the poisons the killer was using? And would there still be a root cellar on Viga-Glúm's land after so much time?

Brynja burrowed beneath the covers and shut her eyes to the fear that welled within her. She would have to wait until morning to talk with Jónas. Maybe he'd be able to make sense of everything she'd learned the past few days.

At the very least, he would console her, just as he had decades ago when Lúkas had disappeared.

Hours later, the smell of smoke wafting through the *vindauga* woke her. Brynja leapt from her bed and ran to the hallway.

"Jónas!"

There was no answer.

She shouted up to her father's bedroom. "Pabbi!" The walls were silent. "Pabbi!"

She bounded up the stairs. The room was free of smoke and Pabbi was sound asleep, his pale face half-buried in his matted hair. Rivulets of drool escaped his dry, cracked lips, and his bony chest rumbled with wheezy gasps of air. Regret squeezed her heart; he was so very thin. Brynja leaned down to kiss him on the forehead and whispered she'd be back in a moment.

She ran down to the kitchen. The door was open. She hurried outside.

Of course. Had she really been in Reykjavik so long that she'd forgotten the sweet smell of birch coming from the smokehouse? She was accustomed to the fresh vegetables and fruits available in the city markets year-round, but here on the farm, life went on as it had for centuries. Jónas insisted on tradition. For centuries, Icelanders had smoked, pickled, and dried their foods for the harsh winters ahead, and Jónas saw no need for change.

She poked her head into the smokehouse. Sure enough, he was tying strips of freshly caught trout to the rafters.

Jónas jumped at the sight of her. "Brynja!" He nicked his palm with the knife he was using to cut the rope. "*Andskotinn!*"

"Oh!" Brynja ran to the kitchen, grabbed a clean dishtowel, and rushed back to wrap the cloth around his hand.

Jónas smiled weakly. "It's nothing, *litla mín*. Don't you worry; I'm fine."

Brynja tied a knot in the dishcloth and put pressure on his hand to stop the bleeding. "There. Come, let's get inside. We need to bandage this up properly, but I think you should keep pressure on it for a while first."

Jónas stomped his boots on the mat before entering the kitchen. "I wish I knew you were coming, *litla mín*. I haven't had a chance to give your father his morning bath yet."

"You need to keep that cut dry."

"I'll manage. Let's make some tea first, though. He'll like that."

Brynja knew better than to argue with Jónas. She put a kettle on the stove, pulled three ceramic mugs from the hooks over the counter, and placed them on the table in front of his typewriter.

"Sit down," she said, pulling out a chair for him.

A half hour later, after they had tea with Pabbi, Brynja was putting away the dishes in the kitchen while Jónas sat at the table. The front door flew open; the house shuddered. Stína waltzed in, a tall figure standing in the shadows behind her.

"So, I'm sitting looking out the window at Amma's just now, checking for black-tailed godwits. Just so happens I've got a bird's eye view of your place and who do I see knocking at your front door?"

Brynja gave her a blank look.

"Óliver, that's who."

The officer stepped forward. "I hope I'm not disturbing you. Wanted to give you a brief update on the situation out at Möðruvellir."

"Please, come in," Brynja said.

"I got your message about a ride down to Reykjavik. I'm afraid I won't be able to give you a lift until this afternoon. Station's short-handed at the moment."

"That's fine. Thank you." She turned to Jónas. "This is Óliver Pétursson, Jónas. One of the officers who's been guarding the church."

"For the book, yes," Jónas said. "Pleasure to meet you."

"And you," Óliver said. "Sorry to interrupt." He turned to Brynja. "I'll be brief. Chief at Akureyri PD is meeting me at the church. We need to question the custodian further about what happened on the night in question."

"What night?" Jónas asked, his eyes darting between Brynja and Óliver. "What happened?"

"There was an incident at the church Sunday night," Brynja said.

"I was just about to tell you."

Óliver glanced at the bloodied dishtowel around Jónas's left hand. "Looks like you've had a bit of a mishap.

"It's nothing, really." Jónas fiddled with the knot, unwrapped the towel, and pushed a flap of skin over the cut. "Just needs a little bandage, that's all."

Óliver stared at Jónas's hand, studying the space where the tips of his fingers and thumb ought to be. "What happened there?"

Behind Jónas's back, Brynja gave Óliver an almost imperceptible shake of her head. She knew Jónas was embarrassed by his deformity.

"Let's get a clean dressing on that wound," Óliver said.

Stína slid open a drawer on the sideboard holding bandages and antiseptic wipes.

"I'm not sure if this is going to need stiches," Óliver said. "Maybe we could take a photo and text it to my sister? She's the doctor at the clinic in town."

Stína handed Óliver the bandages and took the phone from him. "What's your sister's number?" She snapped a picture of Jónas's hand. "Is she at work now?"

"Not sure," Óliver said, giving the number to Stína while bandaging the wound.

"Really, I'll be fine," Jónas said. "I'm not going anywhere."

Brynja knew not to argue with him in front of the police officer. She took a hot kettle from the stove and set it on a pewter trivet in the center of the table.

"Let's sit. I'll keep an eye on Jónas's hand. The bleeding looks under control." She pulled two ceramic mugs from above the counter and set them in front of Stína and Óliver. "I'm glad you're both here. I was just starting to tell Jónas about everything that happened at the church."

"I knew that pastor was trouble," Jónas said. "I hope he didn't do anything stupid. Is the book still there? Is that the problem?"

Brynja shook her head. "People have been murdered, Jónas.

Three people. Poisoned."

Jónas stood up and placed his hand on the table to steady himself. "Why haven't you told me that? Did the pastor try to hurt you when you went to talk to him about the poem? I don't want you—" The color drained from his face. "What if something happens to you? I couldn't bear it."

Óliver jumped in. "Don't worry, sir. We're taking extra precautions to ensure everyone's safety. Unfortunately, the pastor was one of the victims. And the *Möðruvallabók* is missing from the church. The custodian has been taken in for questioning. We let her return to the church for the night but she's due to come back this afternoon."

Brynja placed a hand on Jónas's forearm. "Jónas, sit, you're shaking. Your cut might be worse than you think. This is a horrible situation, but the police have it under control. Why don't you lie down for a while?"

Óliver stepped forward. "If you need anything, sir, you can reach me at the station. In the meantime, I'm going to post a couple of officers outside your door. I don't want to worry you needlessly, but we have reason to believe Brynja might be targeted next. I'm concerned for her safety."

"I can take care of her. We'll keep an eye out for anything unusual. She's safe here. Always has been."

"I'm not so sure," Stína said. "That's why I was on my way over here."

Brynja's eyes widened. "What do you mean?"

"Remember Amma said Viga-Glúm lived somewhere in Eyjafjörður? I stayed up all goddamn night reading that saga. Guess where it turns out Viga-Glúm lived."

Brynja gave her head a sharp shake and leaned forward. "Where?"

"Munkathverá!" Stína said. "Viga-Glúm lived right here at Munkathverá!"

Chapter 30

Brynja struggled to absorb this new shock.

Maybe Jónas didn't know of a root cellar on the farm and maybe Pabbi had never mentioned one, but Brynja was now certain the answer to Lukas's disappearance lay here, on the farm, in an unknown root cellar. *Gloom's root cellar.*

"Viga-Glúm lived here even before the monastery was built," Stína said. "So it was just called Thverá. Just river. Not Munkathverá, monk's river."

The words echoed around Brynja. No matter what the farm was called back then, the fact remained that Viga-Glúm had lived here.

"I have to take a look around," she said, turning toward the door.

Óliver stood up and took a step forward. "You shouldn't leave the house."

Stína grabbed her friend's arm, but Brynja shook her off.

"Now that I know what I'm looking for, I can't just sit around. Don't worry, I'll be careful, but I have to go and search. I have to."

Perhaps some aberration she hadn't paid much attention to in the past would hint at an ancient root cellar beneath.

"I'll stay on here until the two officers arrive to stand guard," Óliver said. "I'll post one on the grounds outside and one inside the turf house."

Jónas argued, not pleased by the intrusion, but after being assured the officers would stay out of his way, he reluctantly agreed to lie down for a while.

Brynja headed for the stable. She saddled up her mare and set off to survey every bit of land at Munkathverá. As she crossed the pasture, she felt the wind kick up, cold and antagonistic. Shadows from the morning's low-lying fog folded into the mountains and a chill settled over the fjord. Brynja zipped her fleece and gave Drífa a gentle kick.

She started in the south, toward Amma's farm, and rode Drífa back and forth over the land, methodically searching for any irregularity in the surface that could indicate an old root cellar: a mound, a depression, eroded soil, unusual vegetation. Nearly two hours later, Brynja had found nothing unusual. But she wouldn't admit to failure, and rode on.

Heading north, Drífa reared her head and bolted toward the sheep corral, just as she had done the evening before. Brynja allowed her to circle the stone paddock before loosening the reins, pushing her heel into the mare's side, and giving her a gentle prod.

The horse nickered, then reared up on her hind legs before galloping north again, toward a cluster of trees that bordered the far end of the farm. Brynja had to let her run. Reaching the small grove, Drífa clawed the ground with her hoof, then snorted and tossed her head.

A gust of wind pummeled them, and Drífa danced sideways.

"Whoa, Drífa."

Brynja pulled up on the reins and tried to steer her from the spot.

The mare wouldn't budge. She pounded her hoof on the dirt and shook her mane from side to side. Never before had her Icelandic horse been afraid of a little weather. It was odd.

Brynja reached over to calm her and caught sight of a bucket of carrots half-hidden in the brush. No wonder Drífa had insisted on leading her to this spot.

Unable to resist giving Drífa a treat, she pulled up on the reins, dismounted, and bent down to pick a couple of carrots from the pail. What were they carrots doing way out here? Drífa accepted the treat but then snorted, ripped the grass from beside the bucket, and reared her head once again. Brynja patted her on the neck and set her loose to graze while she took a look around.

A speck of crimson in the brush caught her eye. In late spring, the fields of Eyjafjörður bloomed with purple lupine, yellow dandelions, and orange poppies. But not red. Red was a rare color in nature, especially here in the north.

She passed it by, but a few steps later, curiosity consumed her, and she returned to investigate.

Brynja squinted to catch a better look. Yes, red.

Why was Drífa so worked up? Most mammals, including horses, couldn't see red at all. But humans had an extra photopigment gene, the long wavelength opsin, so that they *could* see red. Evolution. Survival of the fittest. Humans could see red *because* of its rarity in nature; it screamed survival.

Ripe fruit, poisonous spiders, spilled blood.

Life. Danger. Death.

She looked closer, brushing aside meadow buttercups and sprigs of crowberry.

Somehow, worked into the ground lay a frayed, red ribbon tied in a bow.

The same type of ribbon that, as a child, she had used to fasten her braids. The same type of ribbon she had given Lúkas to hold while she rode the carousel.

She shuddered.

The same type that had been tied around the poem.

What was a red ribbon doing way out here on the edge of the farm? It couldn't be hers. It would have disintegrated years ago in the snowfall, windstorms, and the ravages of time.

Confused, she looked out over the pasture, half expecting an answer from her grazing mare. Drífa returned the gaze but answered only with a deep, fluttering breath before lowering her head again to pluck at the bright green shoots.

Brynja bent over and reached for the ribbon.

The ground shrank as she skyrocketed upward, her neck telescoping far above the wildflowers below. She clenched her fists. *Stay calm,* she told herself, closing her eyes against the tiny barns and turf houses dotting the minuscule mountains in the far distance. She jerked back, staggering on sponges, and waited for the aura to pass. Moments later, her hands and feet retracted, and she spiraled back to earth, falling down upon the cold, damp grass.

Brynja shook away the vision, stood up and brushed herself off.

Again, she bent down to pick up the red ribbon, tugging it loose from the soil. She ran her fingers over the rough fibers and gripped the bow; it unfurled, but the rest wouldn't budge. She looked closer. A knot in the ribbon tied the base to a rusty, metal hook. Puzzled, she brushed away the dirt.

The hook was fastened to the handle of a trap door.

She cleared dirt from the metal slats of the hatch until they opened. She lifted the cover. Steps of packed dirt led down into the earth.

A root cellar.

How many times had she ridden past this copse and never noticed the lay of this part of the land? Why hadn't Jónas told her about this? She looked back toward the turf house in the distance. Maybe the root cellar had been closed up before he came to manage the farm. But, then, who else could have tied the ribbon to the hatch? Pabbi? Amma? Had Lúkas been playing out here so long ago?

Perhaps this wasn't a root cellar after all. Perhaps it was an underground storage bin where, long ago, newly mown hay had been sheltered from the wind. Perhaps it was the remains of an old turf house or even an ancient burial mound.

But no. Her gut told her this had to be a root cellar.

She stepped down into the narrow passageway. The rank smell of decay lifted off the damp walls. Step by step, she descended the dirt stairs. Her boots pressed hard into the earth. She steadied herself with a hand on the earthen walls. At the bottom, she hit her head on the lintel of a doorway. She pushed open a wooden door.

In the dim shaft of light from above, Brynja could make out the outlines of a rustic table. She stepped closer. A scooped berry picker, a hand shovel, and a dozen or so candles were strewn across the tabletop. She felt about for matches, found a packet toward the back of the table, and lit one of the candles.

Her eyes widened in the inky darkness.

On the far side of the chamber, the candlelight cascaded along a dirt wall lined with glass jars. With candle in hand, she read the labels:

ANGELICA
(Hvönn)
Bronchitis, Pleurisy, Incontinence

BEARBERRY
(Sortulyng)
Diuretic, Antiseptic

ICELAND MOSS
(Íslensk fjallagrös)
Sore throat, Cough, Indigestion, Loss of Appetite

These were apothecary jars. Wavy, sea green canisters stuffed with herbs and berries. The underground chill would preserve their organic compounds.

But why were they here? Perhaps she was in some sort of secret storage room for an herbal pharmacy.

Listening to the wind moan above, Brynja passed the candlelight over another shelf. As she moved the containers forward, the fragile glass of the antique jars clinked in the silence of the chamber. She read the labels.

WILLOW

(Grasvíðir)

Toothache Pain

MADDER

(Maðra)

Kidney stones, Inflammation

Madder? Hadn't Pastor Dalmann told her that madder no longer grew in the fields of Eyjafjörður?

LYME GRASS

(Melgresi)

Weight gain

MONKSHOOD

(Sauð-bani)

Nerve pain, Rheumatism

Monkshood? What was monkshood doing here? The aconite in its roots could kill. Its other name—*Sauð-bani*, sheep's death— was plain enough.

Brynja read the label on the next jar:

AMANITA MUSCARIA
(Berserkjasveppur)
Depression, Tics, Epilepsy

Did whoever stocked this pharmacy know just how harmful these mushrooms could be? There was a reason *Amanita muscaria* was called the berserker mushroom. Long ago, it had helped fuel the trance-like fury of Vikings who bit their shields and gnawed at their skin before launching into battle. On top of that, the mushrooms could cause visual distortion and amnesia.

Drífa's hooves thumped above and her loud bray echoed down the steps of the cellar.

She should go. She had to tell Jónas what she had found. Or should she? Did he know about the storage room? How could he *not* know? The cellar was on their farm. He had to know.

Turning toward the steps, she slipped on what felt like a damp, rubber mat. She lowered the candle to check her footing and, in the flickering light, spotted a drawing laid out on top of a chest. Her eyes traveled over the paper. It was a map.

A map of Munkathverá and the neighboring farms.

She recognized the shapes of the pastures, the river as it wound its way toward the fjord, the sheep corral, the barn, the fishing shed. To the south lay Amma's farm—smaller but with its U-shaped property winding around the old Viking cemetery. To the north, beyond Munkathverá's sheep corral, was the farm that belonged to Axel Bragason, Rúnar's brother.

On the map, a sliver of land was outlined in red and filled with bold hatch marks. Among the red markings a cluster of trees was drawn.

That grove of trees—the yew trees that Pabbi had warned her and Lúkas to stay away from—had sunk its roots deep into the earth that lay above her.

She ran her eyes up the wall. Nailed into the compressed dirt was a thick paper, stained with mildew. In the candlelight, she made out the heading: *Transfer Certificate of Title,* and the text below: *It is hereby certified that parcel 13-8467 in Eyjafjörður, North Iceland, bounded by and described as follows…*

Brynja skipped to the bottom of the paper. *Registered in accordance with provisions of Section 107 of the Property Registration Decree in the names of Axel Bragason and Rúnar Bragason. August 24, 1994.*

The beat of Brynja's heart roared in her ears. She was on the Bragason's property. The strip of farmland that Axel—and, apparently, Rúnar—had swindled from her father.

She was standing not *on* the Bragason's land, but *in* their land. Underground, in what must be Axel's storage room. A chill swept the length of her body. She needed to get out of here. And fast. Axel Bragason was not a kind man. If he caught her trespassing on his farm, there was no telling what he would do.

She turned to leave. Looking down to check her footing, she spotted a stack of papers. She leaned down to pick one up. The paper was covered in line after line of dark brown script.

It was rough, not like the thin, flimsy sheets of processed paper she had written on all her life. It was thicker, tough, semi-rigid.

Parchment.

She held the candle over the page. These were not words penned in modern-day script. They were written in the gothic script of Old Icelandic.

A moth brushed against her cheek. She jerked back and the candle flame died in the flurry of her movement. Trembling, she fiddled with a match to light the candle again. She held it up and surveyed several other stacks of parchment lying on the floor. She followed the trail to the rear of the storage room to a table. Torn scraps of bone-white parchment were piled on the tabletop and snow-white quills lay next to a cluster of inkwells. She picked up one of the quills and recognized it as a whooper swan feather. Stína often brought them back after her photography tours in the highlands.

Brynja scanned the wall behind the table and saw a rough-hewn shelf. It was stacked with books. Old, dusty, wood-bound books. *Manuscripts.*

For a moment she stood, immobile, rooted to the packed dirt of the cellar floor. Then she ran frantically across the dark chamber and stumbled up the steps. She gasped for clean, fresh air but the jaws of the coal black mountains pressed downward, and she felt their grasp tighten against her throat.

Chapter 31

Brynja emerged into the open air and fell to the cold, damp grass. The wind howled as the earth gave way. Drífa blissfully munched on a patch of crowberry, unaware that the world had shifted.

What were manuscripts, parchments, inkwells, doing down in Axel Bragason's root cellar? Logic and common sense told her to run, back to Munkathverá and Jónas, but that was too easy. She had to figure this out herself.

She had to go back down those stairs and search for the one manuscript she hoped would not be there—the missing *Möðruvallabók*, containing all three sagas quoted in the mysterious warnings. *Njál's. Egil's. Viga-Glúm's.*

She struggled to understand the whole story as it now lay before her. The Bragason's ancestor, Magnus Björnsson, had discovered the *Möðruvallabók* at Möðruvellir in the 1600s. That much was known. He most likely had taken it to his farm at Hof. Axel and Rúnar's sister Thorunn had lived at Hof before moving to the Westfjords. Tainted wheat had poisoned Tómas, and Thorunn had been the only wheat farmer in Eyjafjördur. Had she poisoned Tómas? Had she poisoned Lúkas?

Was Lúkas buried right here in the Bragason's root cellar?

Brynja looked around at the green landscape, placid even under the wind. What she had discovered was bigger than anything she had expected—too big for her to manage alone. She couldn't go to Jónas and Pabbi. This would be too much for them. But she needed help and she needed it quickly.

She sat up, pulled the phone from the pocket of her jeans, and dialed Ari's number. She desperately needed to hear his calm, sensible advice.

"Brynja?"

"Ari?" Her voice quivered. "I need to talk to you."

"Thank God you called. I've been trying to reach you. Where are you?"

"I found the root cellar—"

"Where? Tell me where."

Even in the chill of the pasture, her palms were sweating. "It's just past the sheep corral on Munkathverá. To the north. Under a small grove of yew trees."

"Stay put. I've just arrived at the police station. Óliver Pétursson's here."

Instinctively, Brynja looked across the fjord toward Akureyri.

"We'll be there in fifteen," Ari said. "Stay—"

The line went dead.

She began to redial his number. The screen was blank.

Why was Ari up here at the police station? Óliver must have told him about Pastor Dalmann's death and that the *Möðruvallabók* was missing. She cringed. It had been so awful the last time they spoke. But now…now, he sounded concerned, caring, the Ari she had fallen in love with.

In the distance, a plume of smoke rose from the chimney of the turf house. Jónas would be wondering where she was. Further north stood Axel Bragason's farmhouse, the small, timber home hidden from view beyond a sheep barn. She took a breath. He wouldn't be able to see her.

She had no idea when anyone had last visited the cellar, or if someone came regularly to work with the herbs and parchments. She could have hours or only minutes to explore what lay below. She had to act fast. She *had* to know if the *Möðruvallabók* was in the cellar.

On hands and knees, she crawled over to the hatch and climbed back down, feeling her way along the dark stairway.

Once inside, she pulled the pack of matches from her pocket and lit several of the candles on the table. The flickering light reflected off the glass jars, illuminating the shelf of dusty books in the rear of the cellar.

Holding one of the candles, she inspected the shelf. She pulled the books forward. One by one, she read the titles on the faded bindings.

The *Möðruvallabók* wasn't among them.

Both disappointed and oddly relieved, she turned her thoughts to the rest of the room's contents. If this cellar belonged to the Bragasons, how had Axel been able to collect all these manuscripts? Did Rúnar know about them?

In the dim light, she scanned the labels on the apothecary jars. On the bottom shelf, she read:

ICELAND POPPY
(Garðasól)
Fever, Analgesic

The Iceland Poppy. Rúnar's passion.

She returned to the map of Eyjafjörður's farms. Again, she read the property deed.

Had the Bragasons' feud with Pabbi escalated to the point of taking his son? Were they that hateful? Or were they covering for their sister, Thorunn?

She slid open the top drawer of the chest. Scraps of parchment, again scribbled on in the gothic script of Old Icelandic, were stuffed inside like medieval Post-its. She opened a second drawer. Inside lay three glass inkwells. Each was filled with black, red, or brown liquid and neatly labeled in the same hand as the apothecary jars.

OAK GALL

MADDER ROOT

WILLOW BARK AND BEARBERRY

Next to the inkwells lay several quills, their hollow shafts sharpened at the tip and stained with ink.

Had Axel written the warnings? Or some other member of the Bragason family? Would Ásta have gotten her hands dirty killing three people? She seemed the most unlikely person to cast as a serial killer. Even if Ásta thought she had the mutation for Paget's—and Brynja had determined that she didn't—she was unlikely to have morphed into a murderer.

Brynja lifted out the inkwell with red ink labeled Madder Root and dipped in a quill. On a strip of parchment, she wrote: *Upon the madder mead.*

She held the parchment up to the candlelight. The text of the poem had looked like this.

She dipped a second quill in the inkwell with black ink, this one marked Oak Gall. She drew a small leaf, similar to one on the poem. She held the parchment up again. The black ink looked the same as that on the poem. But black was black. She could draw no conclusion from this experiment, especially since Theó Friðriksson in the chemistry lab had said the black ink on the poem was made in Denmark, at Ren Blæk Inks.

But she still had another question, a larger one. Why would any of the Bragason clan have written the poem to help her find Lúkas? If they knew something, why wouldn't they have just told her instead of writing a series of cryptic riddles? Had she misunderstood the messages? Had someone written the poem to stir up painful memories? Or had it been Henning's idea—and he'd enlisted Rúnar's help? Was it all a ruse to steer her into such preoccupation with finding Lúkas that she faltered as director of forensics and lost her job? But, then, where did the murders fit in? Every question led to another question that only frustrated her more.

Fiddling with these inks would not give her the answers she sought. It was time to go. The *Möðruvallabók* wasn't down here and if Axel found her, she could be in even more danger.

But Ari had said to stay put. He would be here soon. She would give him a few more minutes.

Trying to stay calm and learn as much as she could before Ari arrived, she took several of the inkwells, quills, and slips of parchment from the chest and set them on the table by the foot of the stairs. She picked up a quill, dipped it into the deep brown ink, and wrote on a second piece of parchment: *At the Thing there is a throng.*

In the candlelight, she squinted at the writing. Every muscle in her body tightened. This ink looked exactly the same as that on the warnings—down to the slightly denser brown at the top of each letter.

Of course, it looks the same. According to Theó Friðriksson, the ink on the warning was identical to the ink the medieval scribes had used when writing the old manuscripts. Whoever was using this ink had probably concocted it from willow bark and bearberry as well.

But why? Why did the new ink have to match the old? Why did it matter?

In the darkness, a mouse skittered across the floor and up the leg of her boot. Brynja stomped her foot to scare it off and dropped the candle, spraying hot wax on her jeans. She jumped back and the heel of her boot hit a large, metal box.

With another candle in hand, she examined the box. It was too heavy to lift. She sat down, cross-legged, in front of it. When she opened the lid, a billow of mold rose up to her face. She sneezed and moved the candle closer.

A thin, leather satchel tied with twine sat within. She lifted it out, wrestled with the knot, and spread its contents on the floor.

These were not parchment. These were paper—a few faded photographs and a newspaper clipping.

She picked up one of the photographs. A young woman lay in bed, clutching a pillow in each arm. Brynja moved the photo closer to the light. No, they weren't pillows. They were two babies, each swaddled in a nursery blanket. The one in her right arm appeared to be sleeping. The one in her left looked directly at the lens, its face half covered by the shadow of the woman's hand.

Brynja picked up a second photo—a tiny picture that must have been meant for someone's wallet—and passed the candle over it. It was the same woman: the same distant smile, the same freckled cheeks, the same part in her wavy hair. Next to her stood a young boy. Brynja squinted to make out his face.

The boy was Lúkas, just as she remembered him.

He stood with his hands on his hips, facing the lens with the same defiant stare she remembered from so long ago.

Who was this woman? And why was she holding Lúkas's hand?

She scanned the background of the pale photo. They were standing in the doorway of a small, yellow house perched atop a hill. It had a red, tiled roof and white-framed windows. A ceramic plaque displaying the words *Højen Fyrvej 3,* entwined in a bouquet of purple flowers, hung above the doorway. In the distance, a wide, flat sea came to rest against a sandy shore.

Brynja didn't recognize the house. Or the beach.

But there he was. Lúkas. She guessed he must be eight or nine in the photo, a year or two older than when she'd lost him.

Lúkas was alive. He was out there. He hadn't died the day he disappeared.

Overcome with joy, she blinked back the tears that welled in her eyes.

Three more photos continued the story. The same woman. The same boy. In each of the photos, Lúkas appeared to be a little older than in the last. In one, Lúkas was maybe ten. In another, a bit older. And in the third, perhaps fourteen or fifteen. But who was the woman? And where were they?

She reached for the newspaper clipping. The fragile slip of paper nearly disintegrated in her fingers as she read the faded newsprint.

Hr. and Fru. Raske
announce the arrival of
Baby Boy Lorens
& Baby Girl Brita
January 11, 1990

Her birthday. The day she and Lúkas were born.

Brynja's eyes darted up to the newspaper masthead: *Dagbladet Dansk.*

Dansk? The Danish Daily?

Brynja read the announcement again. A boy and a girl. Lorens and Brita. Twins.

Lorens and Brita. L and B. Lúkas and Brynja.

It made no sense. She and Lúkas had been born in Eyjafjörður.

As she searched for more photos and clippings in the box, her fingers brushed against a hard board. She held the candle over it.

On the board was painted a Gothic 'M' intertwined with a gilded image of the madder plant, *Rubia tinctorum.* Stems and leaves wrapped about each pillar of the letter, giving way to the delicate petals of the madder flower, all supported by the plant's deep roots.

She had seen this crest before. It was the insignia of the *Möðruvallabók.*

Shaking, Brynja reached for the manuscript. Had it only been ten days since she first ran her fingertips over the page? The first message from this ancient book had lifted her closer to her lost brother than all her memories of him. Instead of being a wisp of hope and an ache in every limb, he'd become real; she had even dared to hope Lúkas was nearby. This book had brought him back to her, more solid than any dream of finding him. Though cryptic, it would lead her where she wanted to go. Her quest no longer seemed quixotic or stubborn, but the proper path of her life. She wrapped her hands around sides of the manuscript, her fingers giving an impulsive squeeze as though a living person could feel her touch.

As she lifted the *Möðruvallabók* from the box, the muted thud of heavy footsteps sounded from above. The cellar door creaked open.

Thank God. Ari had found the root cellar. He must have seen Drífa grazing outside and found the trap door.

Brynja laid the book down, picked up the candle, and headed to the bottom of the steps. "Ari, I'm down—"

The words disintegrated in the tight clasp of a hand over her mouth.

Chapter 32

"Stay still," a man's voice hissed.

Brynja thrust the candle over her shoulder toward the sound of the voice. She twisted away from the attacker as his grip slackened. Once face to face, she punched the man in the gut. He staggered backward against the table, then lurched forward and grabbed her arm.

In the dim light, she saw only a mass of human form. She wrestled free and kneed her assailant in the groin.

He writhed in pain. "Stop, *stop*. I'm doing this for you, *litla mín*. I'm doing this for you."

Brynja froze.

Litla mín. Only one person called her *litla mín*.

She picked up the lone, lit candle from the table and passed it in front of her attacker.

Jónas's eyes shone in the flickering light. She heard a strangled cry—it was her own.

Sirens whirred above. Every instinct told her to flee up the stairs, but her feet were anchored to the floor.

"Why?" she whispered. "Why?"

"I had to do it."

"Do what? You had to do what?"

"The book. It belongs to us. *Guds hjælp, Folkets kærlighed, Danmarks styrke.*"

"Why are you speaking Danish?"

"*God's help, the love of the people.* Don't you see, *litla mín*? The book belongs to us. To you and me and Lúkas. To our family. *Denmark's strength!*"

"What are you talking about? The book's not—"

Jónas stared at Brynja with the crazed desperation of a rabid dog. "You will understand, *litla mín*. You will see. Come. We'll watch out for each other."

His words cut like a knife. *Watch out for each other.*

She was seven again.

Forgive me, Pabbi. Forgive me, Jónas.

Round and round on the carousel.

Smaller and smaller.

I should have watched out for you, Lúkas.

Forgive me, brother.

Ari's voice broke the spell. "Brynja?"

She dropped the candle and stumbled up the stairs. She collapsed in Ari's arms.

He nestled her head against his chest and stroked her hair. "You're safe now."

The spinning lights of police cars sent a kaleidoscope of color across the field. Óliver leapt from one of the vehicles and ran toward them. He motioned for them to stand back, pulling a baton from his belt.

"No!" Brynja screamed, pulling away from Ari. "No! Stop! Jónas is down there. He's not dangerous. He's just gone mad."

Ari held her shoulders tight. "Stay here." He turned to Óliver and nodded toward the cellar.

Óliver moved to the entrance.

A moment later, he shouted up from the cellar. "Call 112!"

The fields swirled around Brynja. A cold, empty terror gripped her gut. She wrested herself free from Ari's grasp and hurtled down the steps.

In the beam of Óliver's flashlight, Jónas's motionless form sprawled across the cellar floor, blood spilling from his mouth. Brynja fell to her knees and put her ear close to listen for his breath. She laid her hand on his chest. His heart was still.

"Why?" She turned to Óliver. "Why? He didn't hurt me." She cradled Jónas's head.

A river of despair coursed through her body. Had she burdened him so much with her need to search for Lukas that he had broken under the strain? Why had she insisted he help her look for Lúkas when caring for Pabbi was all he could handle?

With her scarf, she gently dabbed the blood from Jónas's mouth and cheeks. "I'm sorry, Jónas, I'm so sorry."

She rubbed his pale, lifeless cheek, but the deep red stain didn't fade.

Something wasn't right.

She looked up at Óliver.

"It's not blood…is it?"

He shook his head.

She bowed her head. On the floor, by Jónas's side, lay a shattered, glass apothecary jar. His hand clutched a small, shiny object. As she pulled his fingers apart, a sprig of monkshood tumbled from his grasp, and a vial of red liquid spilled madder ink across the floor.

Late in the afternoon, Brynja sat in the kitchen at Munkathverá. The curtains were drawn, and the room felt cold, empty.

Ari spoke softly. "Brynja, there's no mistake."

Óliver stood next to the door, arms folded over his chest. "I got a good look at Jónas's hand when I bandaged it this morning."

Brynja's eyes darted between Óliver and Ari. "And? What does that have to do with anything? Jónas had an accident shearing sheep a long time ago."

Ari took a deep breath. "Jónas was not who you thought he was—"

"I know who Jónas was," Brynja said. "He wasn't going to hurt me. He…he just cracked."

Ari put his hand on hers. "I know this will be difficult for you to accept. I've got to tell you something you won't want to hear."

"It can't be worse than what's just happened."

Ari spoke in a slow, deliberate fashion. "I'm afraid it is. Jónas was the man responsible for crippling your mother."

"No. You're not making any sense. He would never have done that."

"Your parents were at the Botanical Gardens celebrating the anniversary of the *Möðruvallabók*'s return. Jónas was the person who threw the bomb into the crowd that day."

"No!" Brynja pulled her hand away. "That's not possible."

Óliver filled a glass of water from the tap and placed it in front of Brynja. "When I started at the police academy, I was assigned to explosives. Since bombings are so rare in Iceland, that particular one was always discussed with the new recruits." He opened a manila folder and slid a black and white photograph across the table. "This was taken by someone just before the bomb exploded at the Akureyri Gardens in 1989."

Brynja stared at the image of several dozen men and women applauding a speaker at the podium.

Óliver tapped his finger on a figure in overalls toward the back of the crowd. The person's face was obscured by a large man in front of him, but a raised hand was clearly visible.

"Here," Óliver said, sliding a second photograph across the table. "An enlargement."

The blood in her veins froze.

The hand—a left hand—was missing a thumb and the tips of two fingers.

It was holding a grenade.

"The case was never solved," Óliver said. "The department always suspected that whoever threw that grenade was protesting the return of the *Möðruvallabók*." He pointed at the slightly fuzzy enlargement. "Look here. The leather bracelet on the bomber's wrist bears a medal with the insignia of the Danish Crown. That bracelet was found on the ground later and collected as evidence. It must've fallen off when he threw the grenade."

"It can't be," Brynja whispered.

She struggled to reconcile Óliver's report with her reality. When she had started at Legacy, she'd gotten permission to comb through evidence files at the police station, looking for anything that would shed light on what had happened that day. Time and time again, she had been told by the clerk that no evidence had been collected following the bombing, save for a detonated grenade, a doll with singed hair, a leather bracelet, and several hats and shoes that had been cast off when the crowd dispersed in a panic.

Brynja stared at the photo of the disfigured hand holding the grenade. "I've seen plenty of people with injuries like that. Farmers, fishermen, butchers."

"Brynja," Ari said in a tone that didn't leave room for argument. "When Óliver bandaged Jónas's hand this morning, he suspected Jónas was the perpetrator they'd been searching for all these years. That's why he had the officers posted at Munkathverá. After Óliver ensured Jónas was being watched—"

"Obviously, he wasn't being watched that carefully," Brynja said.

"My apologies. Jónas slipped out when the officer took my call to see how you were." Óliver paused. "At any rate, I called the station down in Reykjavik and asked Henning to confirm what I suspected. He retrieved the photo from the archives. It was never released—we wanted to avoid letting the suspect know what we had. The enlargement shows the same hand as in the photo I took this morning." He pulled his phone from his pocket and opened the image.

"That wasn't your sister you sent the text to? The doctor?"

"No. I sent it to Henning. We're confident that was Jónas's hand holding the grenade. Even down to the slight curve of his pinky finger."

"That doesn't mean anything. Clinodactyly is really common. Even Lúkas had it."

Ari leaned in. "Óliver called me and I flew up immediately. I got here at noon and went straight to the Akureyri police station."

"Why didn't you call me?"

"I did. The officer at Munkathverá said you'd gone out riding. Said he was keeping an eye on Jónas. I tried to reach you all afternoon. Why didn't you answer?"

"I was here all afternoon, out by the fishing shed—" Brynja stopped short. Cell reception on the farm could be spotty, especially down by the river.

"I was so relieved when you finally called me," Ari said. "But then the call dropped. If it wasn't for that horse of yours, I'm not sure we would have found you." He pressed his hands on hers.

"There's more," Óliver said. "After retrieving the photo from the archives, Henning asked the clerk for the leather bracelet."

Ari sat back down. "Henning took it upon himself to have Legacy analyze DNA on the bracelet. Back in the early nineties, that hadn't been done here. Apparently, the police haven't caught up with all the closed or cold cases, and this one was still far down on the list."

Óliver put the photos back into the manila folder. "Henning asked if I could get a sample of Jónas's DNA. Of course, I'd already had the same thought. When I bandaged Jónas's hand this morning, I kept the bloody towel and had one of our deputies fly it down to Legacy. Henning met the deputy at the airport and took it over to the lab."

"Why didn't Rúnar do it? Does he know?" She was bewildered, and then remembered the map in the cellar. "Did he object to any of this?"

"Rúnar's been put on leave pending an investigation of two complaints of sexual harassment."

Ari covered Brynja's hand again. "The lab expedited the analysis. Put everything else aside. Within three hours, they made a match between the DNA on the bracelet and the DNA on the dishtowel. Jónas's DNA was on that bracelet. It would appear that Jónas was the one responsible for throwing the grenade into the crowd at the Botanical Gardens."

Brynja protested. "That can't be. That just can't be. There's *got* to be a mistake. DNA samples get mixed up all the time." She lowered her head. "It's so easy to screw up. Like me giving Legacy Jónas's spoon instead of my father's."

Ari squeezed her hand. "I know this is hard, but Jónas's DNA isn't only on the bracelet." He looked up at Óliver, who stepped back to the door, taking up an official and remote stance. Ari lowered his voice and leaned closer to her. "Brynja, Jónas's DNA is also on the warnings. A one hundred percent match. His DNA is on the parchment that was mailed with the *kleinur*." Ari's voice softened even more. "And it's his DNA on the parchment sent with the rhubarb cake that killed Fríða."

Brynja started to pull away but Ari held her hands in his.

"No. There's got to be a mistake. When I called you from the ferry, you said the DNA on the parchments was mine. First you said the DNA's mine, and now you're saying that it's Jónas's. I won't listen to this nonsense anymore." She pushed away from the table and stood up.

Ari stood also and pulled her close. "The lab results are accurate. They reran the samples and did the analysis twice just to be sure."

"You're wrong. Legacy's wrong. Mistakes are made all the time."

Ari wrapped his arms around her. "You didn't switch the spoons, Brynja. The spoon you gave to Legacy *was* Pabbi's. It was Pabbi's DNA they analyzed."

She narrowed her eyes and gave Ari a scorching look. "See? Wrong again. Stefán said the results meant Pabbi wasn't my father. So, the spoon had to be the one Jónas used."

Ari shook his head. "It *was* Pabbi's spoon."

Her heart was locked in an epic battle with her mind. She couldn't bear to hear what Ari was telling her. But she knew what he was about to say.

"Pabbi isn't your father, Brynja. That's why the DNA on Pabbi's spoon wasn't anything like your DNA." He took a deep breath. "I'm so sorry. The truth is that Jónas was your biological father."

A wave of nausea rolled up from deep within her gut.

"That's why they thought it was your DNA on the warnings," Ari said. "Because, in fact, so much of it *is* your DNA. You've told me yourself that a parent and child share fifty percent of their DNA. The closest match in the database was to you. Jónas's DNA is not in the database. The DNA on the warnings belongs to Jonas."

The hard knot of truth held her. She wanted to run, to tear open the door and race across the field, fling herself into the icy waters of the fjord.

Numb the pain.

Escape the awful truth.

"Jónas was your biological father, Brynja." Ari held her hands in his, gently. "There's more. We're putting the pieces together, detail upon detail, but they all make clearer the role Jónas has played in all this."

Ari glanced at Óliver and the sheet of green wrapping paper visible in the open police folder. He shook his head—it wasn't necessary to show her any more proof.

Somewhere deep within, she felt the painful cut of Occam's razor.

Chapter 33

O'er Earth Huginn and Muninn both
Each day set forth to fly;
For Huginn I fear lest he come not home,
But for Muninn my care is more.

-Old Norse, Anonymous
Poetic Edda, 13ᵗʰ Century

In the space of little more than a day, Brynja mourned the death of Jónas, grieved his deception about her birth, and despaired over the deaths he had caused. But life would not pause for her, no matter how deep her pain, and in the span of the same period she accepted the decline of Pabbi and the inevitability of his end. Ari arranged for him to be admitted to the

Huginn and Muninn Memory Care Home in Reykjavik, and he and Brynja closed up the house at Munkathverá. Amma agreed to watch over the animals. Life as Brynja had known it at the farm came to an end.

While Brynja and Ari sat by Pabbi's bedside filling out paperwork, Stína pinned photographs of puffins, golden plovers, and yellow-bellied sapsuckers to the wall.

An orderly blew into the room.

"It's time for the recreation engagement session," he announced huskily.

"Oh?" Stína wheeled around. "What did you have in mind?"

"Bingo or trivia today, I'm not sure. We like to keep our residents engaged in some sort of cognitive activity at least once a day."

Brynja put down the clipboard and introduced herself.

The orderly walked over to the window and threw open the curtains. Pabbi winced in the sudden stream of sunlight. Brynja leaned down to shield his eyes and a flicker of recognition crossed his face.

"Brynja? My child?"

She felt the same pang every time. She was yanked to one side by her love for the man she had known as her father and wrenched to the other by fury at his betrayal. *Surely, he must have known.* Unless Jónas had had an affair with Mamma? But, then, what was that birth announcement in the root cellar all about? Hr. and Fru. Raske?

Pabbi's eyes glazed over and he let out a long, hollow sigh.

She might never know the answers. Mamma was dead. Jónas had killed himself, taking with him any chance of her knowing why he had inflicted such pain. And Pabbi. She looked down into his barren eyes. Pabbi was gone as well.

Ari came to her side, draping an arm around her shoulder.

The attendant lifted Pabbi out of bed and into a wheelchair.

"We'll be back in thirty minutes or so," he said, wheeling Pabbi out of the room.

Brynja turned to Stína. "Have you heard back from the Magnússon Institute? What did they say about all the manuscripts down in the cellar?"

"One of the curators called just before I got here. Most of the manuscripts are forgeries. It's a mystery why Jónas collected them. Perhaps he created them himself. There aren't many original manuscripts still in existence so maybe he thought he could sell them as the real thing. Maybe that's why he was so determined to get his hands on the *Möðruvallabók*. Pretty extreme, though, killing people and all."

Brynja slumped down on the recliner by Pabbi's bed.

Jónas had not tried to poison *her*—he had sent the doughnuts to her office but had obviously known she wouldn't eat any of them given her gluten allergy.

But that was no consolation. He *had* murdered the others.

"I spoke with Ísak," Ari said. "He called to apologize for Henning's behavior when he questioned me over Fríða's poisoning. And for the poor coordination between police departments. Apparently, the station up in Akureyri never informed Ísak—or me—about the pastor's death or the fact that the *Möðruvallabók* had been stolen. And, worst of all, Ísak wasn't informed about the threat against you, that warning found at the church."

He gazed down at her, the pain of that moment evident in his eyes. A surge of longing flushed through Brynja's body.

"Did Ísak have anything else to say?" Stína asked, breaking the spell.

Ari nodded. "Óliver confirmed that it was Jónas who sent the packages. He must have driven the pickup to the Westfjords where he thought no one would recognize him. Óliver sent a photo of Jónas to the post office and the clerk recognized him, remembered him because of Jónas's deformed hand." He turned to Brynja. "Ísak's also concerned that Henning, without any authorization or discussion, insisted it was your DNA on the parchments. I'm sorry. I never should have listened to him. I shouldn't have questioned for one minute that you could do such a thing."

"I probably would have come to the same conclusion. So much of the DNA was mine, as you say."

"Well, I was wrong."

Brynja's cell phone rang and she reached into her bag. *"Halló?"*

"Brynja? It's Elly. Baltasar's back from his vacation. That stamp? The stamp on the package the scroll was mailed in? You know, the one with the poem about Lúkas?"

Brynja caught her breath. "Yes?"

"It's Danish. It's from Denmark."

"Denmark?"

The birth announcement in the root cellar had been from a Danish newspaper.

Brynja could hear Elly's bangles clatter and clink as she held the phone. "And, Brynja? I found the address of that house in the photo of Lúkas. *Højen Fyrvej 3.* It's Danish for Lighthouse Hill. It's a street in the far north of Denmark. In Skagen, the artists' colony."

Chapter 34

The crunch of tires on the gravel road was all that punctured the calm of late afternoon in Skagen. Brynja and Stína had rented a car in Copenhagen and driven five hours to the remote seaside town in the far north of Jutland. By five p.m., they had checked into a bed and breakfast. Stína headed out to photograph the sea birds, and Brynja set off for the address of the house in the photograph in the root cellar. *Højen Fyrvej 3.*

Brynja pulled up to the small, yellow house and switched off the engine. The dwelling hadn't changed much since the photo was taken two decades ago. Red-tiled roof. White-framed windows. Same ceramic plaque above the doorway, decorated with a bouquet of purple flowers.

A cold breeze lifted off the waters of the North Sea. She stepped outside the car and gently closed the door. The anticipation she had felt since finding the photos of Lúkas grew sharper. As she stood on the doorstep, she clutched at the locket that hung above her pounding heart. If

Lúkas was here, what would he look like? Would she recognize him? Would he recognize her? Would he be happy to see her? Would he remember her? Would he slam the door in her face?

She hesitated, then knocked softly.

A moment later, the door opened and there he stood.

Her knees buckled. She grabbed onto the doorjamb to steady herself. Suspended in a haze of disbelief, trapped between the unspeakable joy of finding Lúkas and the guilt of having lost him so many years ago, she stared at him, unable to speak.

He was taller than her now, strong and sturdy. Same blue eyes. Same curls, now darkened with the years.

"I'm—Brynja."

His eyes widened. "My God—yes, you are. I know you. I'd know you a hundred years from now." His words tumbled forth with a Danish accent.

Shaking, she raised her palm outward. He reached out to place his palm on hers in the secret clasp of their childhood. A flood of tears welled within her. Lúkas wrapped his arms around her, and they stood in an embrace so tight it left no room for the years of painful separation.

He leaned his cheek on the top of her head, then stepped back and looked into her eyes. "Where did you come from? How did you get here?" He steadied her as they walked into the house.

Sunlight streamed into the open living room through a pair of French doors that led to a grassy lawn high above the beach. The walls were stark white. The only piece of furniture was a linen sofa facing a large bay window that overlooked the sea. A watercolor canvas of red-breasted frigates diving for fish rested on an easel in the corner.

Lúkas gently placed a knitted throw over her shoulders and sat down beside her on the sofa. Several books lay on the coffee table in front of them: *Northern Light: The Skagen Painters; Lorens Raske: Watercolors from the Aalborg Museum of Modern Art;* and *Poems of Long Ago, by Hanne Larsen.*

Without a word, Brynja reached into her bag. She drew out a folder, opening it to reveal a child's drawing of seagulls soaring over a shimmering fjord.

"From Stína?"

Brynja nodded. "She's kept it all these years. We never gave up hope we'd find you some day."

A bright-eyed border collie poked its head through the open doorway, panting and pleading to join them. Lúkas patted the edge of the sofa and the dog jumped into his arms.

"I've sat here many times," he said, rubbing the collie's thick fur, "wondering about the life I left behind." He lowered his head. "I can't believe you're here. They told me you died in a fall from the carousel at the carnival."

Her eyes opened wide. "Who told you that?"

"Jónas."

She swallowed. "Jónas? But I was with Jónas looking all over for you. We couldn't find you anywhere."

Lúkas stood up and laid his hand on her shoulder. "Let me get you something to eat. Then I'll explain."

A few moments later, he returned from the kitchen with butter cookies and two small bowls of strawberries topped with cream and grated chocolate. He poured a glass of lemonade and handed it to Brynja.

"Drink this. It'll make you feel better."

She smiled weakly and took a sip. Lúkas took a bite of cookie and passed her a bowl of strawberries.

"It's all my fault, you know," he said quietly. "I never should have gone down into that cellar."

"Cellar?"

"I stumbled upon some kind of underground cellar just before the carnival. It was out past the corral, near those trees that Pabbi told us to stay away from."

"You never told me—"

"I couldn't," Lúkas said. "Jónas was furious with me. I was terrified. He threatened to hurt me if I said anything."

"Hurt you? What do you mean hurt you?"

Lúkas walked to the bay window and gazed out at the white sands of Skagen beach. "I was playing outside, throwing rocks at the edge of the field where the snow had been cleared. I saw a red ribbon. I thought you'd dropped it there, so I went to pick it up, but it was tied to a latch on the ground." He sat back down. "I tugged at the latch and pulled a metal door open. It wasn't heavy. Inside, the cellar was really dark, but I went down the stairs anyway. After my eyes adjusted, I found a stack of huge books at the bottom. I thought it might be some kind of treasure. When I told Jónas about what I'd found, he snapped."

Brynja put her hand on his.

"Jónas's face turned beet red and he bared his teeth like a wild animal. He grabbed the sheets off the clothesline and screamed, 'See these? If you say anything, I'll bury you in these.'"

"My God—" Brynja wrapped the throw tightly around her.

"I was seven and I believed him. A few weeks before I discovered the cellar, I was playing in Jónas's room. I crawled under his bed and saw some old papers. I thought Jónas would be so happy I found them, but he was fuming. That was the only time he ever hit me, but he said he'd do it again if I said anything about the papers under his bed."

A wave of sorrow rolled over Brynja. Lúkas had suffered so much. They both had.

"Tell you what, let's go outside," he said. "The fresh air will do us good."

They walked across the grass and sat down on a bench overlooking the sea. Brynja nestled into the woolen throw and the collie hopped up beside Lúkas.

Below, two young children were running on the beach, playing hide and seek.

"Come out, come out, wherever you are," the boy screamed. The girl squealed with laughter and ducked behind a pile of driftwood.

Lúkas picked up a stick and pointed north to the tip of the peninsula. "You know, Skagen is where the two seas meet. The North Sea and the Baltic Sea. As a kid, I used to come out here and watch the waves crash against one another and then settle back down on the sand. I was sure the sea was talking to me, letting me know that even the worst troubles could turn out okay." He tapped the stick on a patch of dirt. "At least, that's what I used to tell myself."

Brynja put her head on Lúkas's shoulder. "So, you've lived here ever since—"

"Yes." Lúkas said. "Jónas brought me here. To this house. To a woman named Hanne. He said she was my aunt."

She lifted her head. "Hanne? Jónas's sister? Isn't she in a home for the disabled? In Iceland?"

"I'm not sure what you mean. Hanne's not disabled. I lived here with her, in Denmark."

Brynja took a moment to digest yet another of Jónas's lies. But what mattered now was her brother and how he had been treated. "Was Hanne good to you?"

"Yes. Hanne loved me. And I loved her, very much." He drew a series of interlocking circles with the stick. "She called me Lorens."

Brynja froze, picturing the newspaper clipping in the cellar.

"I'd like to meet her," she said.

Lúkas put his arm around her. "She's gone. Hanne died a week ago." He tapped the dirt and put down the stick. "I have something to show you." He pulled a piece of paper from his pocket. "Hanne left me a letter. I think she wrote it for both of us."

"But I didn't know her."

"She knew you, Brynja. She knew you and she loved you."

"I don't understand."

"You will," Lúkas said.

He unfolded the letter and began to read.

June 1, 2017

My dear Lorens,

I'm dying and do not have much longer on this earth. I love you and I have always loved you. But I have shame in my heart.

I hope, in time, that you will forgive me for what I must tell you now.

I was young. Young and foolish and in love.

Jens Raske was his name. I suspect he changed it long ago, just as he changed yours from Lorens to Lúkas to Lorens again. Jens was a cold man. He did not love me as I loved him. In time, I learned his only true love was for Denmark and the vast empire they had once ruled over. For Jens, the enduring symbol of his beloved Danish Crown was the books: the manuscripts he believed belonged to Denmark. You may not even know of them, these medieval books. God knows I didn't.

Centuries ago, the old books were given by Iceland to the Danish Royal Antiquarian as a gift to the Crown. That man was Jens's ancestor. One of the manuscripts—the *Möðruvallabók*—had been passed down ever since from generation to generation in his family. In 1971, the book was returned to Iceland. Jens considered this an unbearable betrayal of his family, of the Crown, of Denmark. He was obsessed, out for revenge.

We were together in Iceland the day he bombed a crowd of innocents in protest. I pleaded with him to stop. How had I fallen in love with a man who could do such a thing? I wanted to end my life. But I couldn't. For I had new life growing inside of me.

Two new lives, it turned out.

Lorens, you have known me as your aunt since Jens brought you here. You were just seven, and I heard you cry "Jónas" as he drove away.

My darling boy, I am not your aunt.

I am your mother.

Chapter 35

The clouds, the sea, and the sand swirled together in a tumult of emotion. The photo of a woman holding two babies flashed into Brynja's mind.

"Hanne was our birth mother," Lúkas said.

Brynja bowed her head and was silent for a moment. Pabbi was not their father and, now, Mamma not their mother. She clutched the silver locket so tightly that her nails dug into her palm. Had her twenty-seven years been a lie? Betrayed by not only one set of parents, but two?

She looked up at Lúkas. From Hanne's letter, he already knew Jónas was their father. How could she tell him that Jónas was dead? Worse, much worse, that he was a murderer?

Every question led to another, each more painful than the last.

"I'm still confused," she said. "Why did Jónas bring you here?"

"He said I'd be better off with Hanne since Pabbi wouldn't be able to cope with your death from the carousel accident. That Pabbi was already so distraught over Mamma. Of course, at the time, I thought Jónas was just watching out for me. But now, after reading Hanne's letter—"

The tune of Iceland's national anthem rang through the open window of the house.

Lúkas started. "What's that?"

"My cell phone. I'm sorry. It's my fiancé. I should answer it." Brynja walked inside to answer the call. "Ari?"

"Brynja, I'm here at the facility and they've updated me about your father's condition. I'm glad you gave them authorization to do so because I've got some news."

Brynja's throat tightened. Now, every time she heard that word—father—she had to stop and think just whom it referred to.

"Is Pabbi okay?"

"Yes. He's more than okay."

"So, it's a good place for him?"

Brynja looked over at Lúkas and motioned through the open door that she'd be right back.

"Brynja, the doctor says your father's recovering."

"Recovering? People don't recover from dementia."

"Well, your father has. His memory's coming back."

Brynja shook her head. She was sure any facility named after Odin's ravens, Huginn and Muninn—Thought and Memory—liked to pride itself on doing all they could for their residents, but, really...

"Your father's memory is coming back. Once he settled in, the doctor asked him about his situation up at Munkathverá, including who took care of him, what his daily routine was. Exercise, diet, that kind of thing. Páll told the doctor just how well he'd been cared for, how well Jónas had fed him. He said the one exception was the mushrooms that Jónas insisted he eat. He said he hates mushrooms but Jónas practically forced them down his throat."

Mushrooms? *Amanita muscaria.* Brynja had seen them down in the root cellar. If that's what Jónas had been feeding him, no wonder Pabbi had spiraled so rapidly. *Amanita muscaria* were known to cause memory loss and hallucinations.

"So, it wasn't dementia, after all," Brynja said, and Ari agreed, repeating more of what the doctor had told him.

She recalled the first signs of Pabbi's fading. Had Jónas started feeding Pabbi the mushrooms once she'd told him about the poem? Had he intentionally poisoned Pabbi to stop him from helping in her search for Lúkas? Or did Jónas poison Pabbi to keep him from talking about what he knew?

Did Pabbi know what had happened to Lúkas? Did he know that Jónas had taken Lúkas from them? *Impossible.*

And yet...

"Will he be okay?" she asked.

"Yes. The doctor says he's going to be fine."

"Thank you. Thank you so much for being there."

"Absolutely." Ari paused. "Listen, the director of *Thor's Hammer* invited me out to a shoot this afternoon."

"Great. Sounds like fun. Thank you for calling right away about Pabbi."

"I also wanted to make sure you knew about the movie shoot. I know you worry, and it's a love scene between Sif and Thor. With Ásta as Sif."

She smiled slightly. "Not a problem, Ari. Have fun. You don't need to ask me."

She glanced toward the window and her brother playing fetch with his dog. "*Elskan,* can I call you when I get back to the B&B? I'm with Lúkas." Her eyes swam with tears. "I found him. I found Lúkas."

She went back outside. It was time to tell Lúkas about everything that had happened. The poem, the warnings, the poisonings. How would her brother react, knowing he had inherited the genes of a man who had murdered three people? He would never be able to free himself of Jónas. But neither would she. Their father's DNA lurked in every cell of his body, as it did in hers.

Lúkas was calling to the border collie, who was happily sniffing for the ball in the bushes.

Brynja walked across the lawn. "Lúkas—"

"Everything okay?" He bent down to wrest the ball from the dog's mouth. "Let me finish reading Hanne's letter. You need to know the whole story."

Brynja nodded, knowing full well she would have to tell him the ending.

They sat down on the bench. Lúkas pulled the letter from his pocket and continued to read.

I have kept this secret buried in my heart since the day you were brought back to me. I hope I did the right thing by not telling you.

Lorens, Pabbi isn't your father. Jónas is.

When I threatened to leave, he tried to poison me. After I recovered, he saw how broken I was. Afraid to betray him, I never told a soul.

I feared for your life as well, and for the life of my daughter. Your sister. I named her Brita. When you first arrived, you cried for her day and night, believing she had died. Lorens, she's alive. Your sister is alive and living in Iceland.

And now I must tell you a deeper secret, a secret I have buried beneath the layers of a mother's love since the day you were born. Did I do the right thing, Lorens? Did I have a choice? I don't know. I can only hope that you will forgive me.

When Jónas threw the bomb into the crowd that day, a fragment tore through the womb of the woman you knew as Mamma. It killed her unborn baby and her chances of ever conceiving again. The only witness was the woman's husband, a farmer. You remember him as Pabbi.

Pabbi threatened to turn Jónas in to the authorities. I don't know what they said to each other, but the result was an agreement. Pabbi had seen my pregnant belly and vowed not to turn Jónas in if he agreed to give up his unborn child. He was desperate that Mamma become a mother.

Jónas agreed, but on one condition: he stay on as Pabbi's farm manager. I was devastated. My only consolation was that, in spite of himself, Jónas became extremely fond of you and your sister as you grew. At the same time, he never gave up hope he could retrieve the *Möðruvallabók* for his family and bring it back to Denmark.

In the early years, Jónas stayed in touch with me. He sent me photographs, drawings, and letters with news of you. Perhaps he was not completely heartless.

I learned that, over the years, he retrieved many of the old Icelandic parchments from libraries, bookshops—anywhere he could—and stashed them in a root cellar. But I knew he would never be satisfied until the *Möðruvallabók* was back in his hands.

When you found his trove of parchments in the cellar, he brought you here. He needed to make sure that you could never divulge his secret. Even the words of a small child could be dangerous.

I had to do it, Lorens. I had to give you both up. Jónas threatened to kill me, and the lives growing inside me. I chose life over death.

I only have a few days left and Jens cannot threaten me any longer. I have cancer of the ovaries, the very organs that gave life to you and your sister. It is a fitting end for my sins.

Lorens, I have written to your sister and sent it to the police station in Reykjavik, hoping they could track her down. I wrote a poem as a riddle, hoping the clues would lead her to the cellar and what became of you. I could not tell her directly, as I feared Jónas would harm you both.

I love you, Lorens. And I love your sister, the daughter I never knew.

As I take my last breath, my dying wish is that you find happiness together.

Your loving mother,

Hanne

Lúkas rested the letter in his lap. "Hanne was taking a lot of morphine when she wrote this letter to me and the poem to you. If she had been in her right mind, she would have realized you would immediately tell Jónas and Pabbi about the poem."

Brynja sat in stunned silence. So, that's why Jónas had cracked. The moment she had read the poem to him, Jónas had known that Hanne was trying to reveal his past.

"After Hanne died last week," Lúkas said, "I found the letter tucked beneath her pillow. I wish you had known her."

"Me too." Brynja smiled through her tears. "But we've found each other, Lúkas."

"The first thing I did after the funeral yesterday was book a flight to Iceland. I'm glad you found me first. But how? How did you know where to look for me?"

"I found the cellar. I was out riding. Remember our mare, Drífa? She led me to the cellar. I saw the red ribbon on the latch. The same red ribbon you must have seen. I climbed down and found photographs of you. We tracked down this house from the photos."

The waves crashed onto the shoreline below.

"I've been looking for you since the day you disappeared, Lúkas. I always believed you were alive, but there were only ever false leads. Then I received the poem a couple of weeks ago. The poem that Hanne wrote."

They sat in silence for a while, listening to the children playing below.

Brynja stood up. "What do you say we walk down to the beach?"

A smile crept up Lúkas's face. "I don't know. The last time we walked somewhere together it didn't turn out so well."

"I promise I won't let go this time," she said.

Lúkas jumped up and took her hand. "Come."

He led her down the path through tufts of marram grass that sprang from the sandy hillside. Reaching the beach, he wrapped his sweater around her. They walked to the water's edge and stood side by side, silently watching the waves roll in from the west.

Brynja inhaled the spray of salt air and, for the first time since Lúkas disappeared, when she was a seven-year-old girl who didn't yet know what the world was like, she felt whole again.

A colony of gulls soared high above, carrying with them the last traces of the Blue Hour, that time of day when the sky meets the sea and becomes not air and water, not wind and waves, not the path of the sun nor the road of the whale, but the light in which the two become one, the light in which the past fades into the future and gives way to the present.

Author's Note

Although based on historical truths *Double Blind: The Icelandic Manuscript Murders* is a work of fiction and poetic license was liberally employed to enhance the story line. For instance, the medieval Icelandic manuscripts are Iceland's most precious treasures and would never be couriered around the country simply for someone to have a look at it. Whenever the manuscripts are transported anywhere, they are put in locked, heavy duty cases with light and humidity controls under high security measures. Among other such examples, the physical description of the *Möðruvallabók* (there is no gilded 'M' on the cover) and the composition and access to the DNA database are not to be considered entirely factual.

Concerning the medieval Icelandic family sagas, these were written down in the thirteenth and fourteenth centuries, and are essentially family stories, based on tenth- and eleventh-century events in the lives of

Iceland's earliest settlers. The sagas contain many short poems written in a precise, demanding, "courtly" form, often nearly impossible to render at all closely into English. (For a brief discussion of this form, see Chapter 20.) Allusions abound, riddle-like in nature. Translations of these poems, understandably, vary widely. Still, all may be considered valid. I have limited my quotations from such poetry to versions which our characters might have had access to and confess to having cherry-picked the versions best suited to my tale, even to having made small changes in some: e.g. the ash-tree (for ale-horn) goddess in Chapter 27. If you wish to discover more about Iceland's sagas, most if not all of can be found at www.sagadb.org and *The Complete Sagas of Icelanders, including 49 tales* (Leifur Eiriksson Publishing).

Acknowledgements

To the many Icelanders who shared unforgettable moments so necessary for the realization of this book, I am eternally grateful.

Thank you to Guðvarður Már Gunnlaugsson, the manuscript master at the University of Iceland's Árni Magnússon Institute, and Ásdís Hermanowicz, then a graduate student in Medieval Icelandic Studies, who allowed me access to the medieval Icelandic manuscripts, including the *Möðruvallabók*. They enlightened me with the history and significance of these world treasures.

Gísli Rúnar Víðisson toured my family through the north of Iceland. He, his wife Alma Björg Almarsdóttir, and their children have since become great friends. Thanks also to Helgi Guðmundsson for showing me many of saga locales as we explored the south and west of the country.

Special thanks to Erica Green and Eliza Reed, co-founders of the Iceland Writers Retreat, for sharing the great literary tradition of Iceland to those across the globe. In fact, my attendance at the first IWR event inspired me to write this novel.

Deep gratitude for the insight of several Icelandic readers: Guðmundur Heiðar Frímannsson, professor at the University of Akureyri, Ingibjörg Björnsdóttir, Helgi Guðmundsson, and Dagný Thorgilsdóttir, who taught me much about the language and customs of her native land.

Many thanks to editor Sara Litchfield of Right Ink on the Wall, mystery author Susan Oleksiw, and literary agent Michelle Richter of Fuse Literary for their expertise and encouragement. Medical professional and author Serita Stevens provided me with expert consultation on plant poisons. Hyla Troxell—chemist, numismatist, and scholar—was a tireless and exacting editor throughout the many revisions of this project. Thank you, mom.

I am grateful for the insight and commentary of many readers, including Deborah Gaal, Johan Brahme, Gersony Hildebrand Troxell, Denise Sakai Troxell, Emily Troxell, Larry Winokur, Vicki Ziegel, Jon Roy, KC Mulligan, Emily Kerr, Chris Shultz, Shellsy Ashen, Coral Ashen, Cindy Tolles, Beth O'Brien, and book club members Kim Anderson, Jill Behrle, Linda Bovee, Kathy Browning, Paula Carpou, Meg Casalaspi, Vicki Czapla, Cathie D'Itri, and LaNel Shimano. Thanks also to the invaluable mentorship of Lou Nelson and input from writing group members Herb Williams-Dalgart, Deborah Gaal, Susan Angard, Timothy Twombly, David Collins, Beverly Plass, Brad Oatman, and Kristin James.

And to my beautiful family—Rob, Cole, Olivia, and Wyatt— my heart is filled with love for you. Thank you for traveling this journey with me.

9 781733 452809